IMAGES
of America

SPEEDWAY

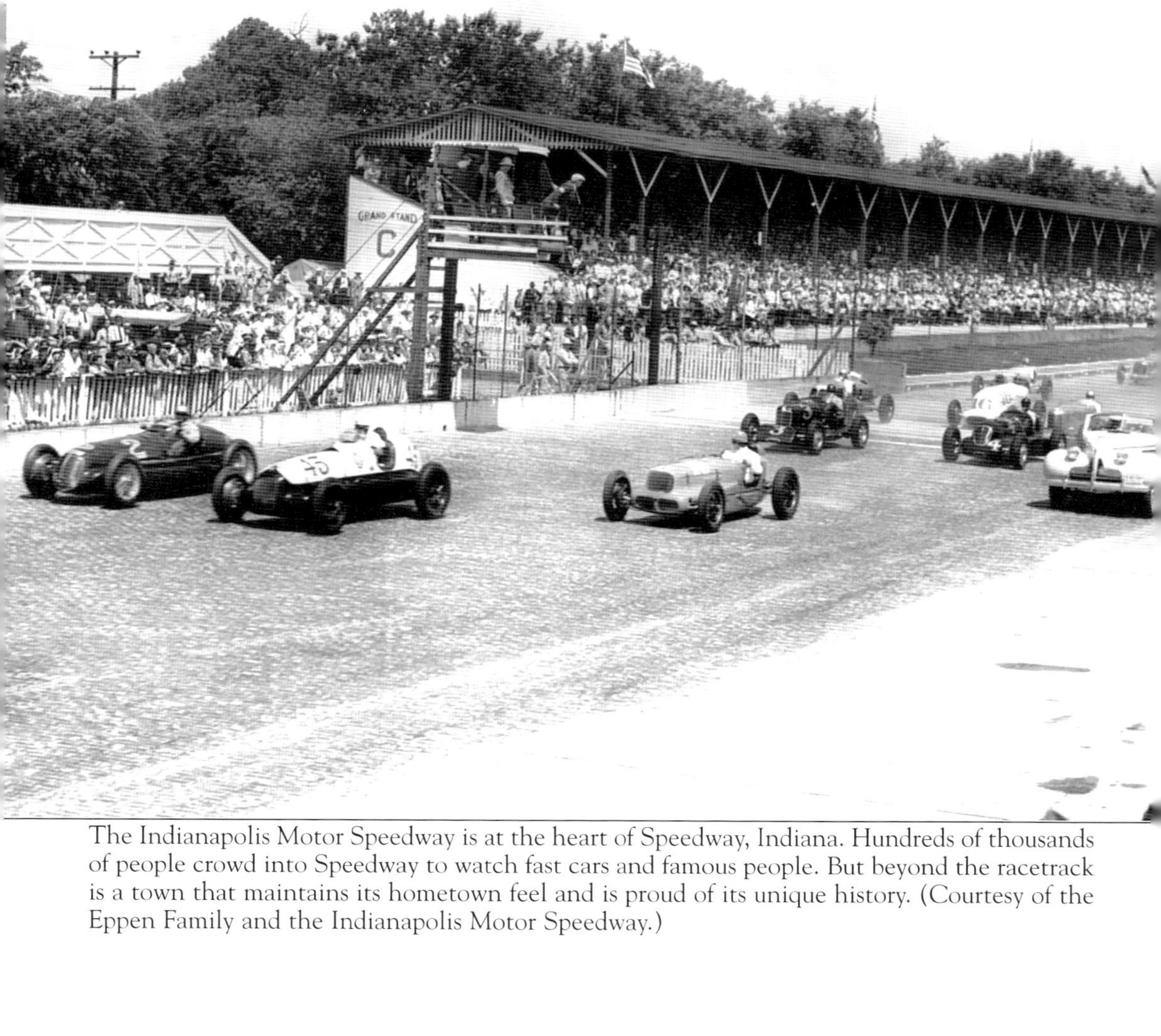

The Indianapolis Motor Speedway is at the heart of Speedway, Indiana. Hundreds of thousands of people crowd into Speedway to watch fast cars and famous people. But beyond the racetrack is a town that maintains its hometown feel and is proud of its unique history. (Courtesy of the Eppen Family and the Indianapolis Motor Speedway.)

IMAGES
of America

SPEEDWAY

Jane Carroll Routte

ARCADIA
PUBLISHING

ISBN 978-0-7385-3332-2

Published by Arcadia Publishing
Charleston, South Carolina

Printed in the United States of America

Library of Congress Catalog Card Number: 2004108742

For all general information contact Arcadia Publishing at:
Telephone 843-853-2070
Fax 843-853-0044
E-mail sales@arcadiapublishing.com
For customer service and orders:
Toll-Free 1-888-313-2665

Visit us on the Internet at www.arcadiapublishing.com

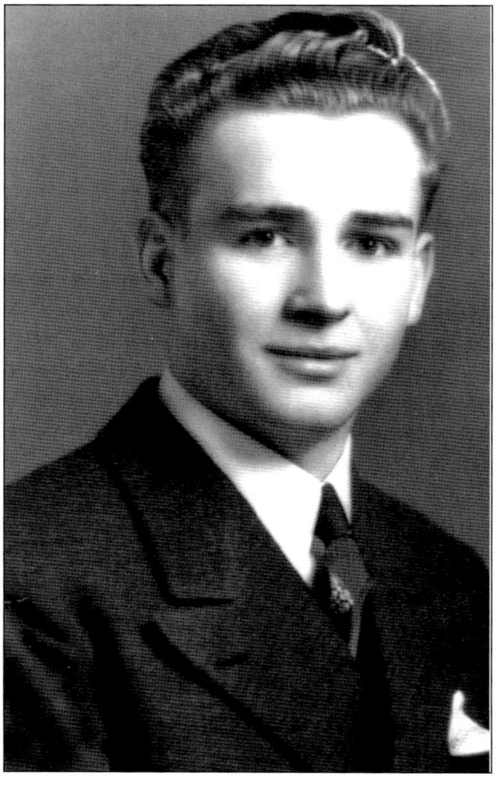

Carl Pieper was a lifelong resident of Speedway. He and his wife Rosemary were very generous in lending pictures for this book and for sharing historical information. Carl will be kindly remembered.

CONTENTS

Acknowledgments

I would like to give very special thanks to the following groups and individuals:

The Indianapolis Motor Speedway and especially Dave Hilberry and Mary Ellen Loscar
Mr. and Mrs. Carl Pieper
The Eppen Family and especially Marcia, Ernest and Louise
Edith Spencer
Elizabeth Frazier
Mary Ann O'Neal
Don Katterhenry
Charles Bennett
Sister Rachel West and Marian College Archives
Robert and Pauline Grothe of the Speedway Bed and Breakfast
John Otte
The Old Speedway Neighborhood Association
Dick Jordan
American Legion Post 500 and Gene Tsariff
Sara Sanderson

I also want to thank my husband Steven and the rest of my family for supporting my efforts.

INTRODUCTION

Speedway's history is wrapped around the two-and-one-half mile oval of the Indianapolis Motor Speedway. The track was established in 1909 as a testing ground for Indiana's booming automotive economy. The city of Speedway followed along in 1926, building its future on the track and the automotive-related industries that followed it to the remote country spot six miles west of Indianapolis. Now, for three months of the year, racing fever takes over, and the population of this Indiana town swells from 12,000 to hundreds of thousands as racing fans from all over the world rush into the area to see the fast and the famous.

Speedway has played host to Clark Gable, Amelia Earhart, Paul Newman, several Presidents of the United States, and countless other famous faces. These famous people came to watch race car drivers make history every year. These drivers included Mario Andretti, A.J. Foyt, Bobby Unser, Dale Earnhart, Michael Schumacher, and others who set the standards for speed and racing endurance.

Now, Speedway's 2.4 square miles have become surrounded, but not swallowed, by the great encroaching amoeba of Indianapolis. Even though the city surrounds it, and Indianapolis gives its name to Speedway's biggest race, Speedway has managed to maintain its distinct and unique identity in Hoosier history and life.

Speedway is more than a town that surrounds the most famous auto racing track in the world. The city is proud of its quality schools, and the residents have prospered from the businesses of the area. Civic pride runs strong through a community where generations of families have remained in the same neighborhoods, and sometimes in the same houses. Speedway was originally the dream of Carl Fischer, who, in 1926, envisioned a "horseless city just opposite the Motor Speedway, an industrialized city devoted to motorizaton of all traffic." He did not want to see the shacks that were sprouting up near other industrialized areas, but instead, a well-planned and comfortable city of cleanliness and pride. With the help of Lem Trotter, a visionary developer, he was able to make this dream come true.

During World War II, while racing was suspended and the track fell into disrepair, the city of Speedway was actively employed making engines for military tanks and aircraft. The Allison Transmission plants churned out jobs and the equipment to support the war effort.

The Prest-O-Lite Corporation, the first business to move to Speedway in 1912, was the first producer of a practical headlight for the new automobiles that were hitting the road. It was through the efforts of Prest-O-Lite's owner that the speedway track came into being. But Carl Fisher's vision did not stop with the Indianapolis Motor Speedway and the city of Speedway. He was also the man who developed Miami Beach into the famous tourist attraction that it became before WWII.

The post-war boom brought new life to Speedway, and the names of many streets reflect the patriotism of the citizenry: Patton, Eisenhower, MacArthur, and Truman. The Ben Hur line of the interurban train brought people to see the new home sites that were being offered for $10 down and $10 per month. The dirt roads were turning into paved streets. Eddie Rickenbacher, the World War I flying ace who owned the track, sold it to Anton "Tony" Hulman Jr. who, with the help of Wilber Shaw, revived it from near death to become the great racing venue of today.

Speedway citizens continue to be proud of this American town with a unique history and heritage, and visitors continue to crowd into this town in search of speed and excitement.

One

THE TRACK

Before the town of Speedway existed, the speedway did. Incorporated on February 8, 1909, the Indianapolis Motor Speedway Company began building the automobile racetrack that would become the first name in racing throughout the world.

Carl Fisher was the man with the dream. He designed the track as a testing ground for the rapidly developing automobile industry of the early 1900s. Along the way, the track also became the testing ground for speed and endurance. Motorcycles, gas-filled balloons, and airplanes were raced and exhibited during the very early years of the track. In 1911, the first 500-mile race lasted 6 hours, 42 minutes and 8 seconds with an average winning speed of 74.6 miles per hour. The track tested both man and machine to the limits of the day.

Since those early years the Indianapolis Motor Speedway has played host to the fast and the famous. The Indianapolis 500 is the world's largest annual single-day sporting event. In 1994, Nascar added the Brickyard 400, and the Formula 1 United States Grand Prix made Indianapolis its home in 2000. It is no wonder that the nickname for the town of Speedway is "The Racing Capital of the World."

All of the pictures in this chapter are used through the courtesy of the Indianapolis Motor Speedway. All statistics quoted are from *The Indianapolis Motor Speedway, A History*, by Donald Davidson, IMS Historian.

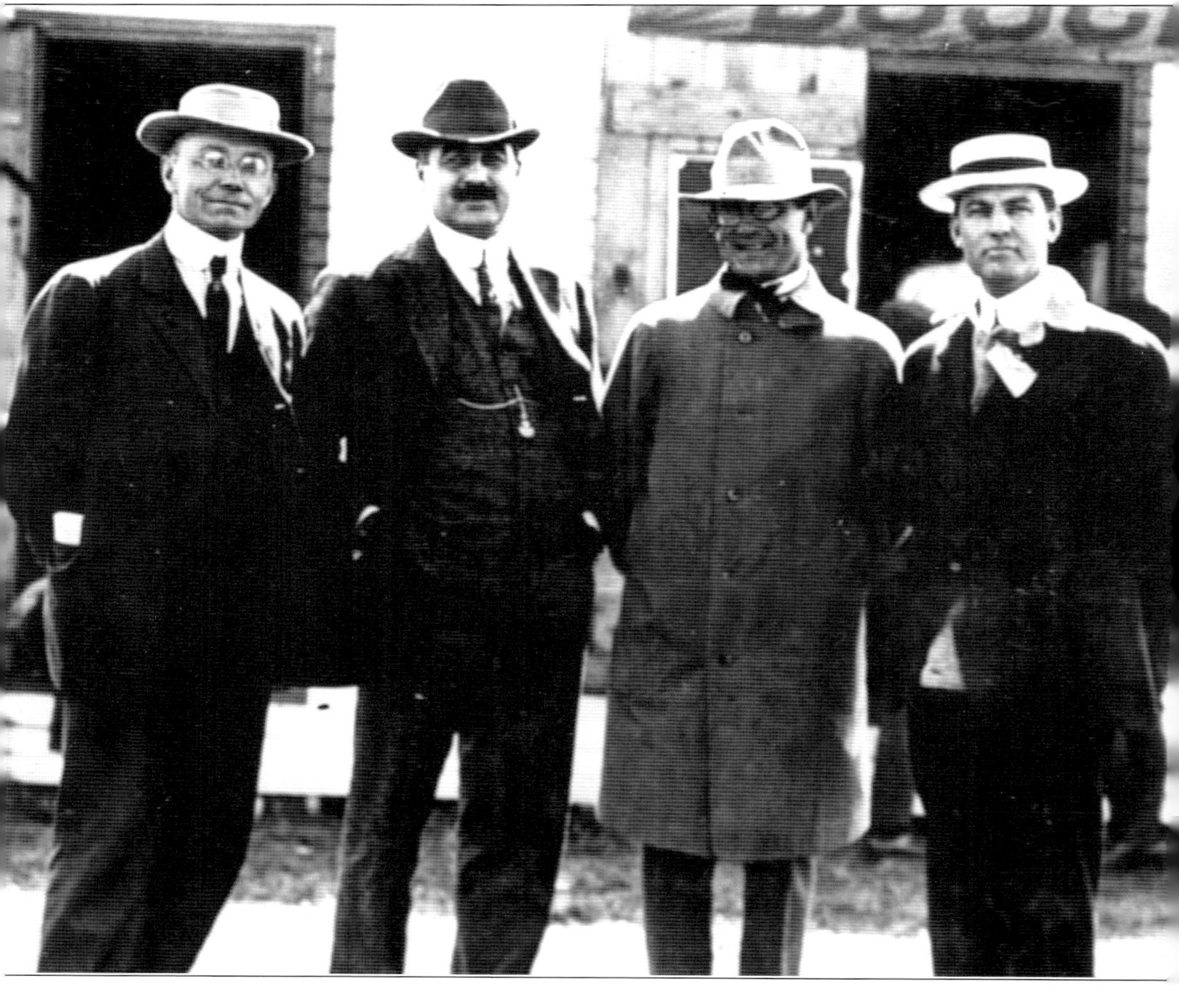

Arthur Newby (1865–1933), Frank Wheeler (1864–1921), Carl Fisher (1874–1939), and James Allison (1872–1928) were the founding fathers of the city of Speedway and the Indianapolis Motor Speedway. It was their vision and planning which brought the vision of Speedway—the horseless city, the industry, and the racetrack—into being. Their vision revolutionized the automobile industry and automobile racing in the United States.

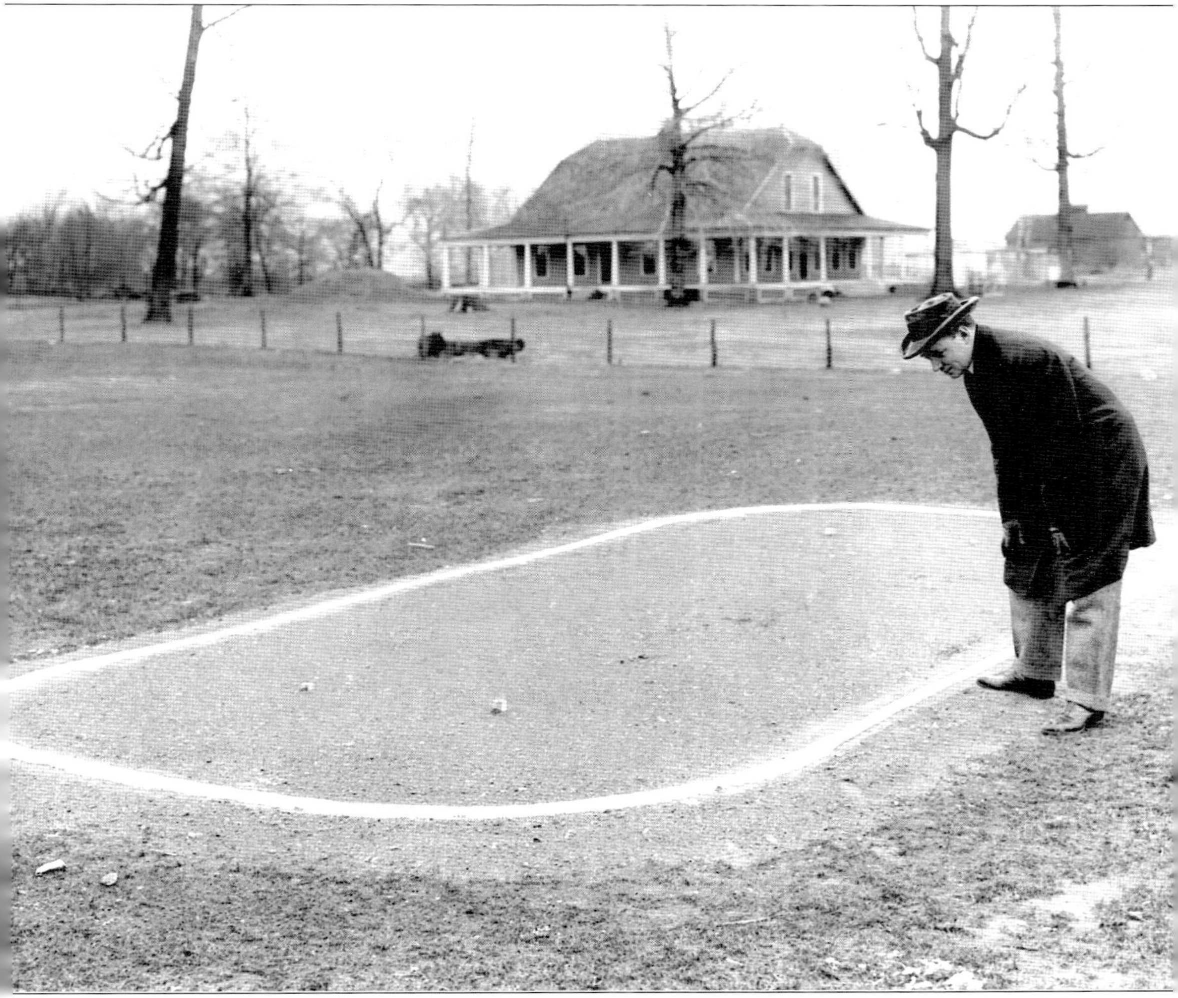

"The Vision" is the popular name of this photograph. Louis Strange looks over the layout of the track before it was built. The farm in the background belonged to Asa Morgan, and the barn in the far back still stands on the grounds of the Indianapolis Motor Speedway today. Louis Strange was the first pole sitter at the first Indianapolis 500. He had the pole position because he was the first to sign up for the race.

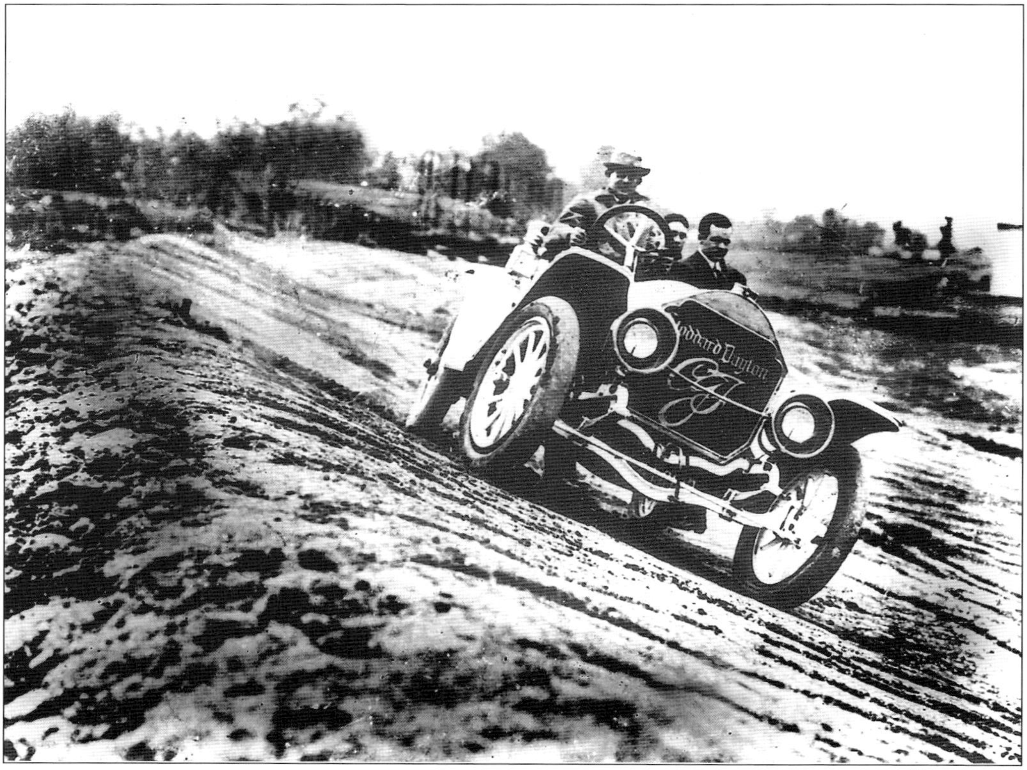

Carl Fisher tries out the Indianapolis Motor Speedway while it was under construction. He is driving his personal Stoddard Dayton automobile. The Stoddard Dayton was the make of car chosen for the first pace car for the 500. Notice the right-hand steering wheel on the car.

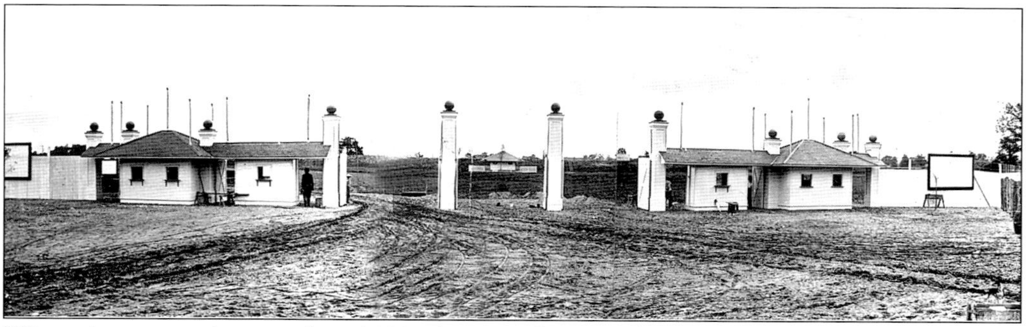

When the racetrack opened in 1909, this was the gate that greeted visitors. In early years, the Indianapolis Motor Speedway was used for air shows, balloon races, and several different automobile races. The first Indianapolis 500 was held in 1911 and was won by Ray Harroun, with a relief driver, Cyrus Patschke.

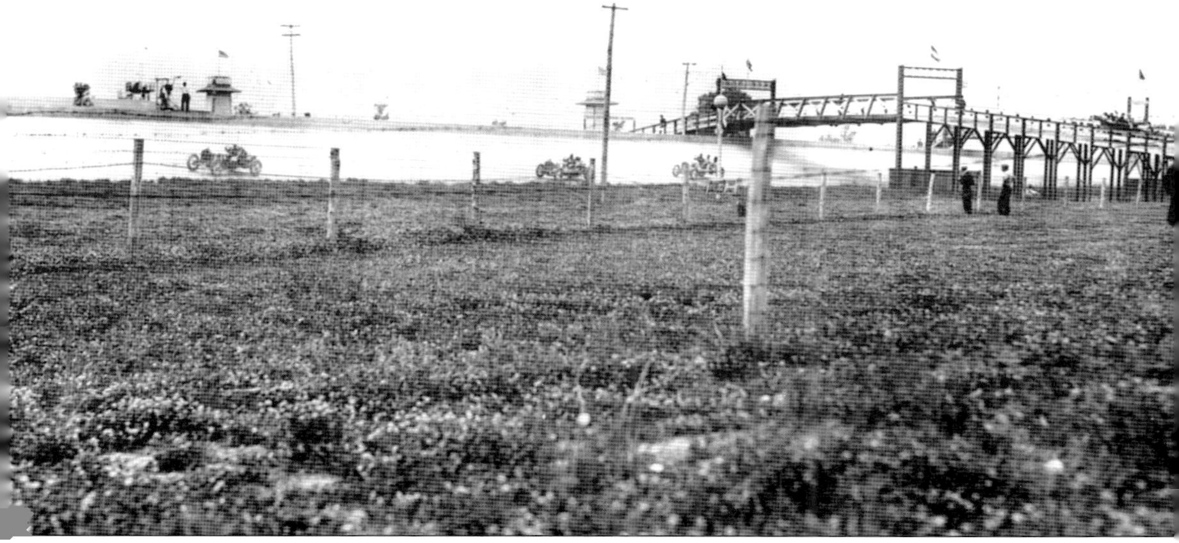

This very early view of the track shows the inside of the first turn. Notice the gate posts on the other side of the track and the bridge that spanned the track to the infield. In 1912, a tunnel was built under turn two and in 1913 a second tunnel was added under the main straightaway north of the start/finish line. Other tunnels were added in later years to allow access to the infield without crossing over the track.

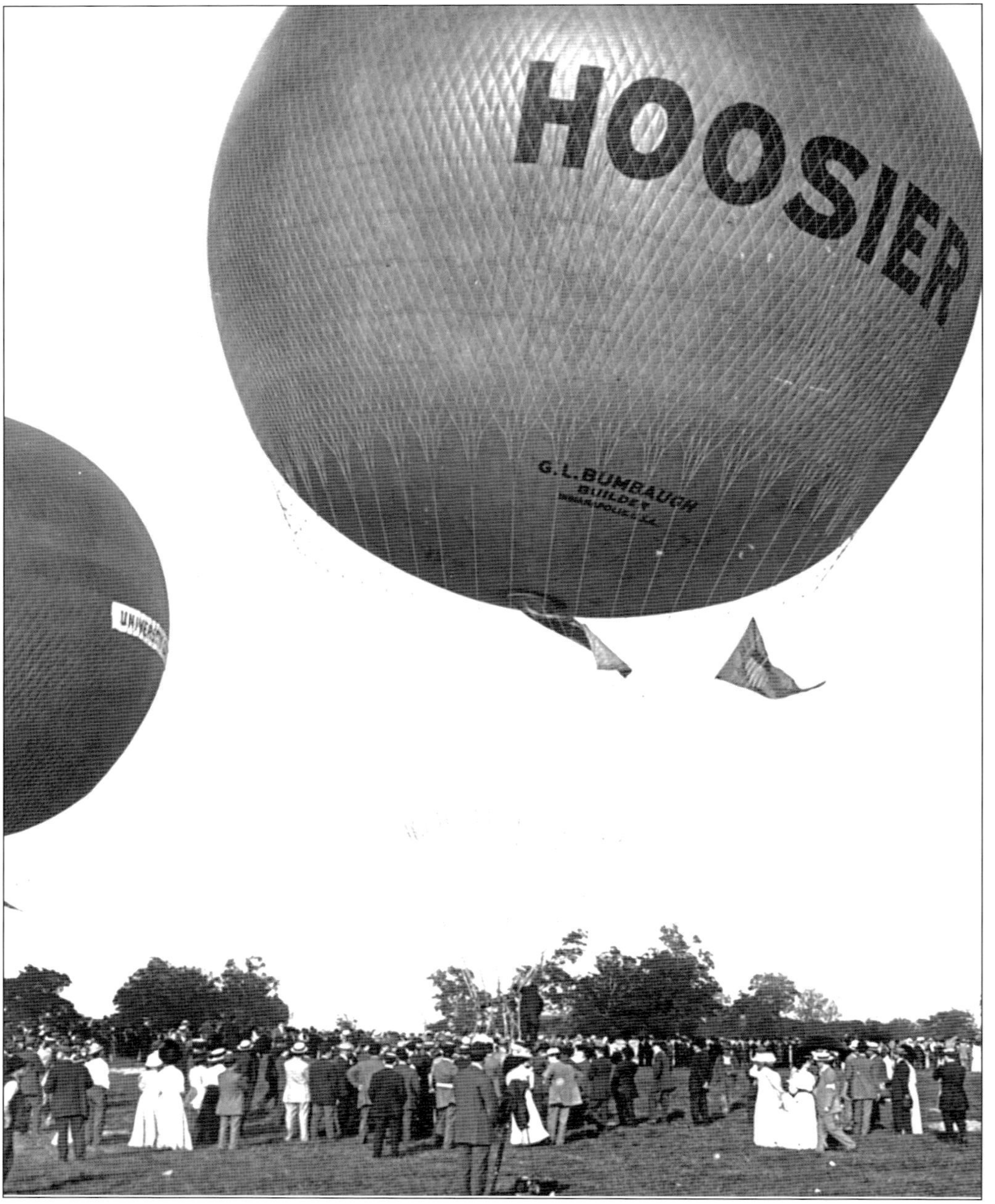

Few people associate the Indianapolis Motor Speedway with anything but automobile racing, but the first competitive event at the track was the National Championship for gas-filled balloons. This event took place on June 5, 1909. Other non-automotive events at the track included motorcycle races and a 1910 air show.

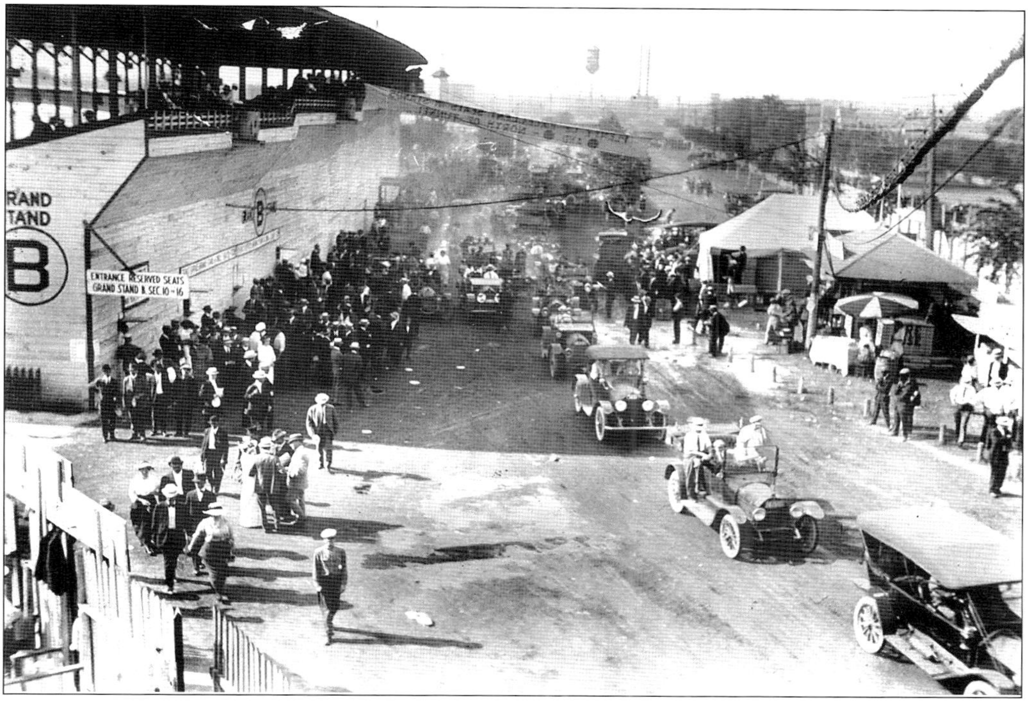

Race fans at the track in 1912 walked along Georgetown Road to get to the stands. The sign over the road reads, "Plenty of excellent seats in stands C and D north of tunnel." Notice the water towers and chimneys of the Speedway city industries.

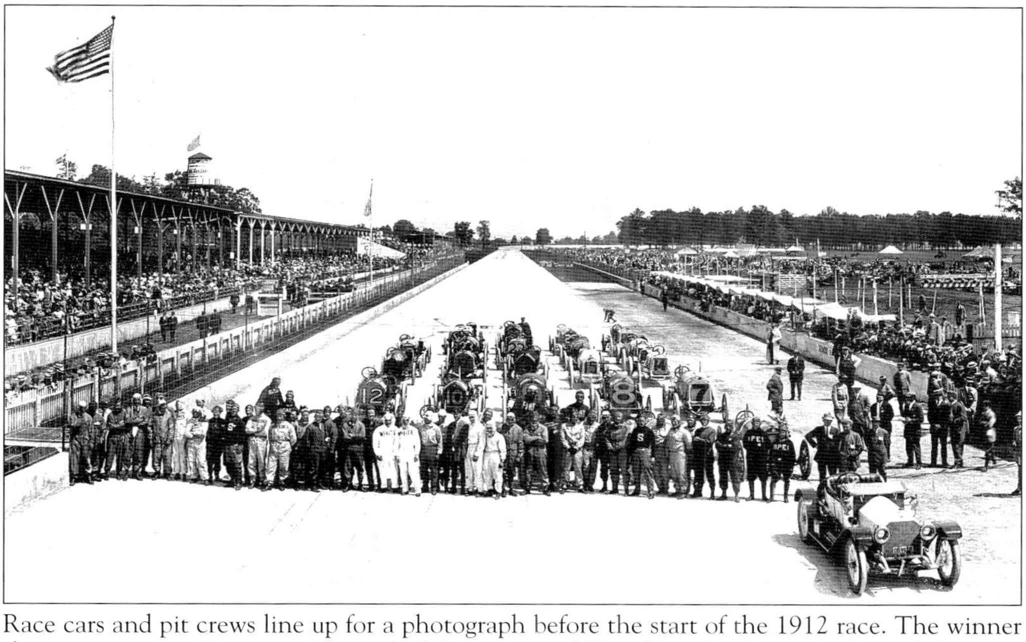

Race cars and pit crews line up for a photograph before the start of the 1912 race. The winner that year was Joe Dawson with a relief driver named Don Herr. In the early days of the race, two men rode in the cars. The average winning speed was 78.719.

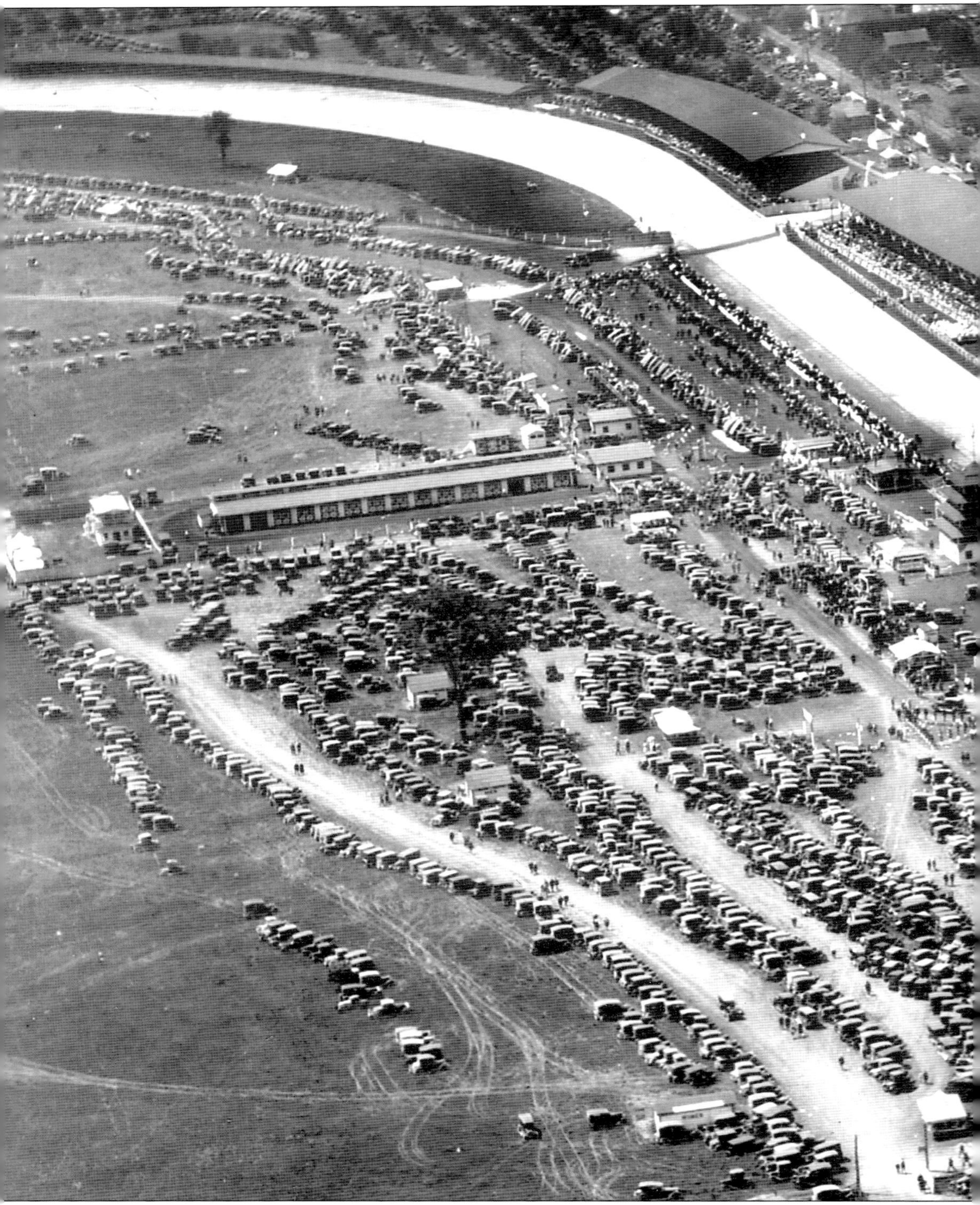

As cars lined up for the 1922 race, the crowds filled the stands, and the automobiles filled the infield. Outside of the stands the farmlands stretch away to the west. The Eppen truck farm is

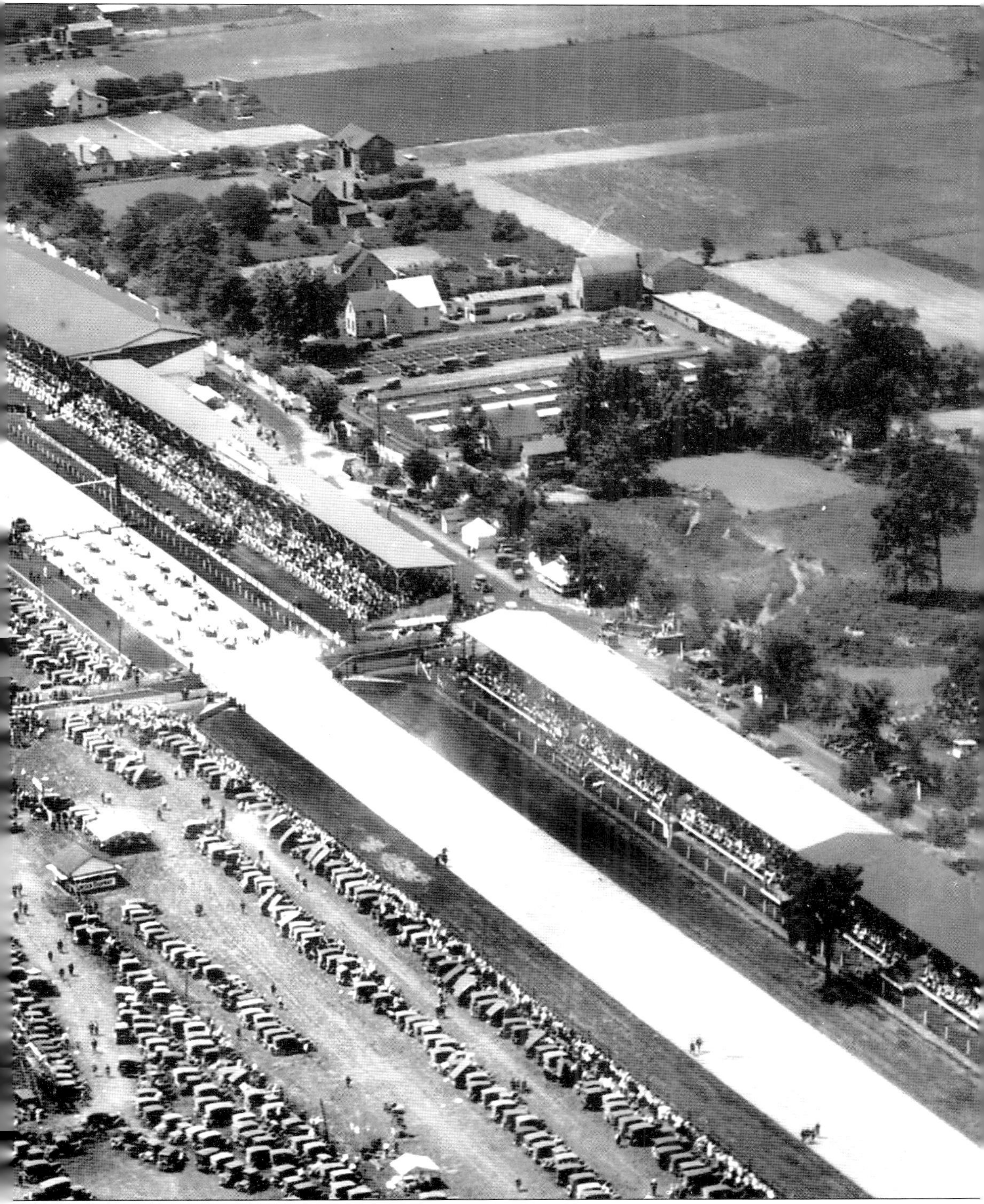

visible along the country road that became Georgetown Road. The garages are contained in one building, and the pagoda stands south of the location of today's tower.

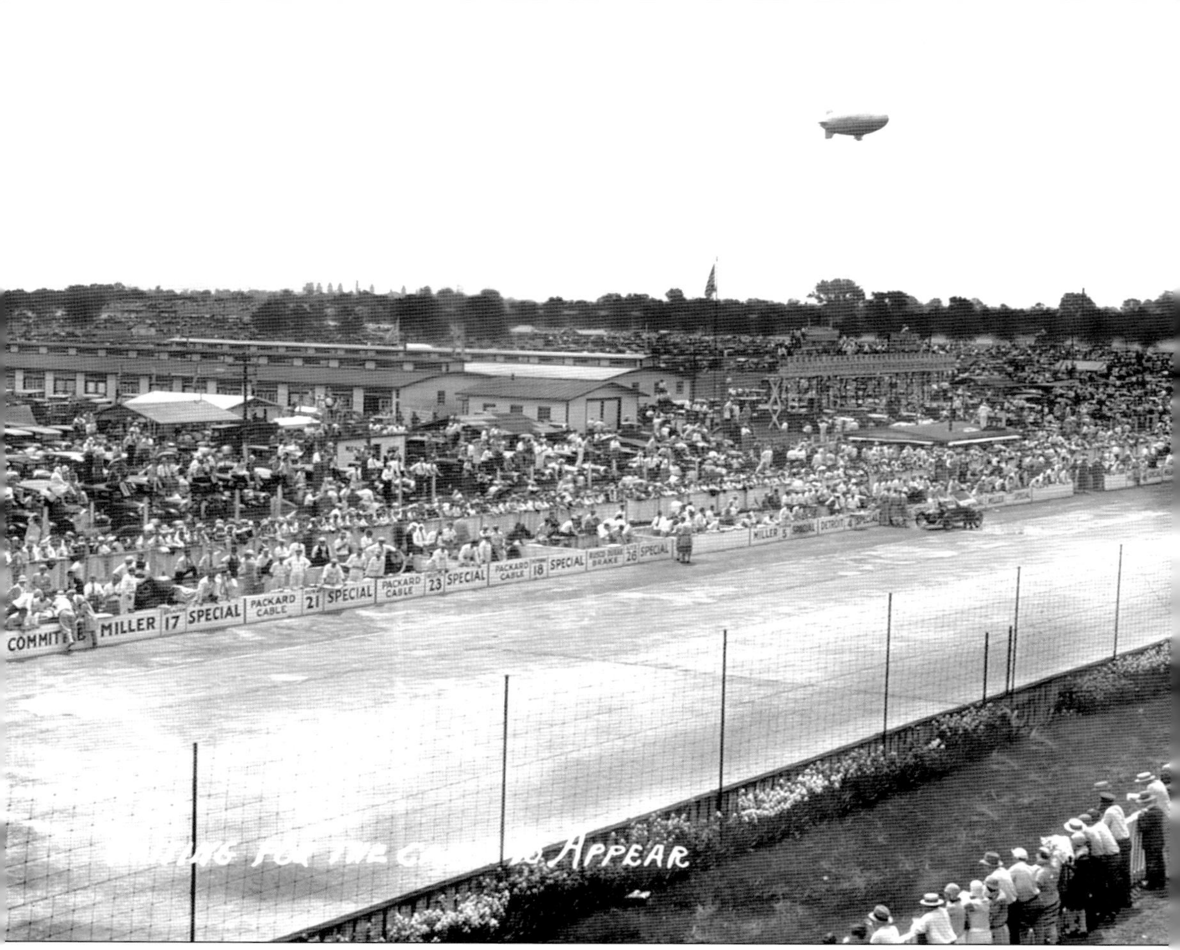

The pit teams wait for the cars. In 1929, pit row was marked with names of the teams. By this time there were two long garages on Gasoline Alley. Notice the blimp above the track and the Indianapolis skyline in the distance.

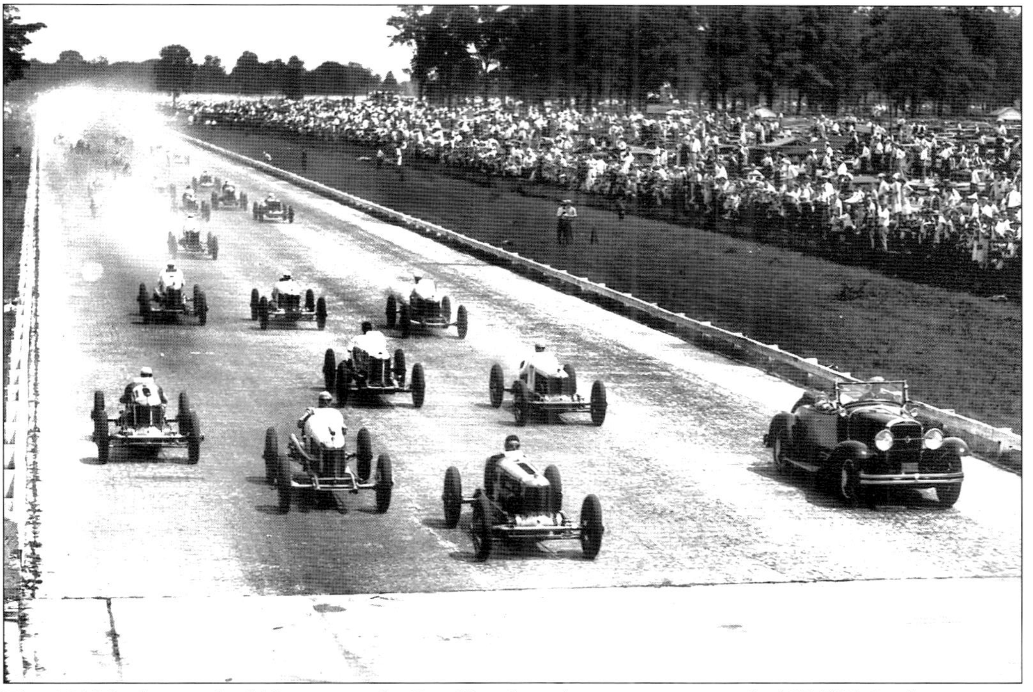

The 1929 Indianapolis 500 was won by Ray Keech with an average speed of 97.585. In this picture, crowds cheer from an infield which contains many trees, limiting the view of the track on the opposite side. Notice the brick surface which gave the Speedway its nickname, "The Brickyard."

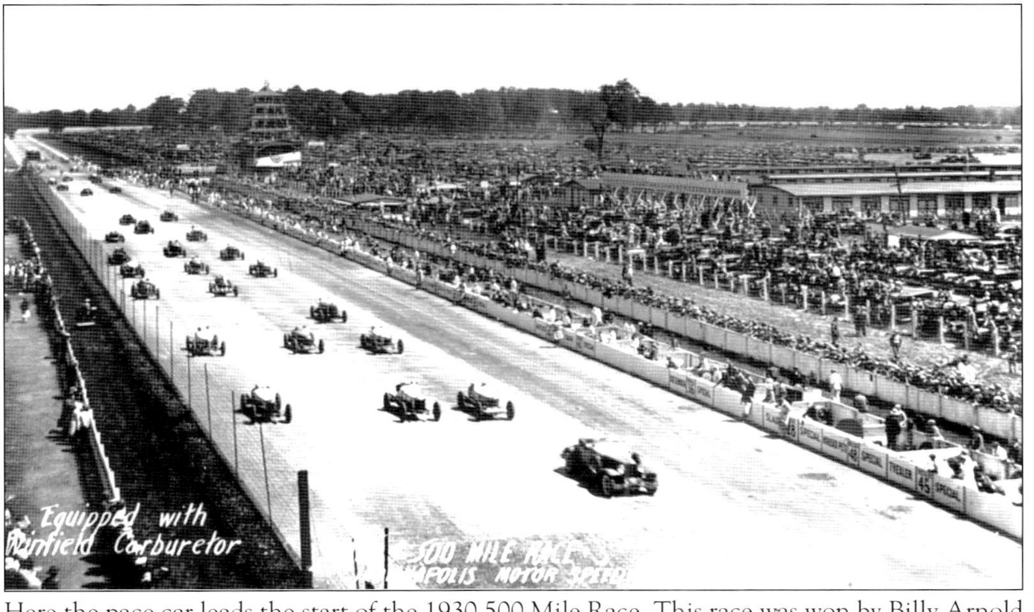

Here the pace car leads the start of the 1930 500 Mile Race. This race was won by Billy Arnold with an average winning speed of 100.448. This was the second time that 100 miles an hour had been broken as the winning speed of the race. The first time was in 1925 by Peter DePaolo with a winning speed of 101.127.

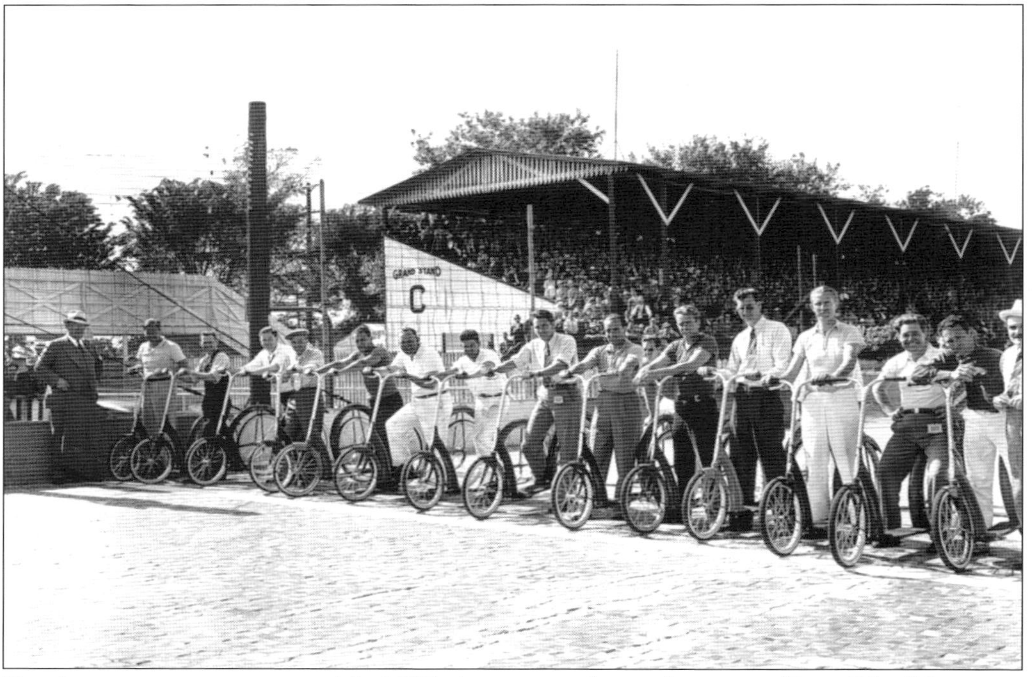

Gentlemen, start your scooters! In 1937, the race car drivers line up on "Ingo Bikes" for a pre-500 race of a different sort. This was apparently a one-time event, probably for a promotion of some kind.

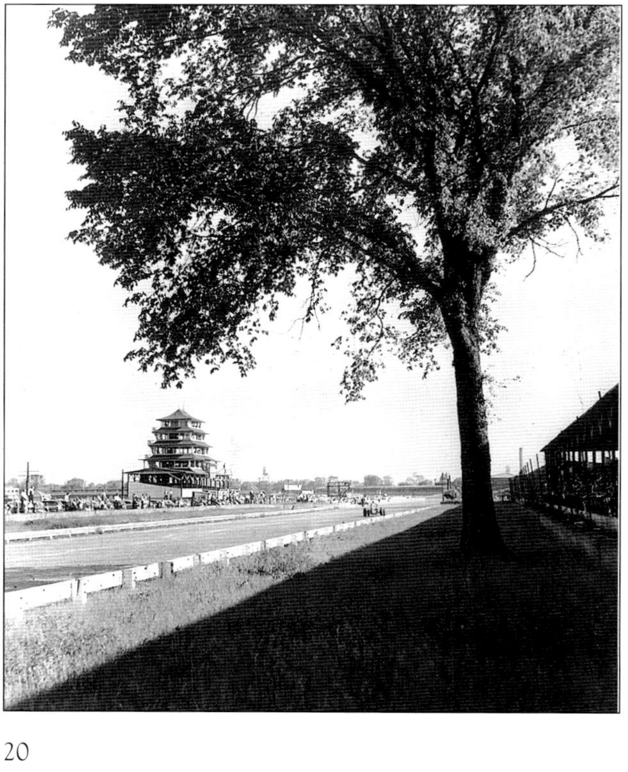

The main straightaway and the pagoda of 1941 are pictured here. This pagoda was built in 1926 after the original one burned on the day after the 1925 race. Here the stands are separated from the track by a width of grass and a tree. Fans must have been upset when they found themselves in seats behind the tree for the race.

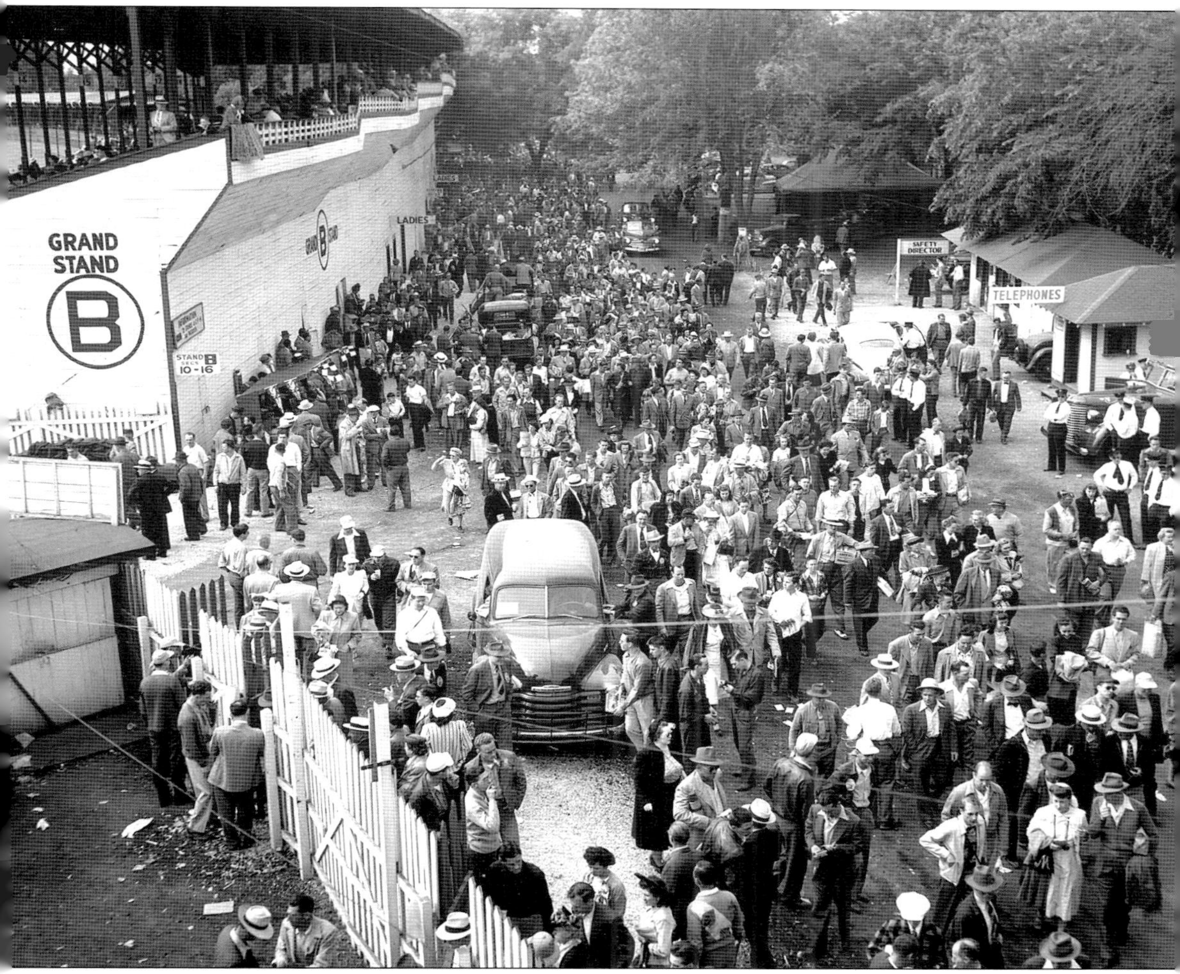

Fans hurried along Georgetown Road in 1948. After WW II, race fans hurried back to the races. The track was closed during the years between 1942 and 1945, but was rescued by Wilber Shaw who talked Anton Hulman Jr. into buying and saving the track. Wilber Shaw served as president and general manager. Races restarted in 1946. The race was also suspended in 1916 and 1917 during WW I.

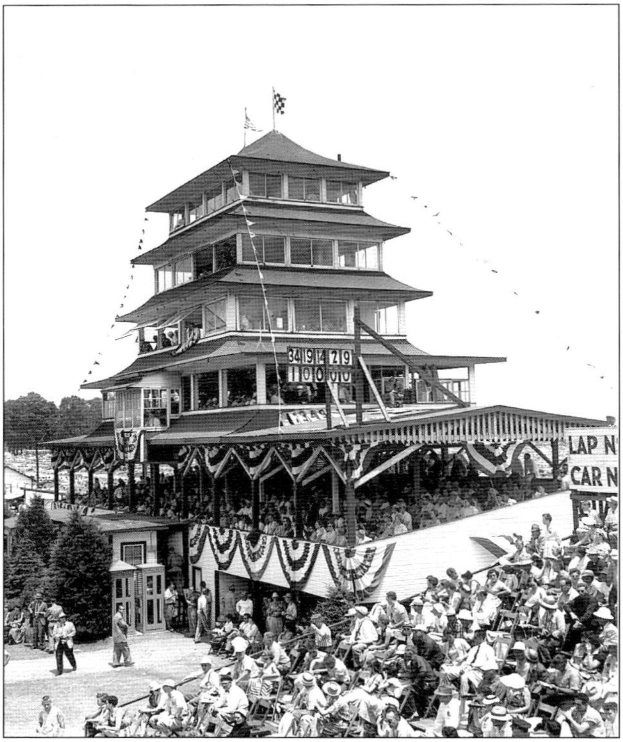

The pagoda of 1954 was built in 1926, but windows that opened and closed were added. In 1956 this pagoda was replaced by the Master Control Tower, in use from 1956 to 1996. Today the 10-story control tower is the landmark of the Speedway.

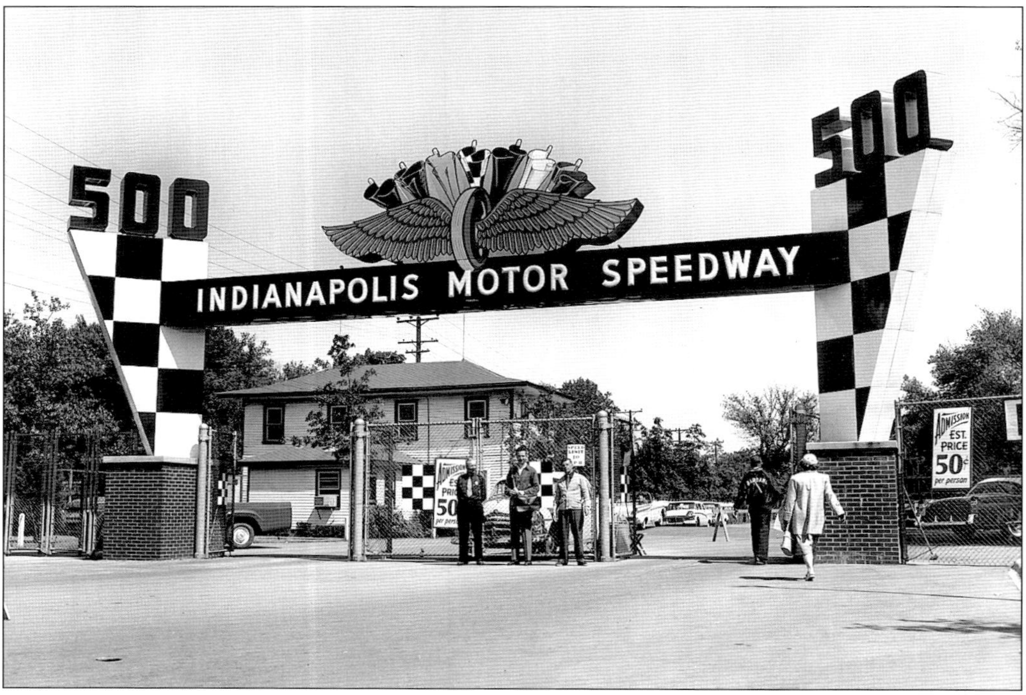

Visitors to the Indianapolis Motor Speedway in 1958 were greeted with the winged tire and flags logo that has become famous in automobile racing. Admission was only 50 cents.

Two

Race Fans

Race fans pour into Speedway, Indiana, from all over the world to watch the "Greatest Spectacle in Racing" every May. The Memorial Day weekend Indianapolis 500 is still the biggest draw for the fans, but Nascar's Brickyard 400 has its own loyal following that grows every year.

The residents of Speedway welcome the fans with open arms, and often open yards, as they park thousands of cars in the front and back yards of their homes. Many fans return year after year to the same houses for parking and friendship. Long-term associations have been formed across the country and around the world with Speedway residents who have shared their homes with the race fans.

The tradition of entertaining race fans goes back to the very beginning of the town's history. In fact, race teams stayed in the homes of Speedway natives for many years. People around the town are happy to tell tales of the race car drivers and teams who would return year after year to sleep in their guest rooms. When Speedway was a small town, miles from Indianapolis, hotels and accommodations were hard to come by.

Perhaps this generous sharing of their town is what makes the people of Speedway such friendly and kind neighbors.

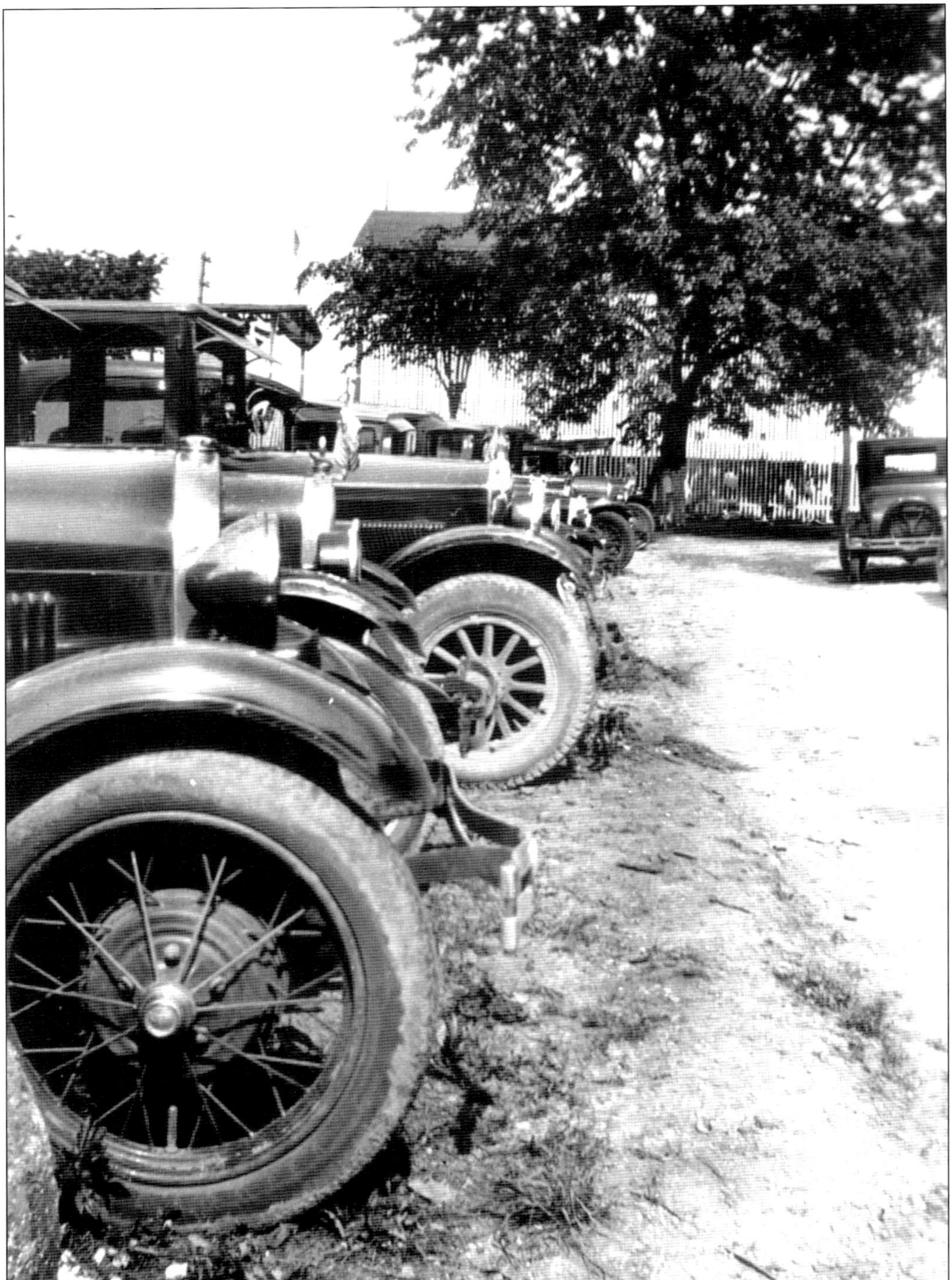

Race day parking is an old and honored tradition for the people of Speedway. Many families from the very early days have boosted their incomes by parking cars in the yards of their homes. (Courtesy of the Eppen Family.)

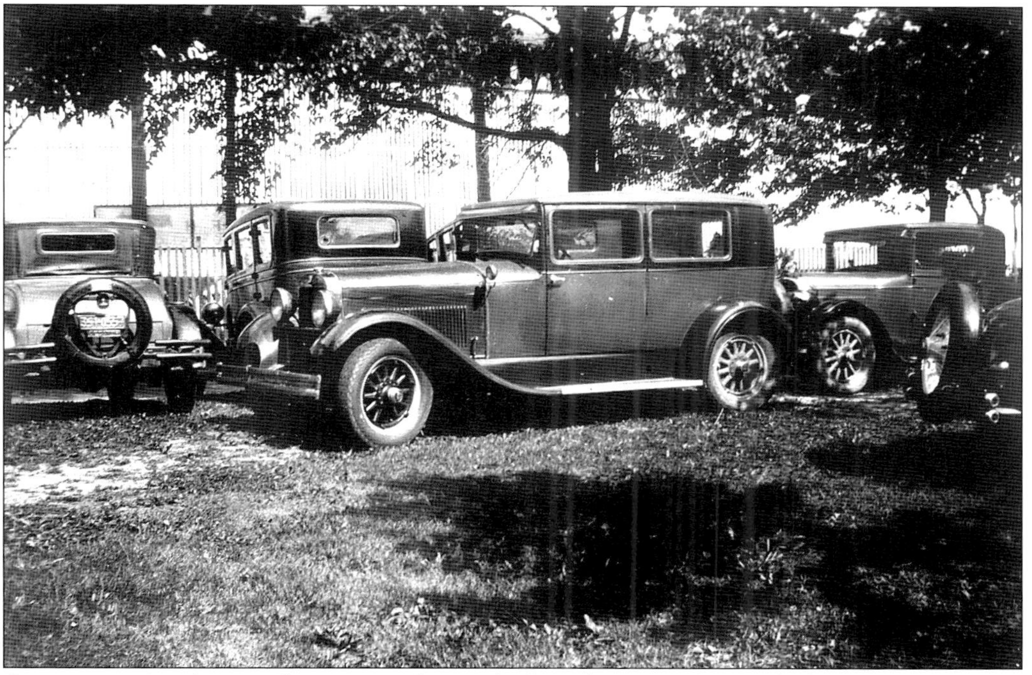

Georgetown Road was still a country dirt road when these race fans parked at the Eppen farm. Notice the white fence that used to run behind the track. (Courtesy of the Eppen Family.)

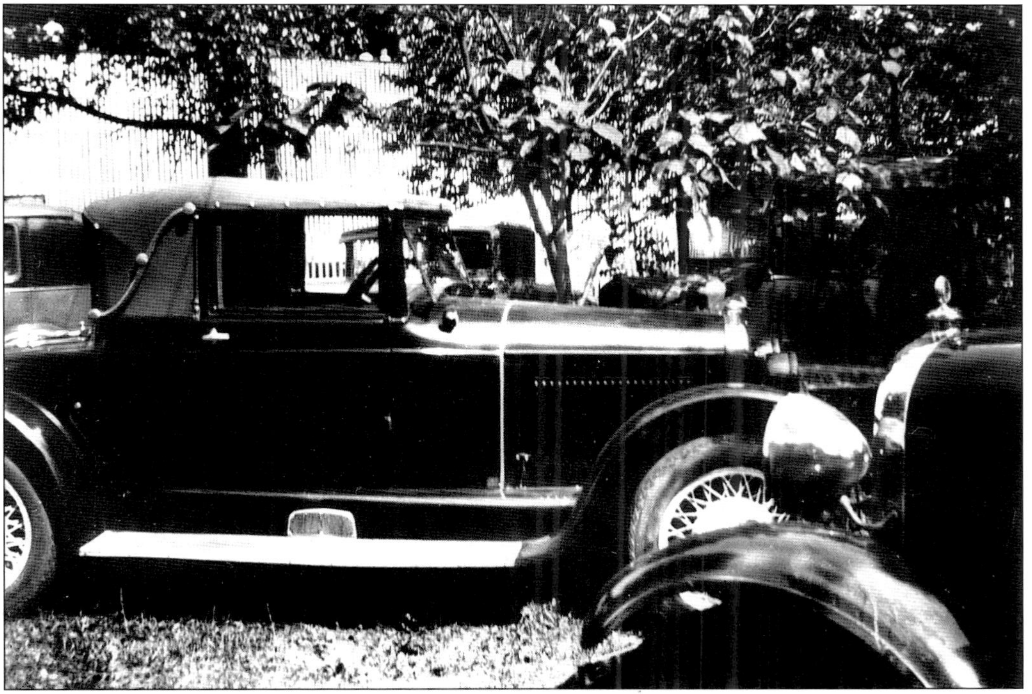

Parking on race day was 50 cents when these fans parked in the early days of the race. (Courtesy of the Eppen Family.)

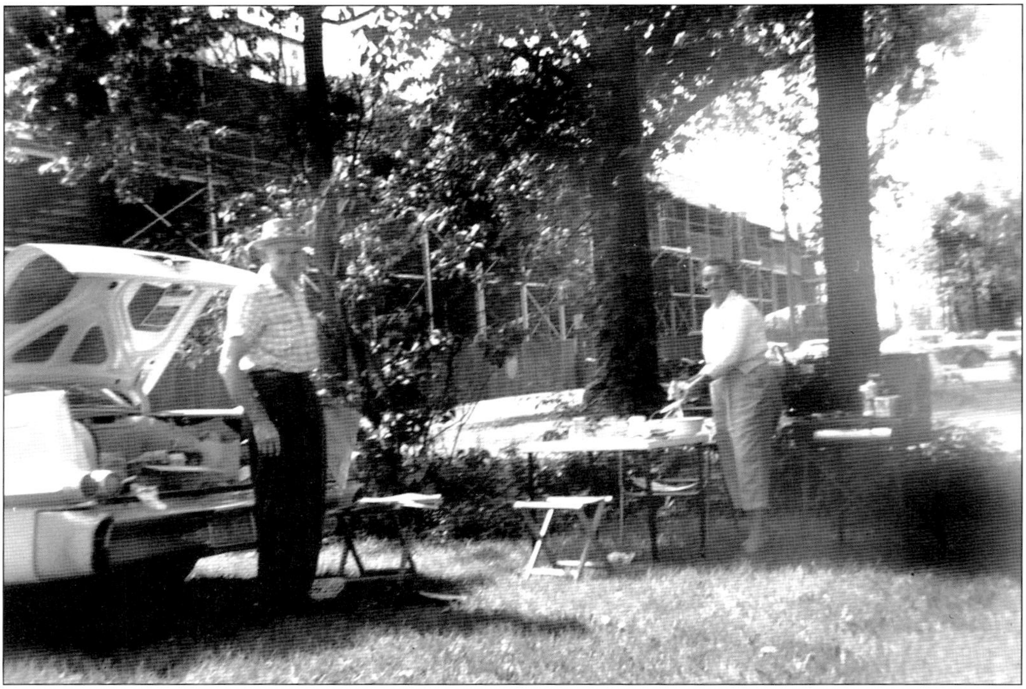

Tailgating is nothing new to Indianapolis 500 fans. Here race fans enjoy the pre- and post-race tradition from the trunk of their car along Georgetown Road. (Courtesy of the Eppen Family.)

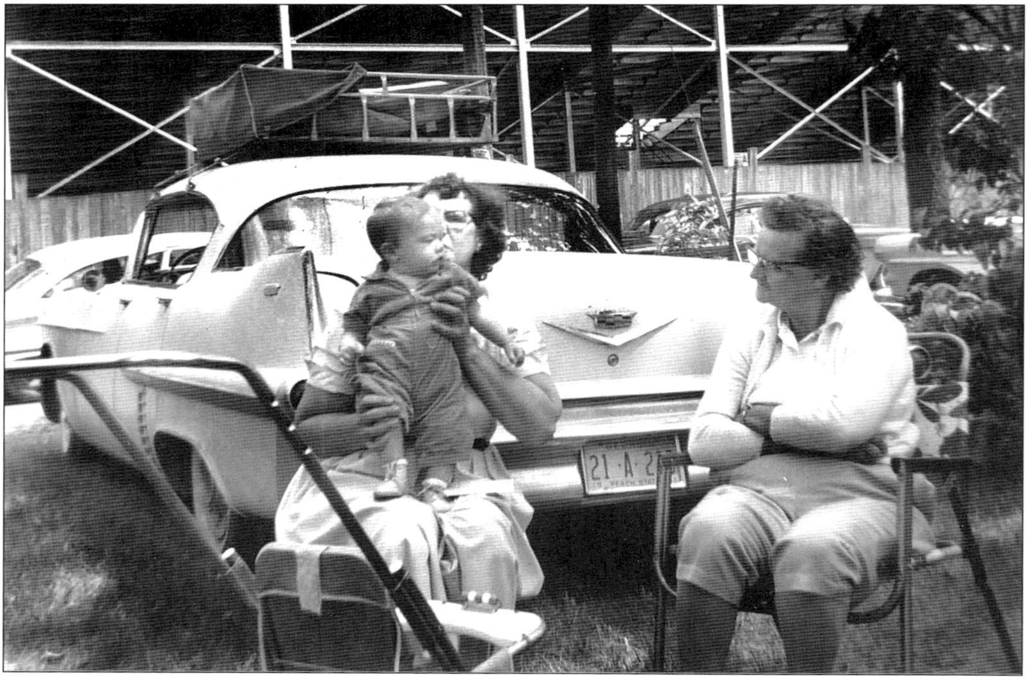

Young and old fans hang out during the month of May in Speedway. (Courtesy of the Eppen Family.)

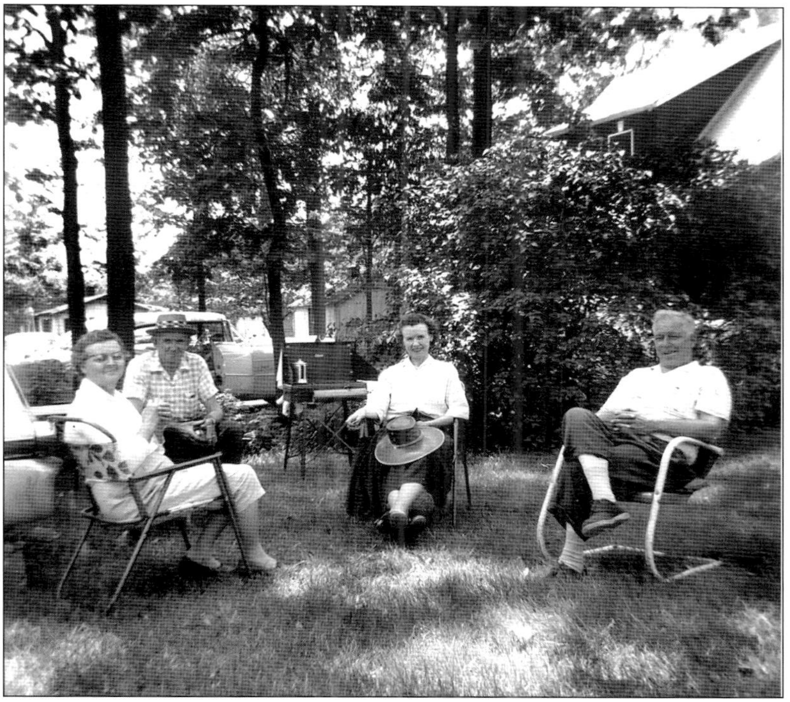

The location of the Eppen home across from the Indianapolis Motor Speedway made it a popular place for parking and parties. (Courtesy of the Eppen Family.)

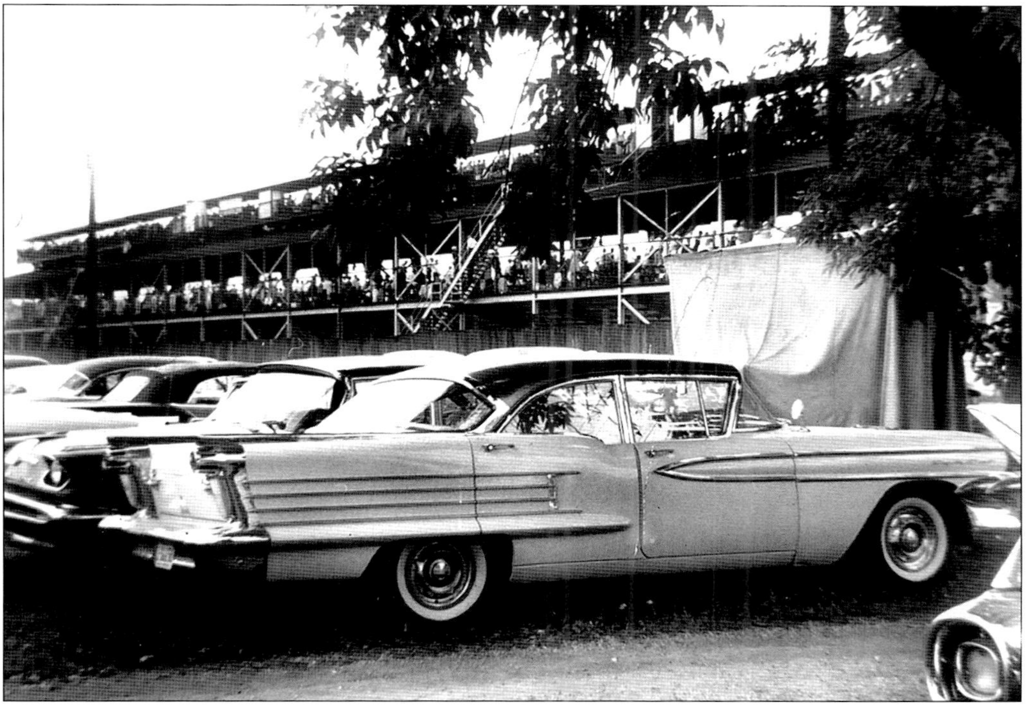

Tents popped up from time to time for race fans who spent the night before the race. Many fans would sleep in cars to have a chance to get into the track early on race morning. (Courtesy of the Eppen Family.)

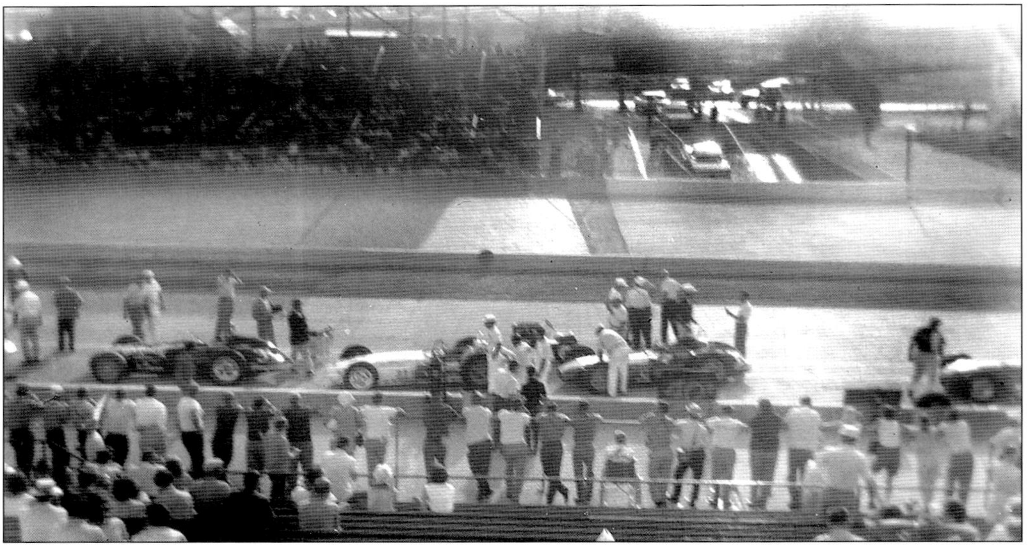

Race fans watch as cars are readied in preparation for the 1960 Indianapolis 500. (Courtesy of the Eppen Family.)

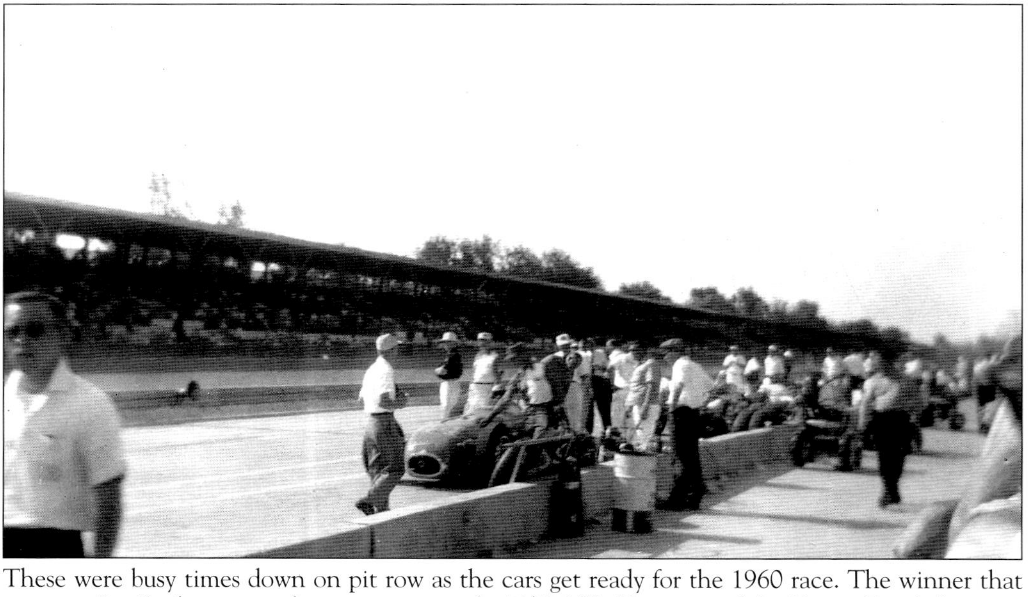

These were busy times down on pit row as the cars get ready for the 1960 race. The winner that year was Jim Rathmann with a winning speed of 138.767. (Courtesy of the Eppen Family.)

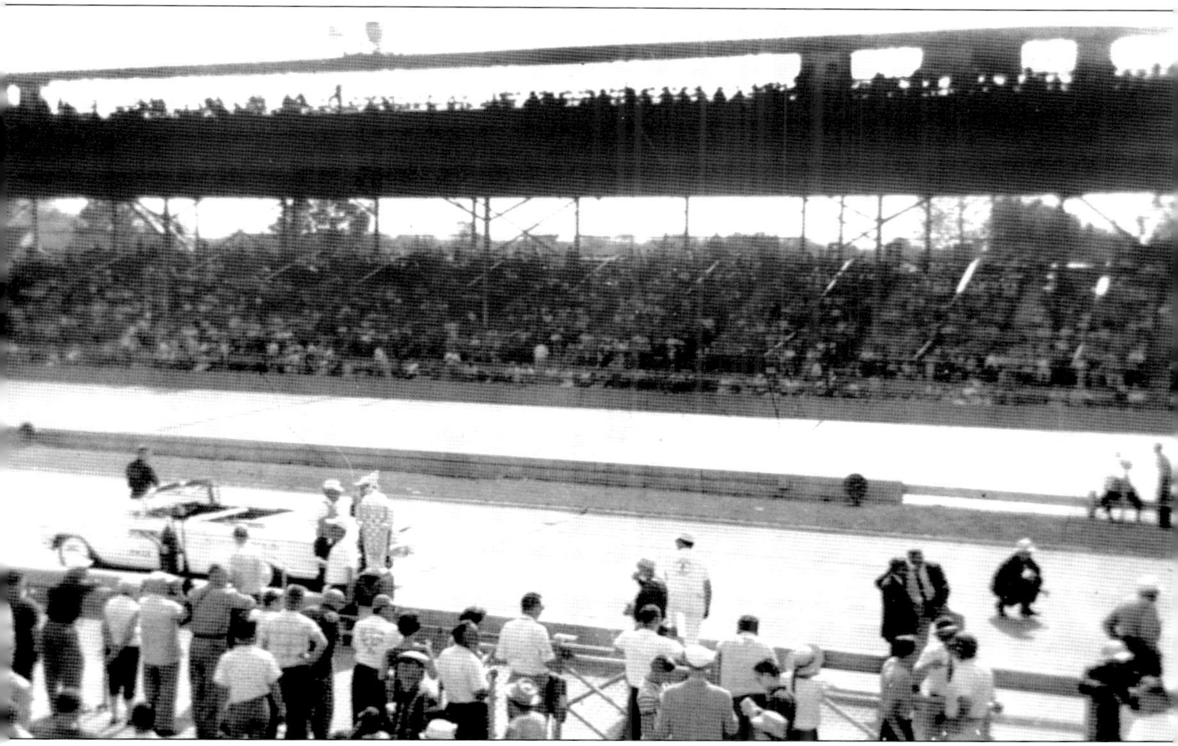

Fans and track officials take a look at the 1960 Oldsmobile convertible pace car. (Courtesy of the Eppen Family.)

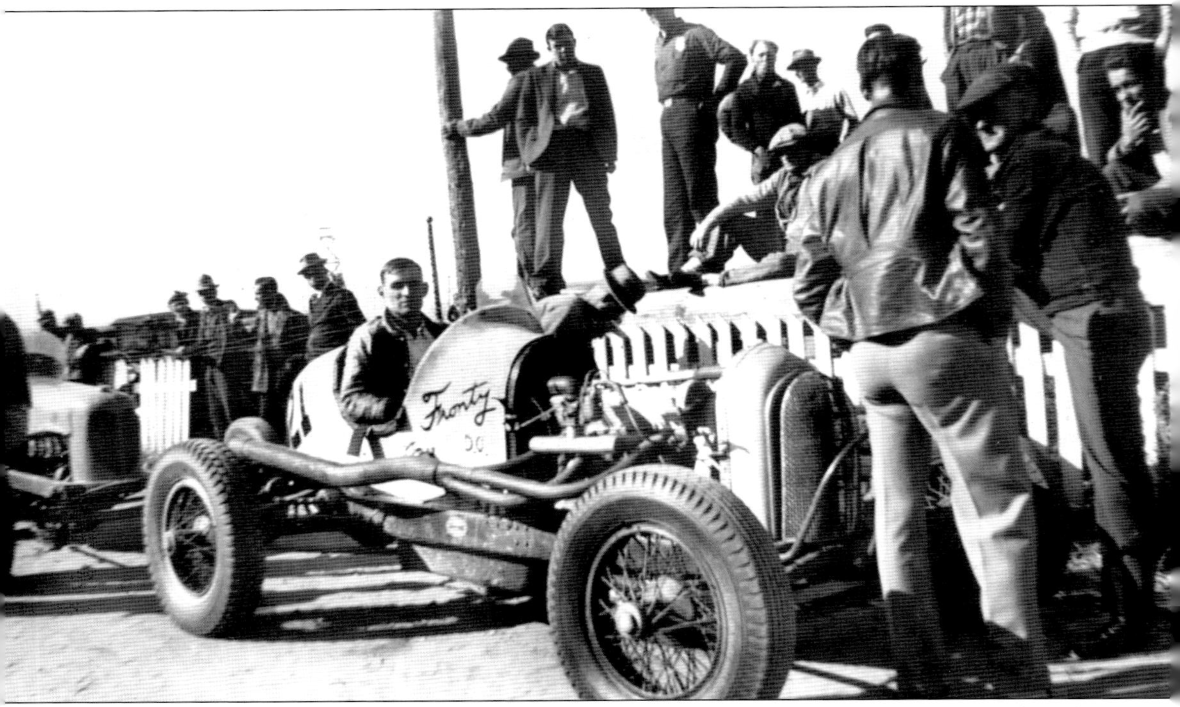

Racing was not restricted to the Indianapolis Motor Speedway in Indiana. Race fans from Speedway would go to outlying towns to watch "wildcat" races at small tracks. Ernest Eppen and his brother watch as fans look over a racer. (Courtesy of the Eppen Family.)

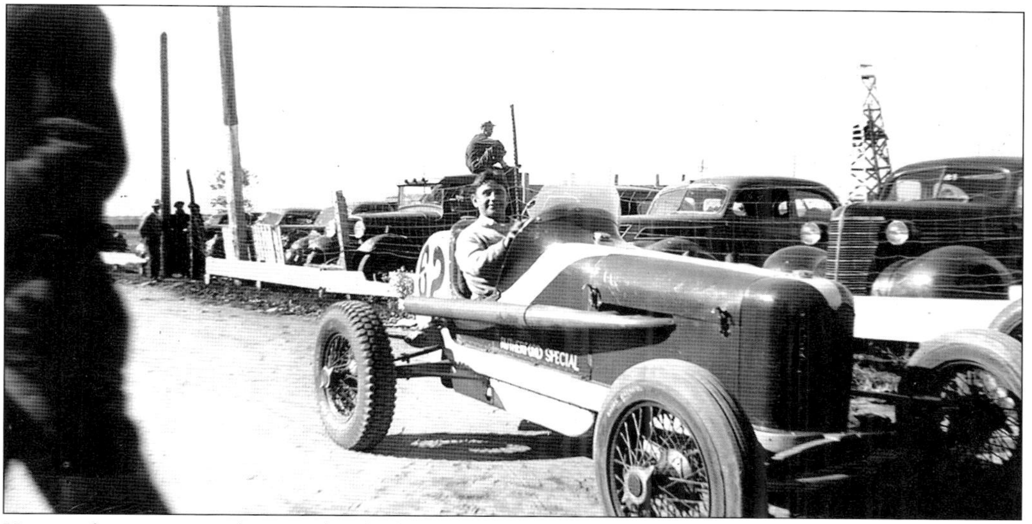

Here a driver sits in the "Rutherford Special" while awaiting the beginning of a wildcat race. (Courtesy of the Eppen Family.)

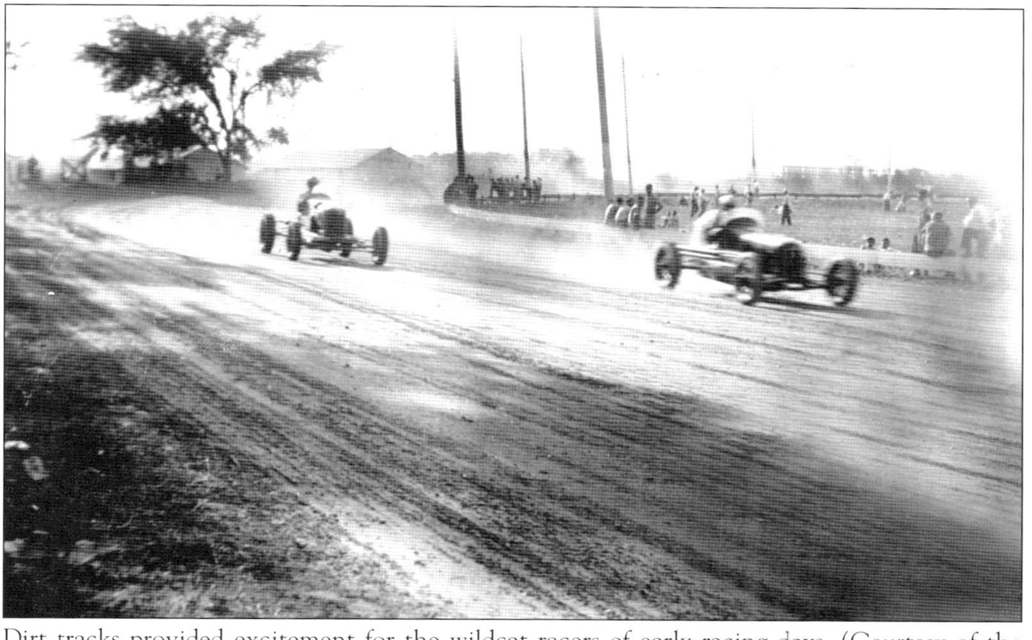

Dirt tracks provided excitement for the wildcat racers of early racing days. (Courtesy of the Eppen Family.)

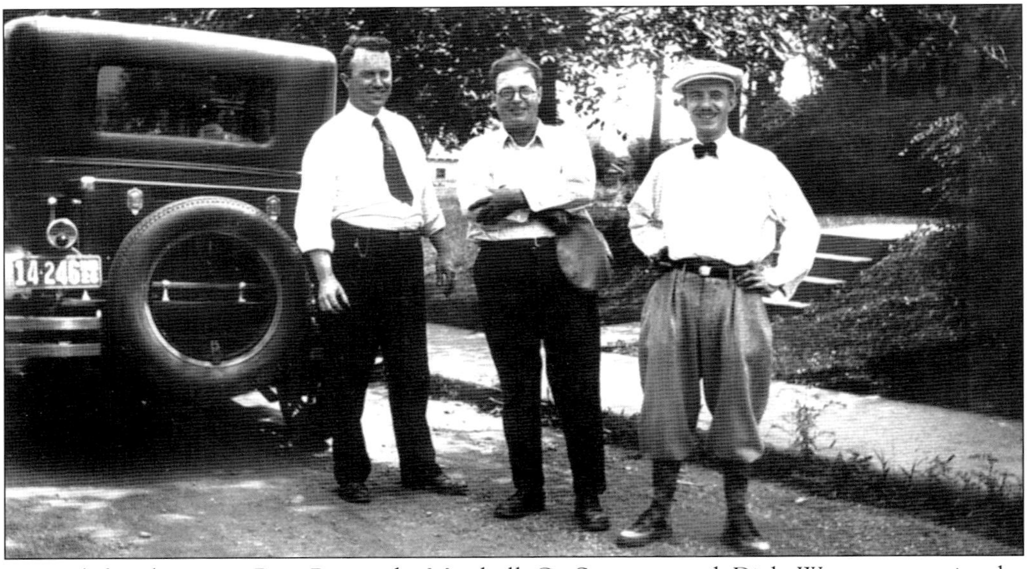

Dressed for the race, Rex Bostwick, Marshall G. Spencer, and Dick Wagner pose in the appropriate dress to attend the Indianapolis 500 in 1929. (Courtesy of Edith Spencer.)

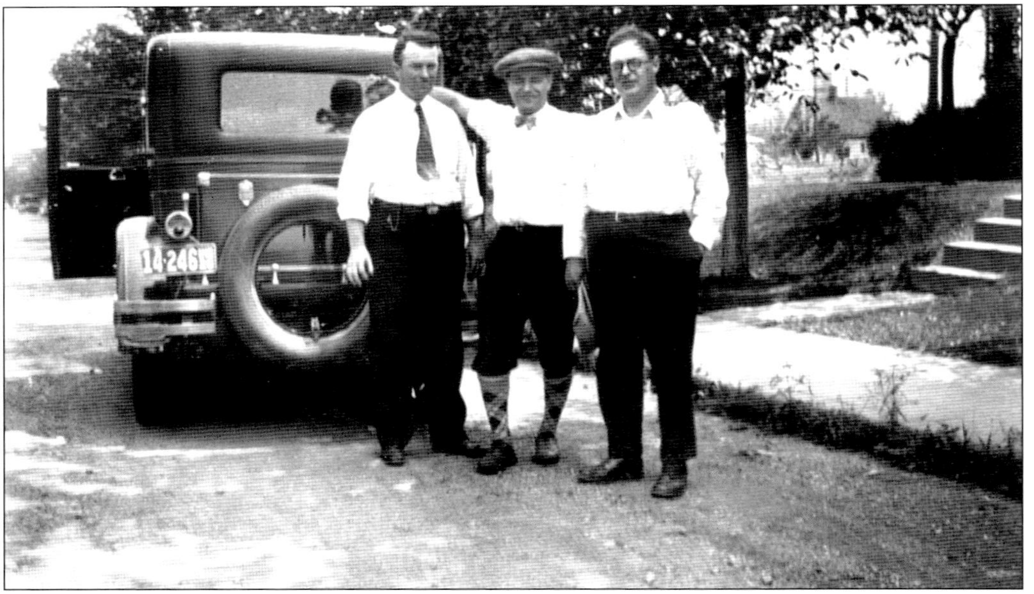

Before the start of the 1929 Indianapolis 500, these fans posed together on 14th Street. Pictured are Rex Bostwick, John Brant, and Marshall Spencer. (Courtesy of Edith Spencer.)

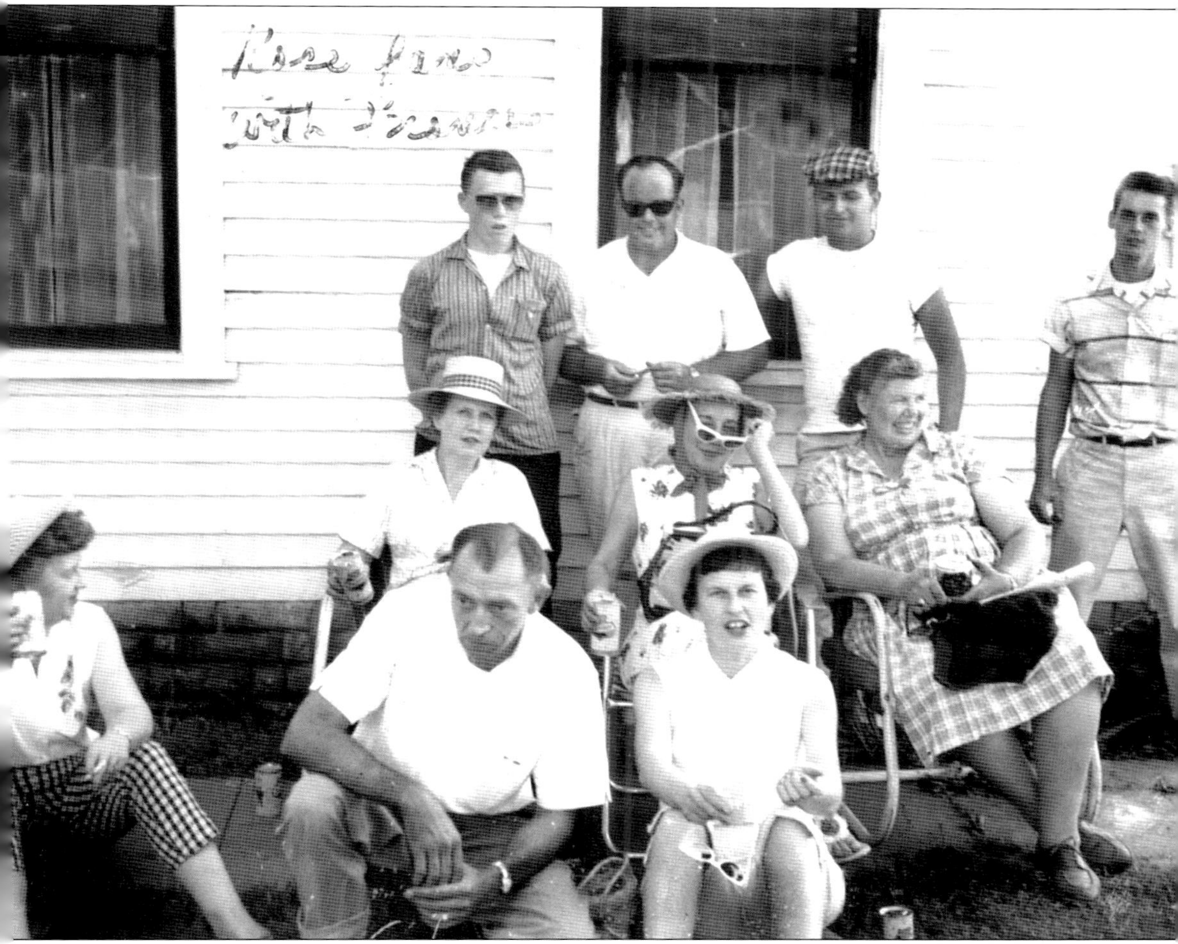

Annual visitors are dressed for the Indianapolis 500 as they pose here with Francis Eppen. (Courtesy of the Eppen Family.)

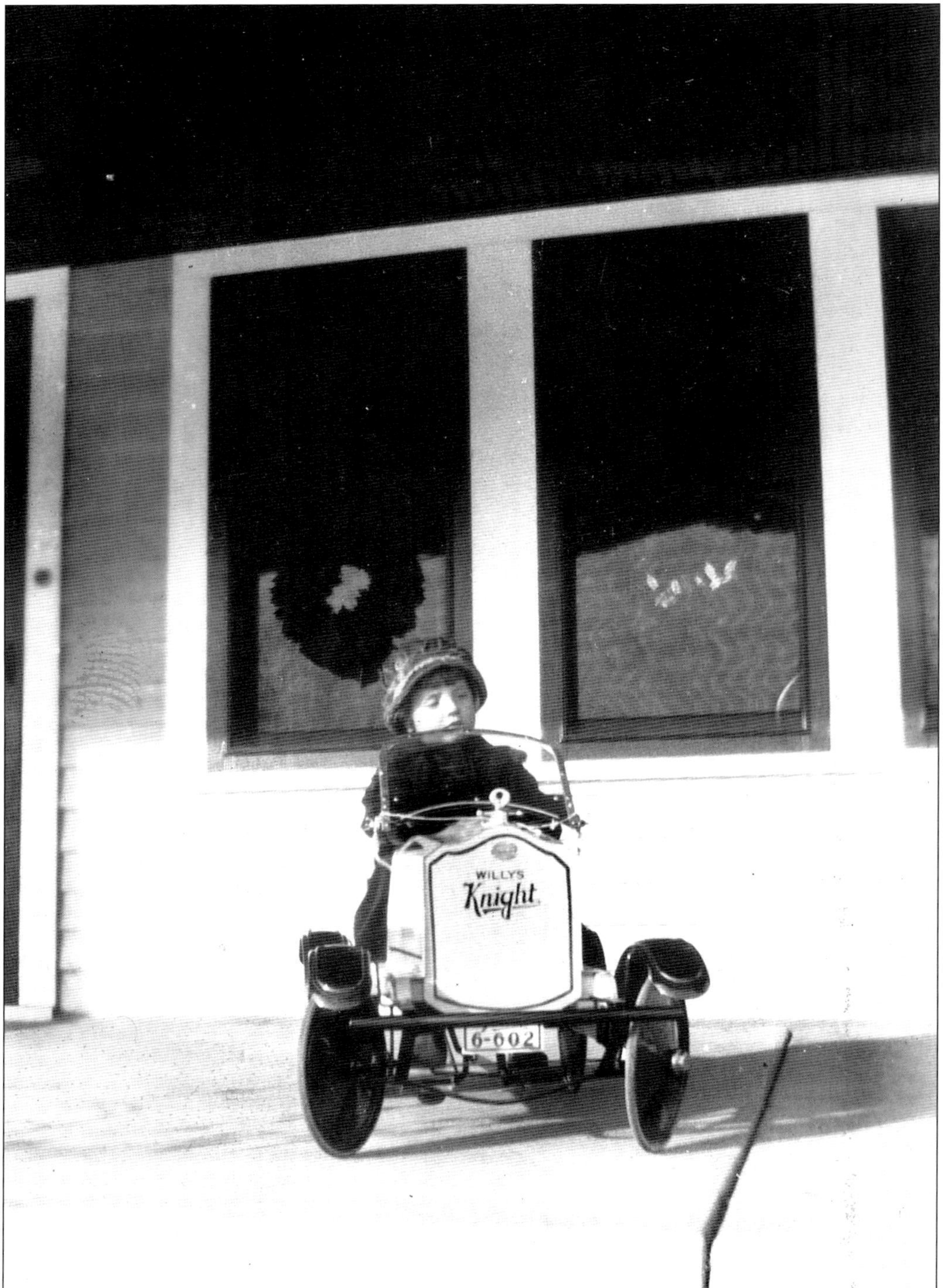

Racing fans start young in Speedway. Here, Edith Spencer enjoys her toy model of the 1924 Willys Knight on the porch of her home on 10th Street. (Courtesy of Edith Spencer.)

Three

THE TOWN AROUND THE TRACK

You have only to read the street names in the town of Speedway in order to get a sense of the history of the area. Names of people like Allison and Fisher, along with names of automobiles such as Cord, Winton, and Auburn remind the residents that their city was a dream built by men obsessed with automobiles and industry.

The building boom after WW II brought with it a housing addition that has streets named for American generals. Veterans came home from the war and used the GI bill to buy houses on Patton, Eisenhower, and MacArthur.

The town was dreamed of by Carl Fisher as a "horseless city...devoted to motorization of all traffic...the homes would be homes and not the kind of shacks that usually infest an industrial center." The town was platted by Lem Trotter, and the people worked in factories nearby while enjoying the pleasantries of small-town life.

Linked by the Ben Hur line interurban to Indianapolis and Crawfordsville, Speedway was a convenient stop for race fans and workers. But long after the interurban station across from the track disappeared, and the trains were replaced by automobiles, the people of Speedway still enjoy talking over the backyard fence and the small-town feel of their neighborhoods. The town of Speedway may be surrounded by the sprawling city of Indianapolis, but the identity of Carl Fisher's dream town still remains intact.

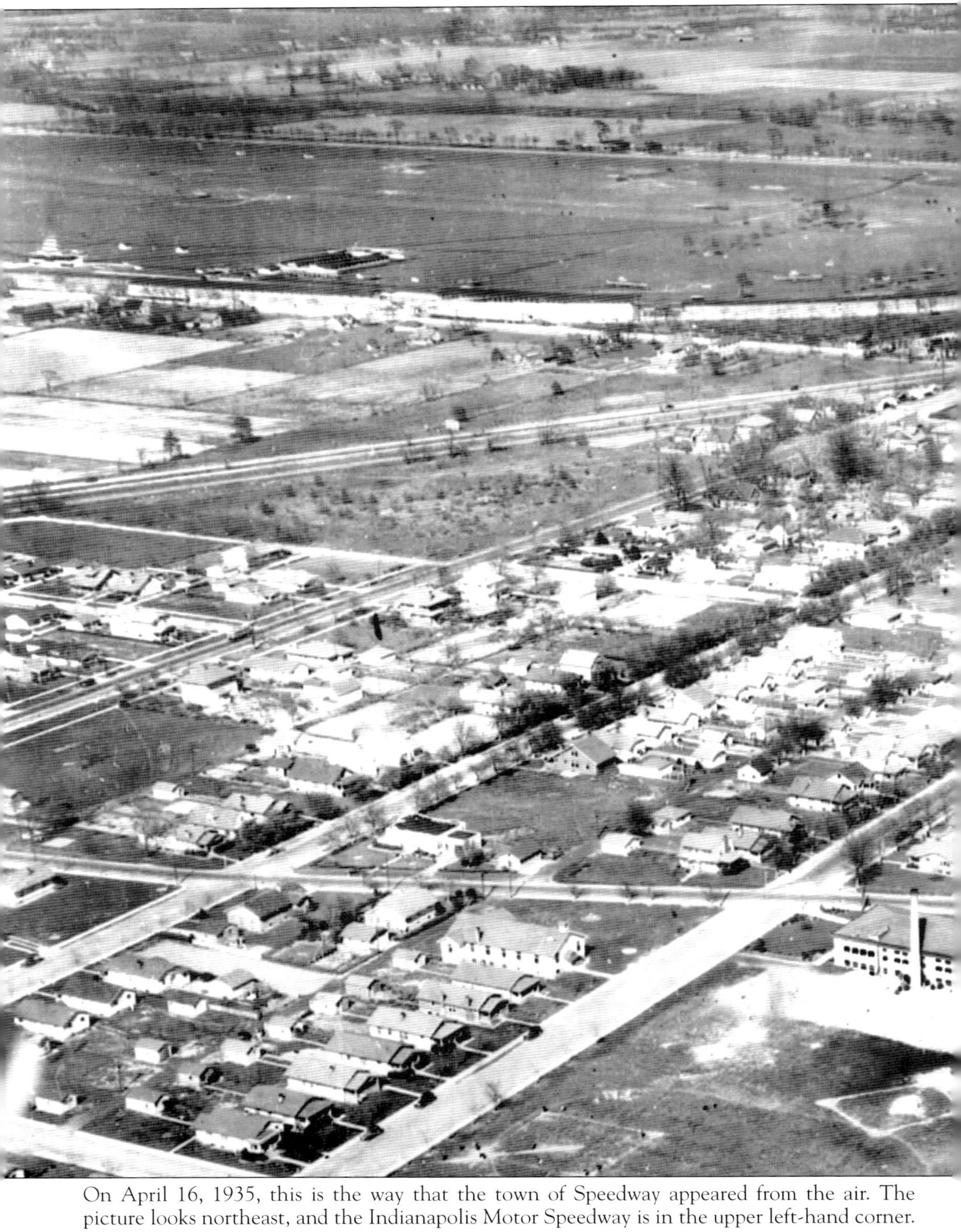

On April 16, 1935, this is the way that the town of Speedway appeared from the air. The picture looks northeast, and the Indianapolis Motor Speedway is in the upper left-hand corner.

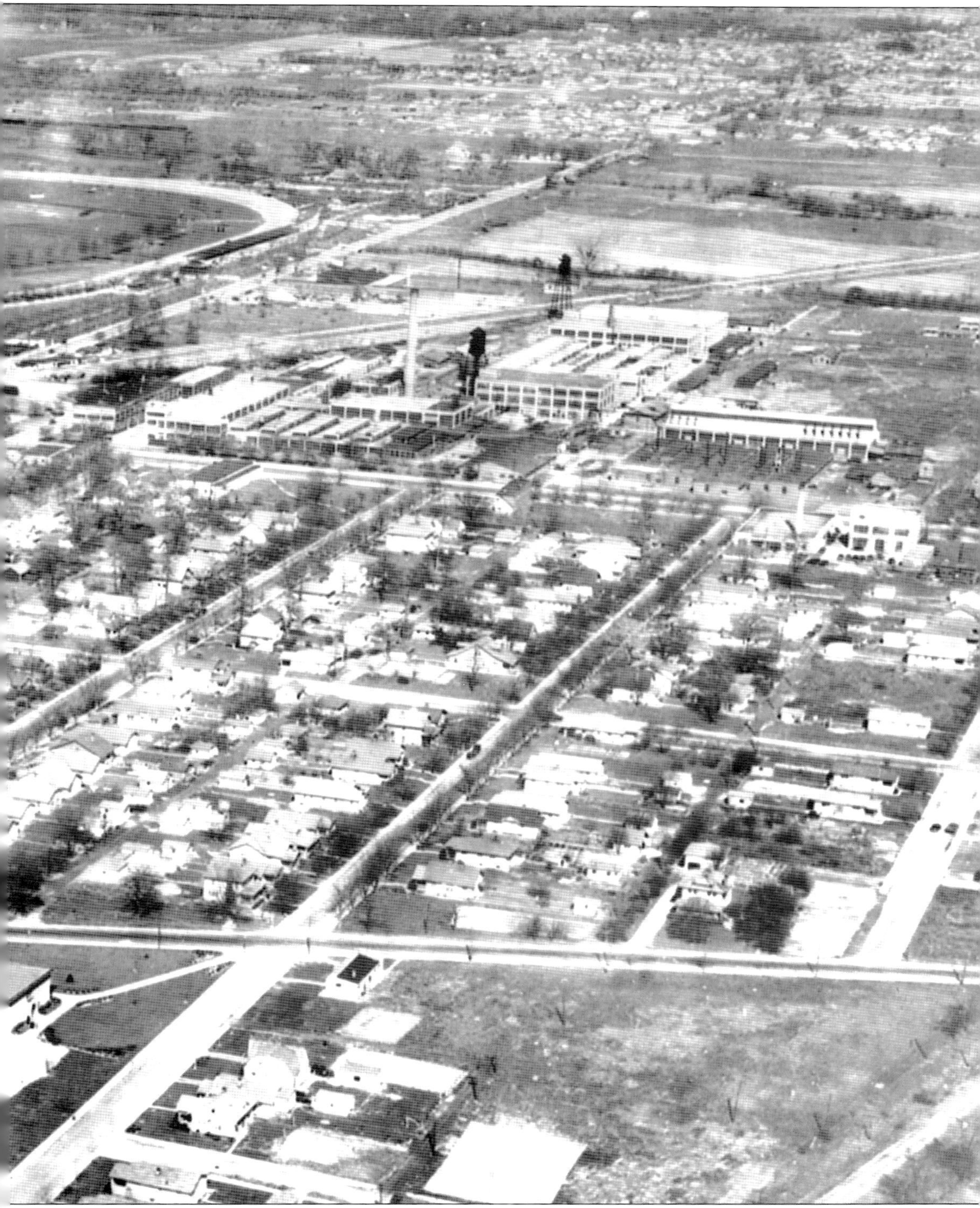

The factories of Speedway are upper right. In the foreground is the Speedway School. The residential area is the original "horseless town." (Courtesy of Elizabeth Frazier.)

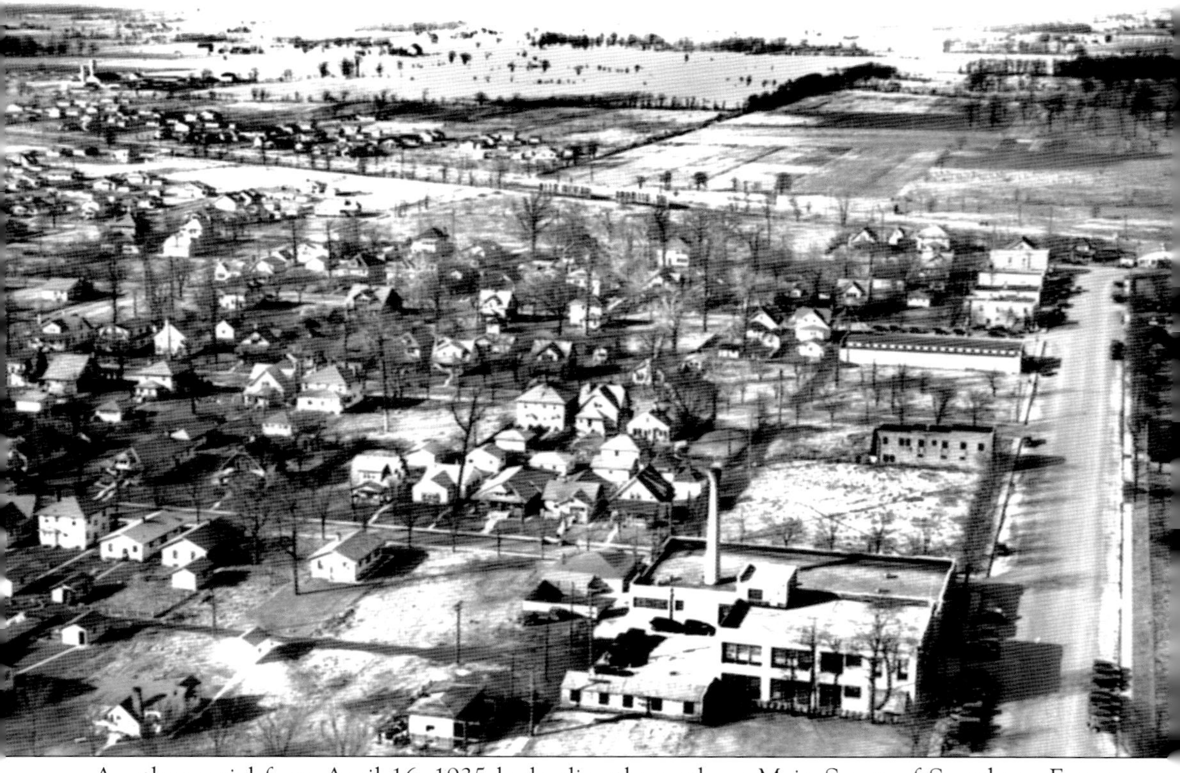

Another aerial from April 16, 1935 looks directly north up Main Street of Speedway. Farms stretching north gave way to housing divisions as the town grew rapidly after WW II. (Courtesy of Elizabeth Frazier.)

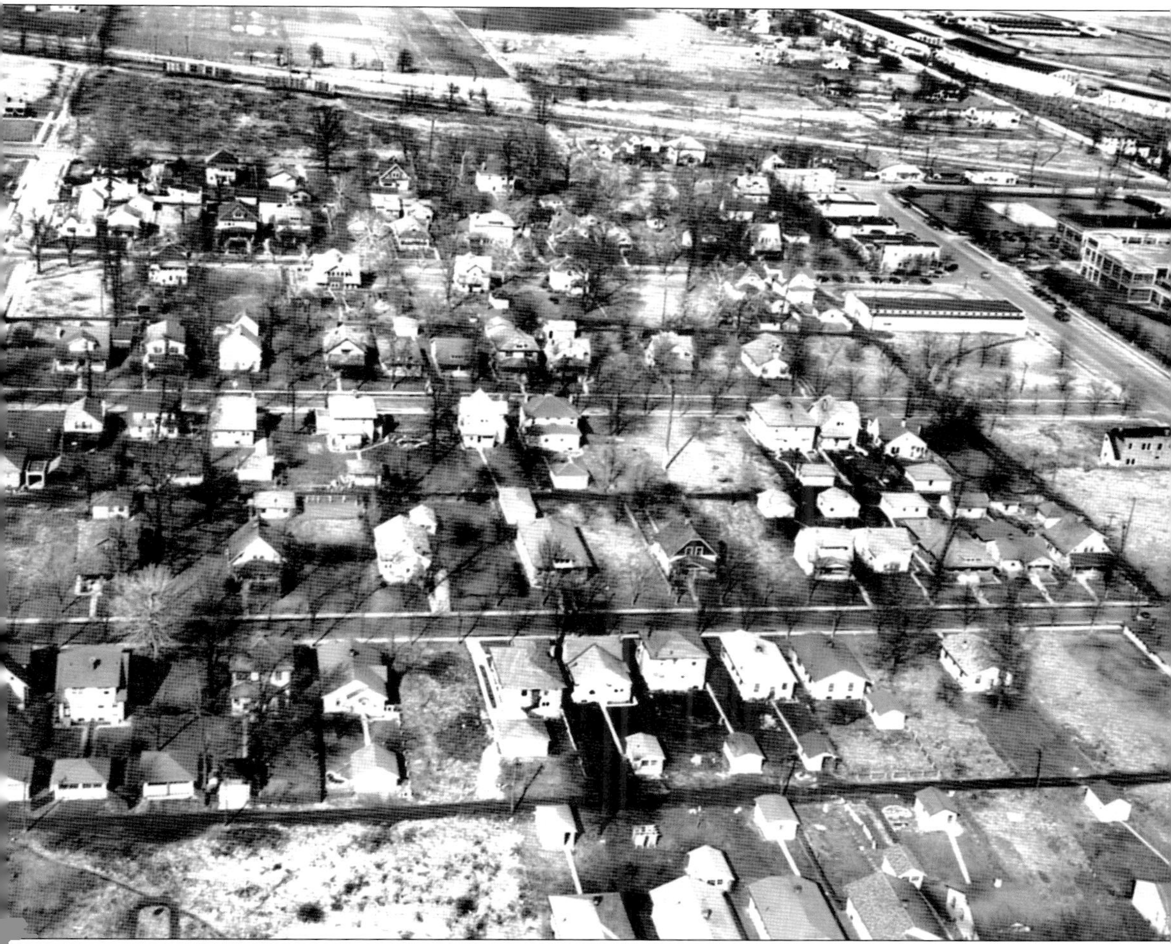

This aerial looks north, showing a corner of the Indianapolis Motor Speedway in the upper right-hand corner. The neighborhood was designed with garages on alleys. The empty lots soon filled in as the neighborhood grew. This section of Speedway became known as the Old Speedway Neighborhood. (Courtesy of Elizabeth Frazier.)

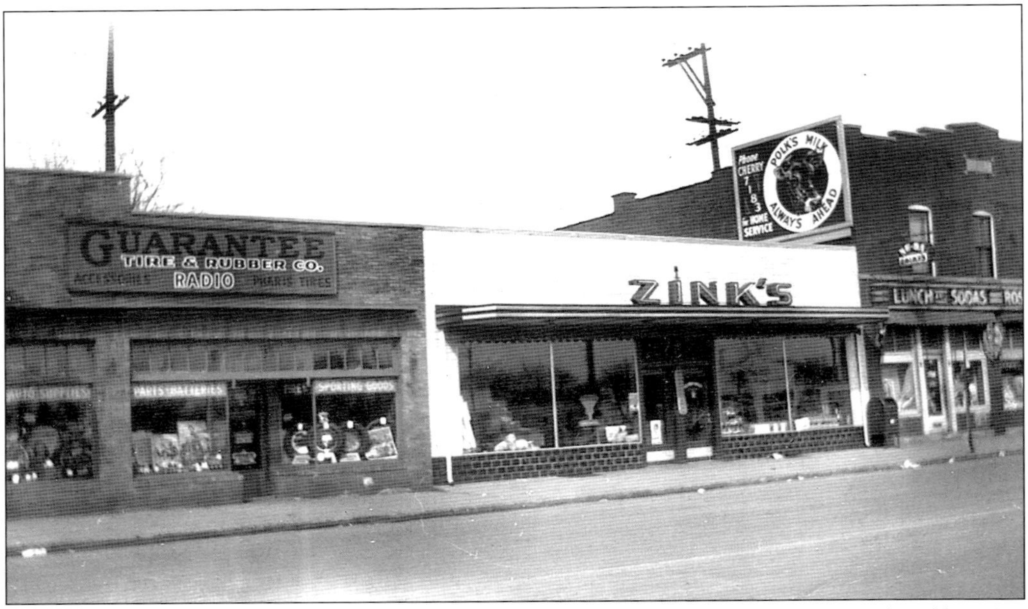

Rosner's Drug Store (far right), Zink's grocery store, and the Guarantee Tire and Rubber Co. were landmarks on Main Street in the 1940s. (Courtesy of Elizabeth Frazier.)

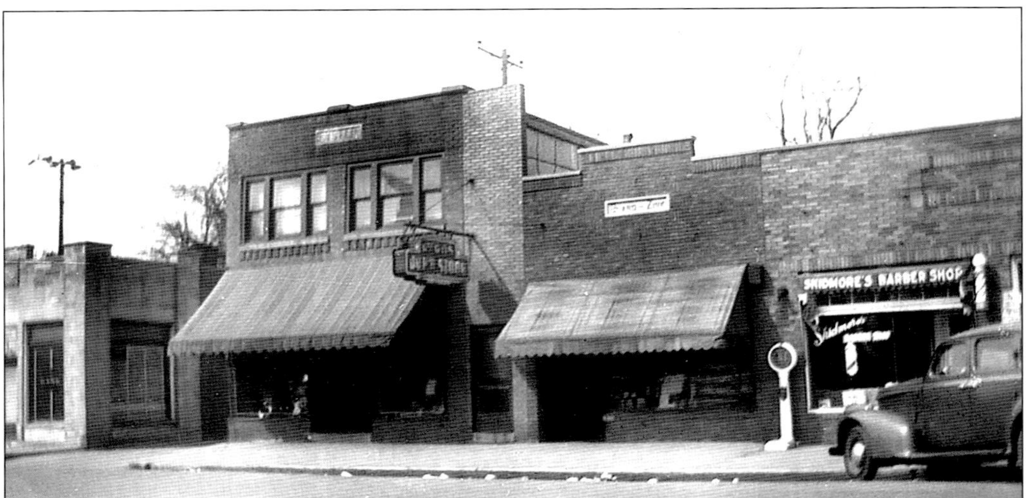

Skidmore's Barber Shop was a popular gathering place on Main Street. (Courtesy of Elizabeth Frazier.)

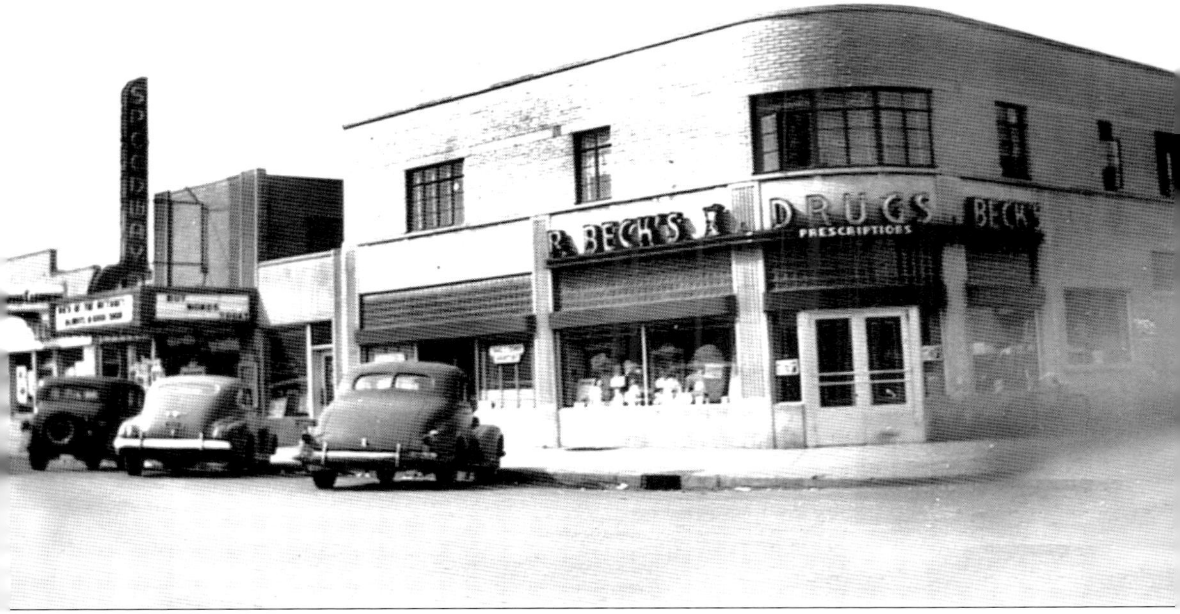

Beck's Drugs stood at the corner of 15th and Main Streets. The Speedway Theater became a fixture in town in 1937.

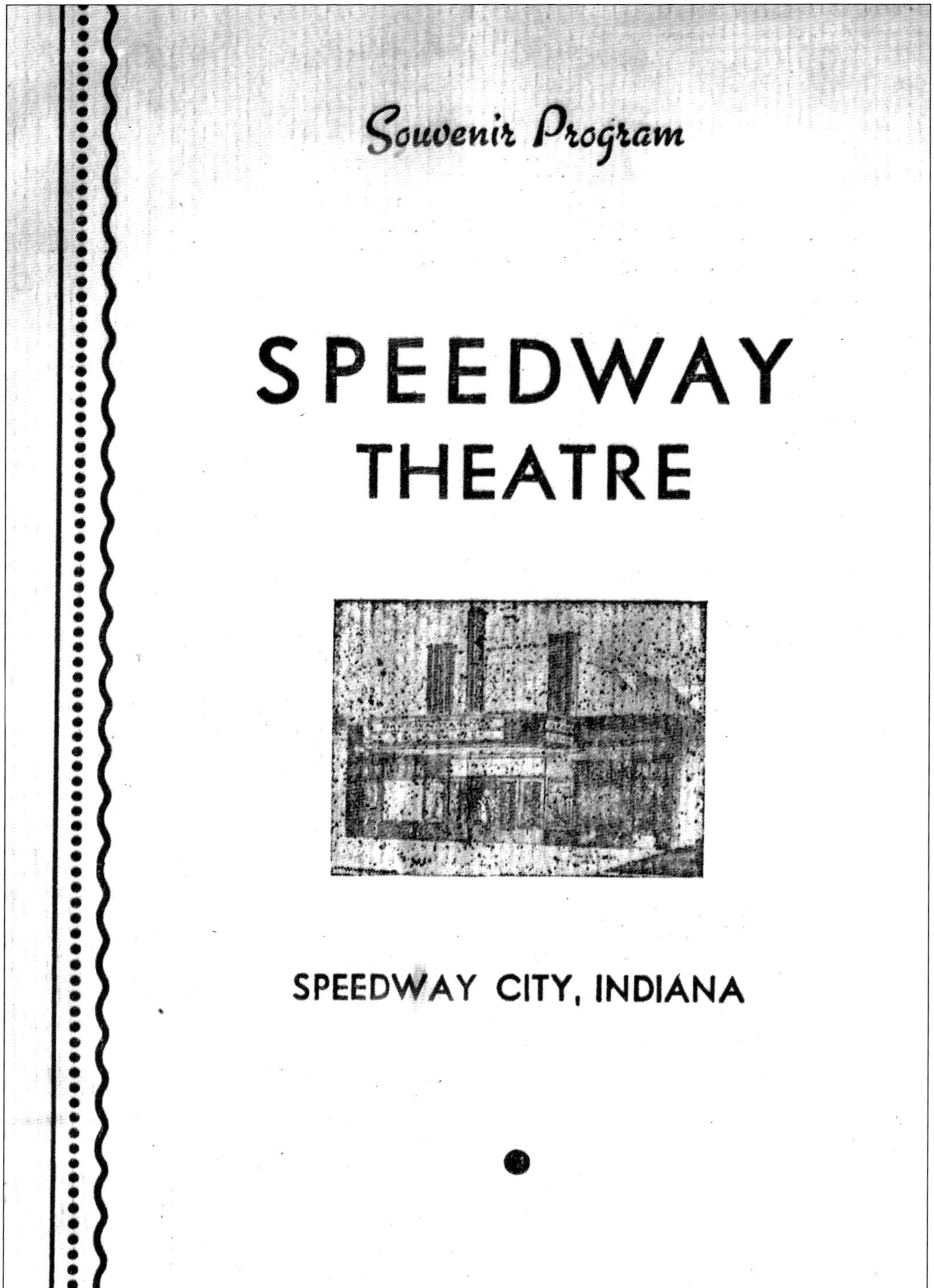

The souvenir program for the Speedway Theatre announced the current program for the eagerly awaited movie house in growing Speedway City. (Courtesy of Elizabeth Frazier.)

SPEEDWAY
• THEATRE •

MAIN STREET at 15th   SPEEDWAY CITY, IND.

PROGRAM

Tues., Wed. **Oct. 12—13**

MARION DAVIES — ROBERT MONTGOMERY *in*

EVER SINCE EVE

and

GLENDA FARRELL — BARTON MacLANE *in*

FLY AWAY BABY

SELECT SHORT SUBJECTS

Thurs , Fri. **Oct 14—15**

JEAN ARTHUR — EDWARD ARNOLD *in*

EASY LIVING

and

WALTER CONNOLY — JEAN HERVEY *in*

The LEAGUE of FRIGHTENED MEN

SELECTED SHORTS AND NEWS REEL

Saturday **October 16**

JACK OAKIE — ANN SOUTHERN *in*

SUPER SLEUTH

and

WILLIAM BOYD — JIMMY ELLISON *in*

BORDERLAND

CARTOON COMEDY

Sun., Mon. **Oct. 17—18**

JACK BENNY — GAIL PATRICK *in*

ARTISTS and MODELS

and

DOROTHY WILSON — CHAS. QUIGLEY *in*

SPEED TO SPARE

Tues., Wed. **Oct. 19—20**

WARREN WILLIAM — MADY CORNELL *in*

MIDNIGHT MADONNA

and

GEORGE BRENT — BEVERLY ROBERTS *in*

GOD'S COUNTRY and the WOMAN

Thurs., Fri. **Oct. 21—22**

EDWARD G. ROBINSON *in*

THUNDER IN THE CITY

and

JACQUILINE WELLS — PAUL KELLY *in*

The FRAME UP

PARAMOUNT NEWS

Saturday **October 23**

JACK HOLT — GRACE BRADLEY *in*

ROARING TIMBER

and

TEX RITTER (The Singing Cowboy) *in*

TROUBLE IN TEXAS

COMING SUNDAY -:- OCTOBER 24

GARRY COOPER -:- FRANCES DEE -:- GEORGE RAFT

in **SOULS AT SEA**

No doubt the lineup of movies coming to the Speedway Theatre caused excitement for the residents. Probably many of them flocked to see "Speed to Spare," a daring racing movie featuring a speedway and racing similar to what took place just down the street in real life. (Courtesy of Edith Spencer.)

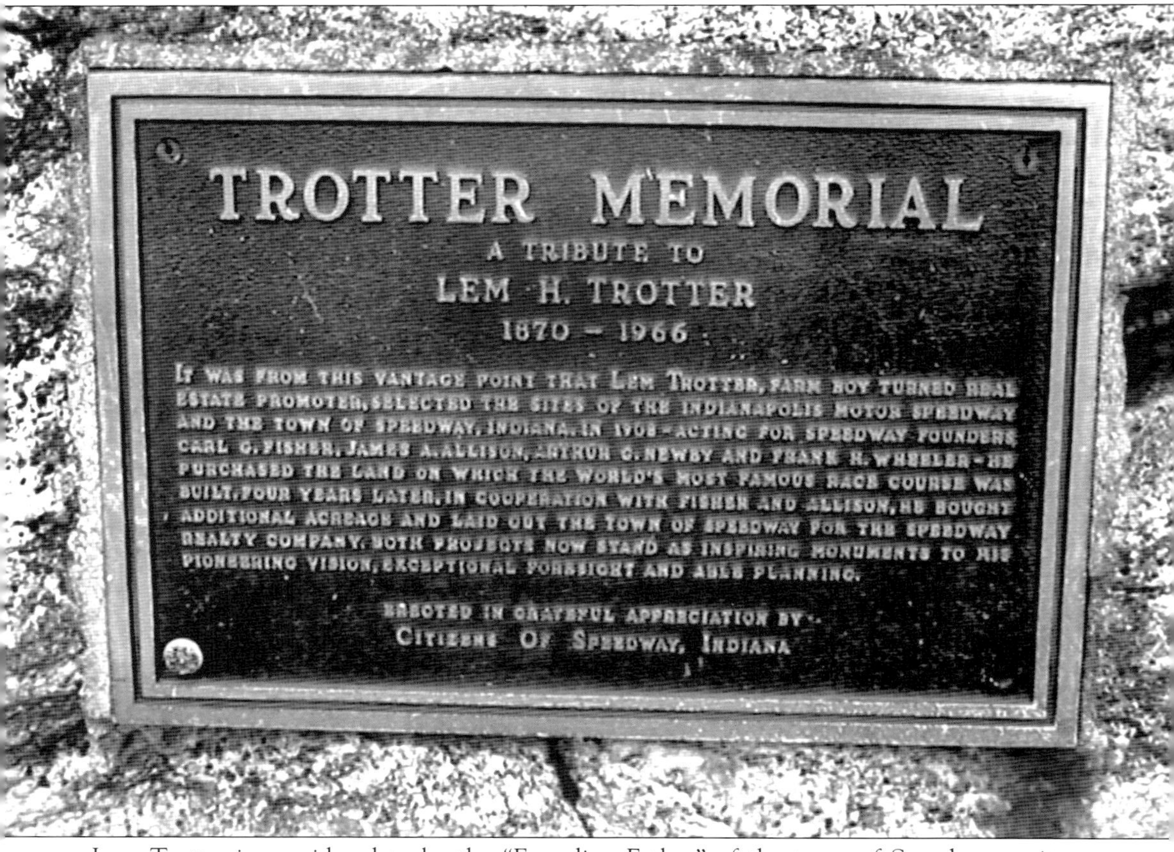

Lem Trotter is considered to be the "Founding Father" of the town of Speedway as it now stands. Born in Danville, Indiana, on February 15, 1870, he became the real estate genius who selected the property for the future Indianapolis Motor Speedway and the "horseless" town of Speedway. (Courtesy of Don Katterhenry.)

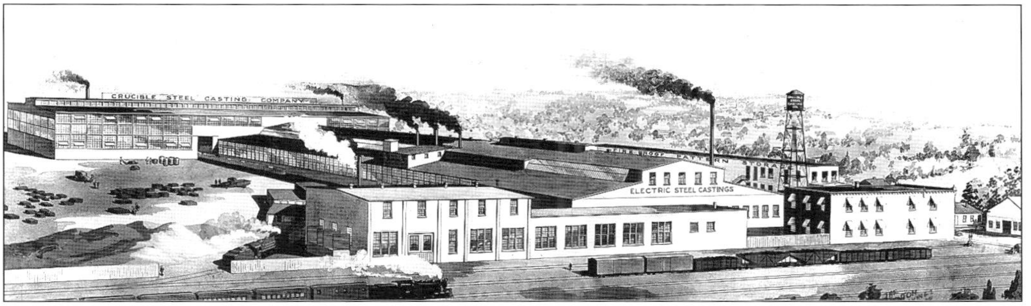

This photograph shows an artist's rendering of the layout of Electric Steel Castings Company. The picture was distributed by the Canton Engraving Company of Canton, Ohio. (Courtesy of Edith Spencer.)

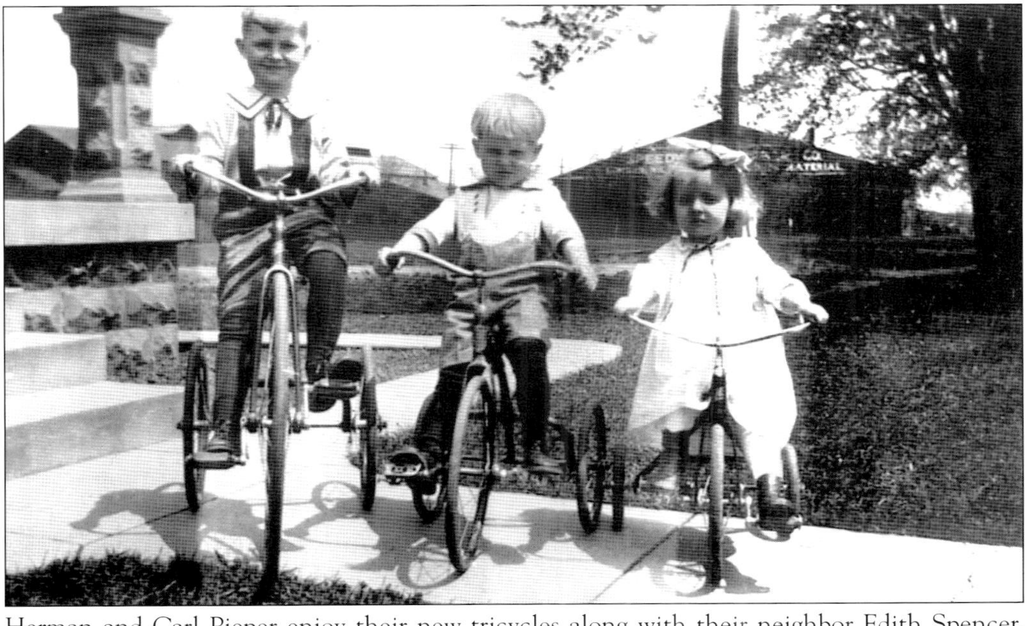

Herman and Carl Pieper enjoy their new tricycles along with their neighbor Edith Spencer. (Courtesy of Carl Pieper.)

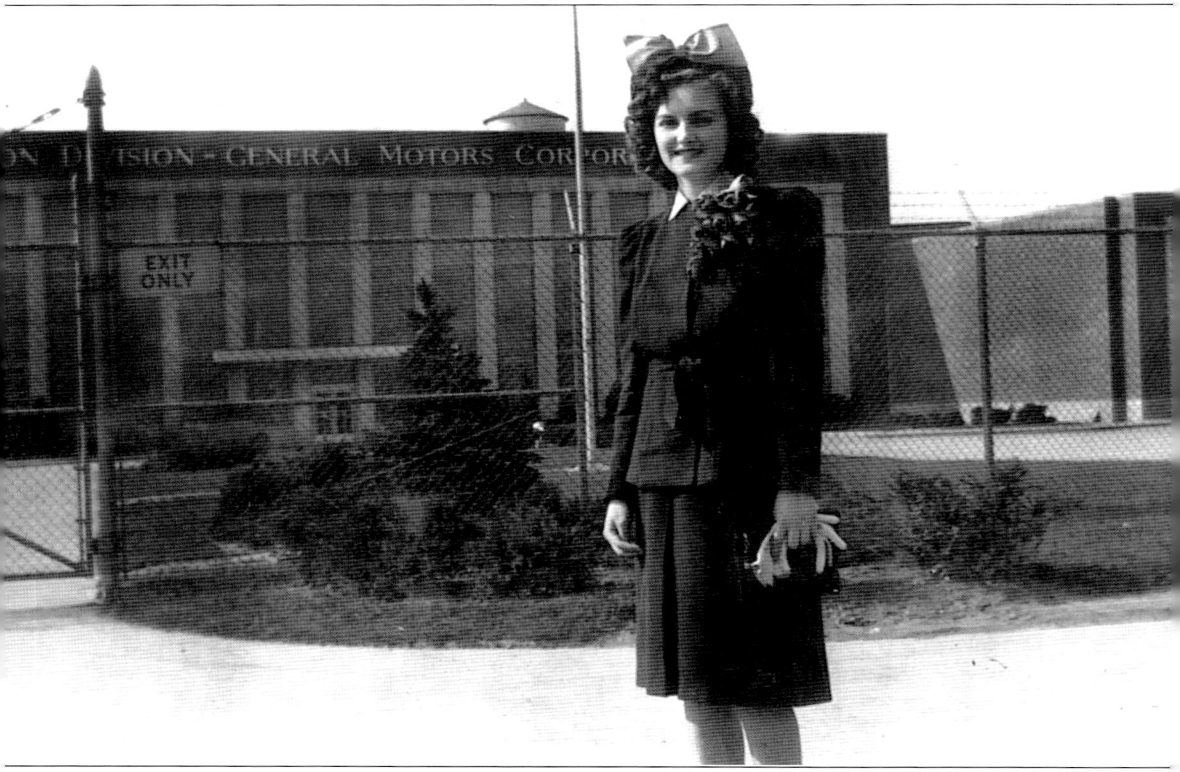

During the 1940s, the Allison Division of General Motors Corporation played an important role in the winning of WW II through its production of aircraft engines. In this picture Rosemary Pieper poses in the latest fashions of the day. (Courtesy of Carl Pieper.)

Agnes Spencer, long-time teacher in the Speedway schools, poses with her younger sister Edith in this picture taken on 14th Street. (Courtesy of Edith Spencer.)

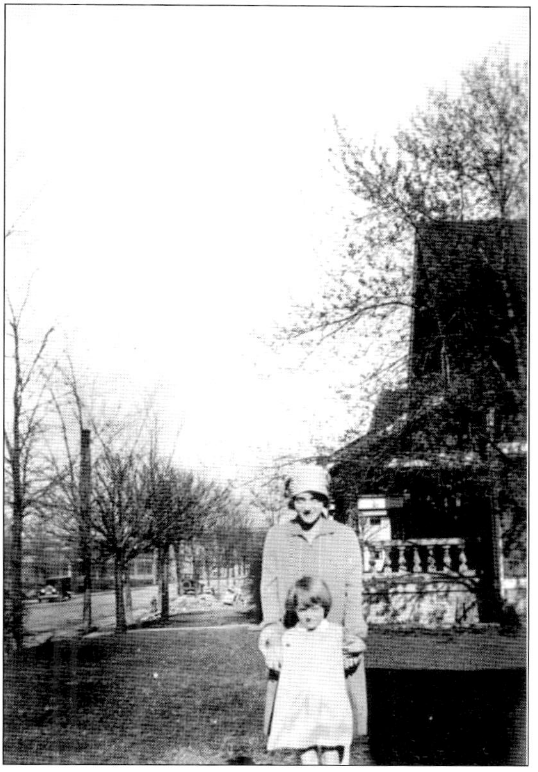

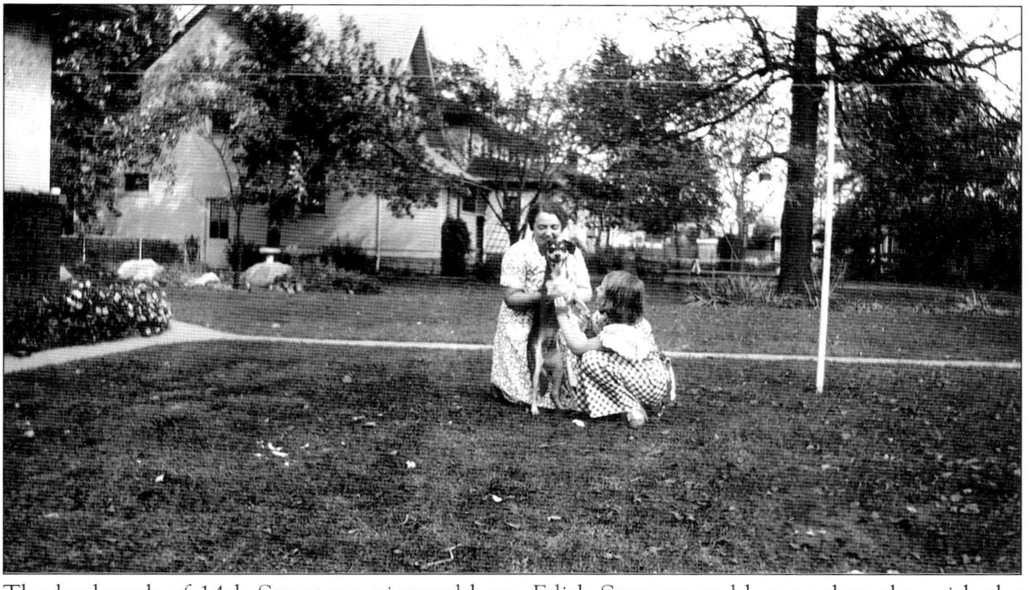

The backyards of 14th Street are pictured here. Edith Spencer and her mother play with the family dog. (Courtesy of Edith Spencer.)

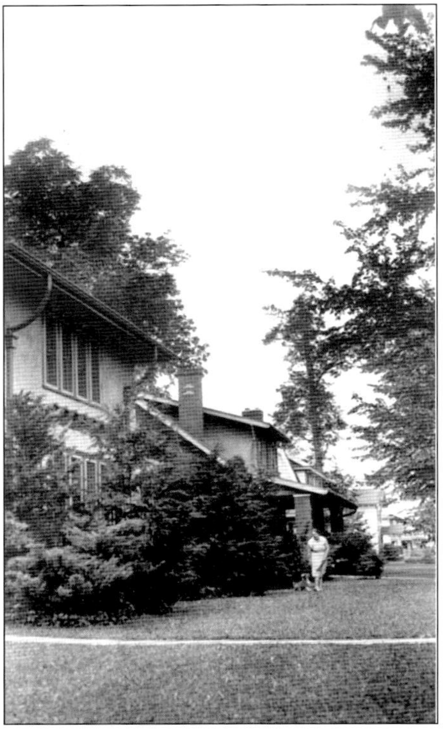

This view of the 4900 block of 14th Street, taken in the 1930s, looks west. (Courtesy of Edith Spencer.)

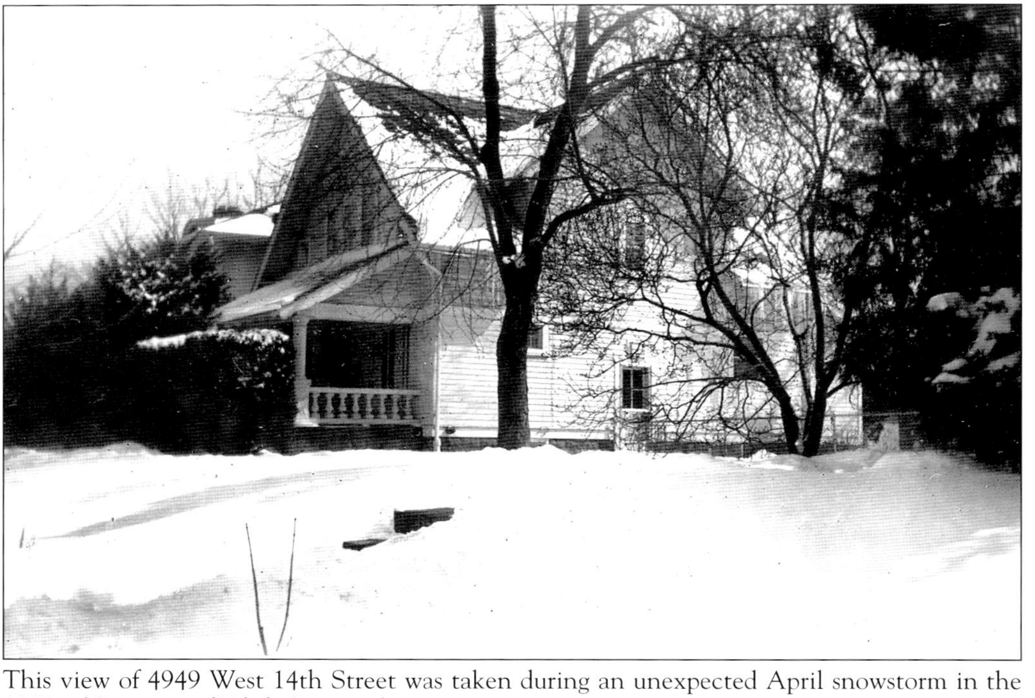

This view of 4949 West 14th Street was taken during an unexpected April snowstorm in the 1930s. (Courtesy of Edith Spencer.)

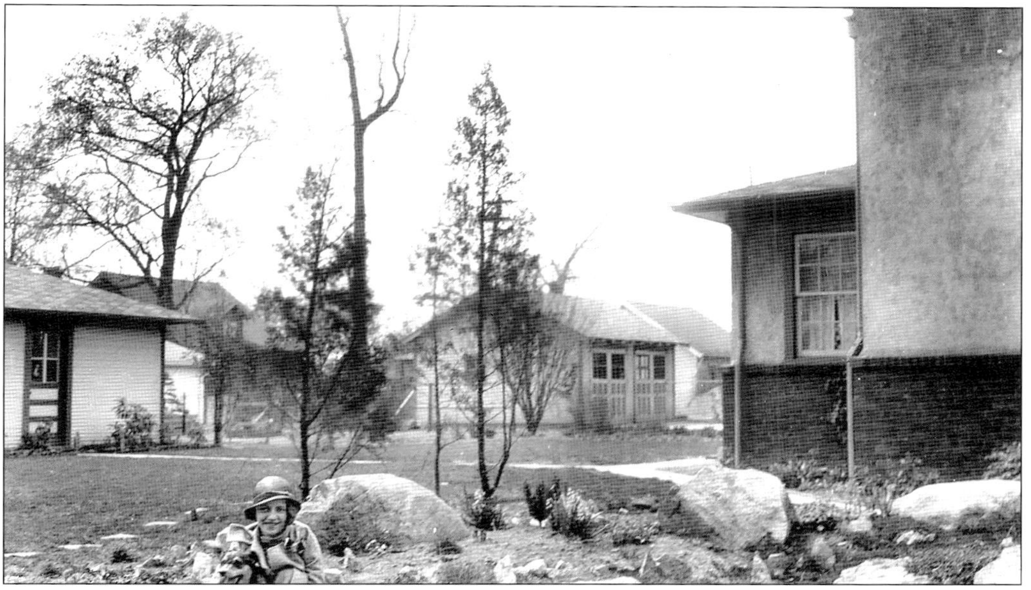

This shot behind 4957 West 14th Street shows the trees and garages as they were in the 1930s. (Courtesy of Edith Spencer.)

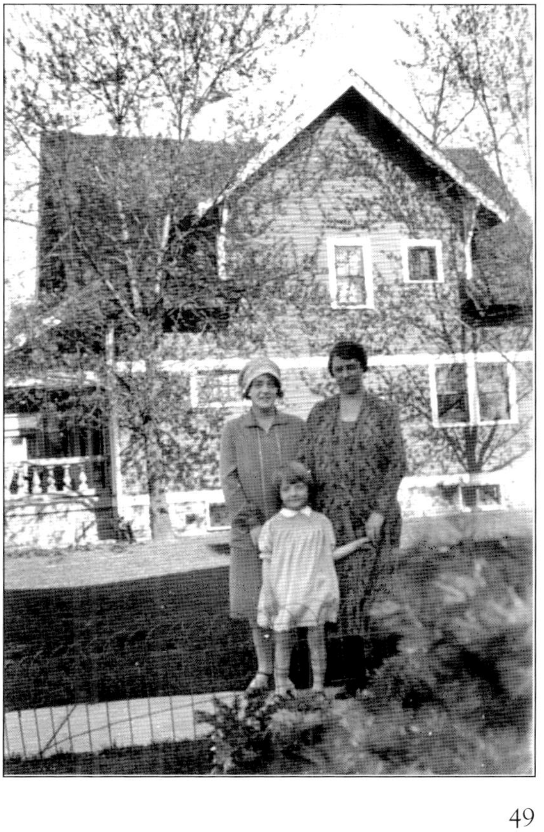

Here Agnes, Edith, and their mother Edith Spencer pose. They are beside 4957 West 14th Street. The picture is looking east. (Courtesy of Edith Spencer.)

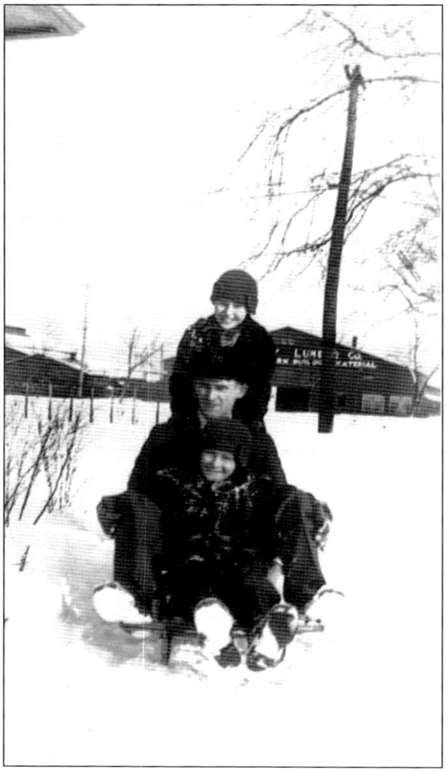

Two winter views of the front yard of 4922 West 10th Street in the 1920s show the old Speedway Lumber Company in the background. Notice the Flexible Flyer sled that Herman and Carl Pieper shared with their father Herman. (Courtesy of Carl Pieper.)

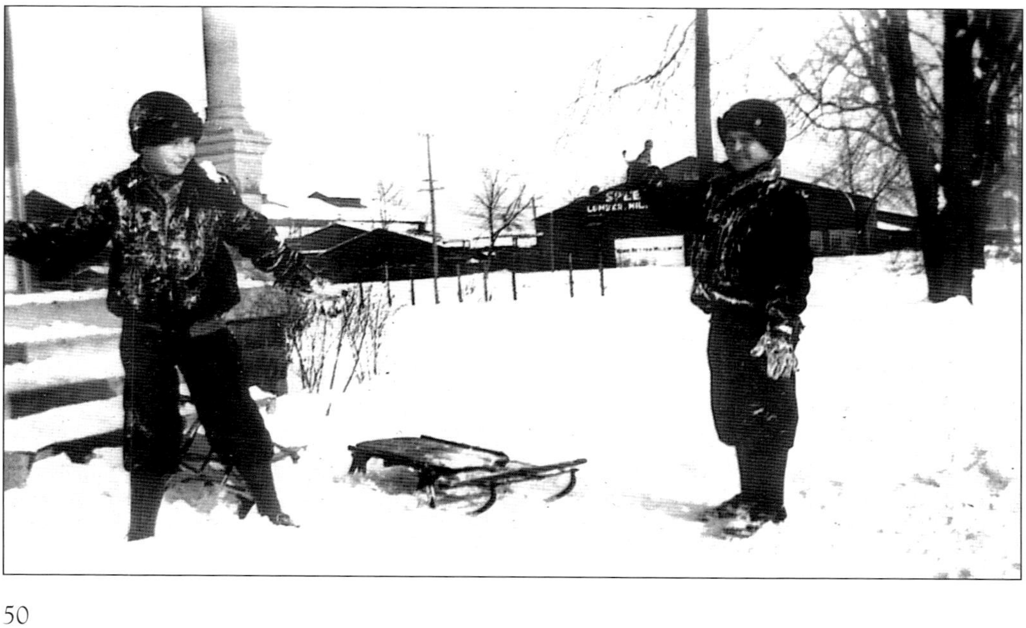

Edith Spencer takes her dolly for a stroll along West 10th Street. The view is looking south where the Allison Plant stands today. (Courtesy of Carl Pieper.)

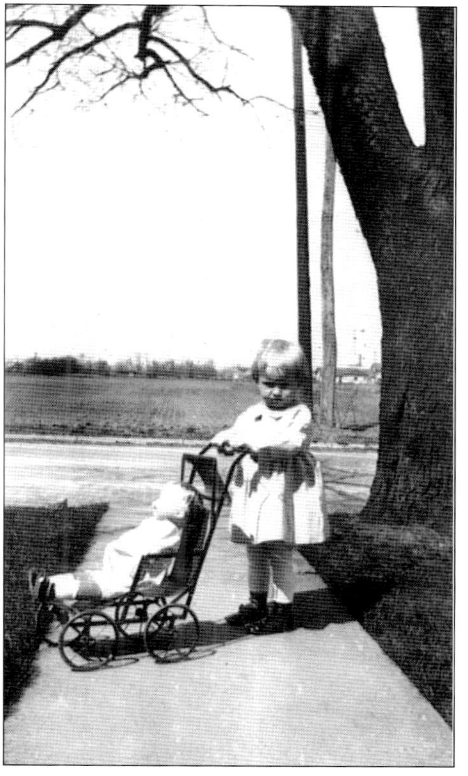

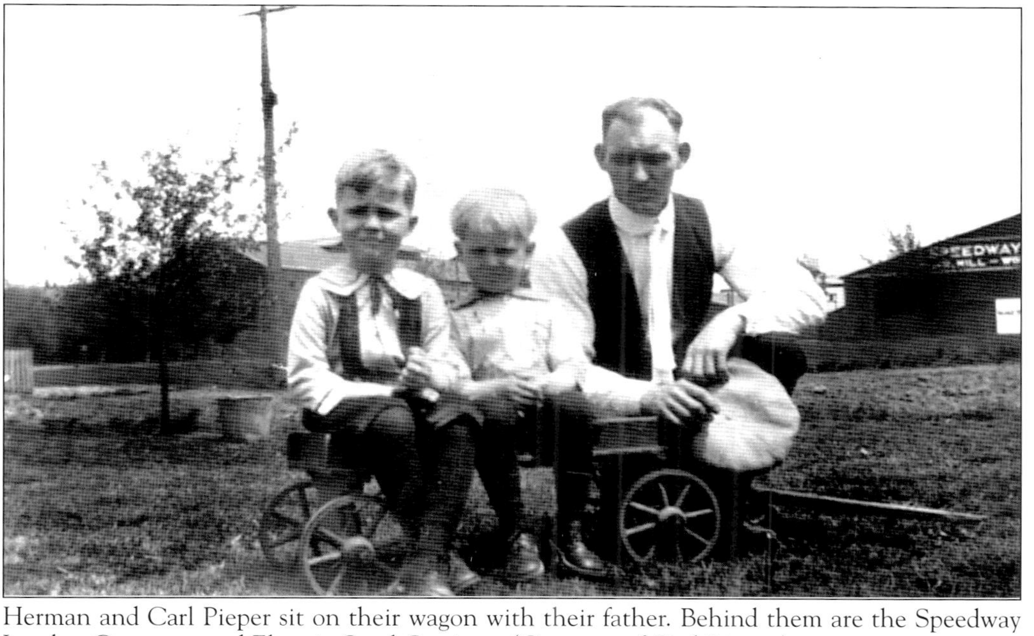

Herman and Carl Pieper sit on their wagon with their father. Behind them are the Speedway Lumber Company and Electric Steel Castings. (Courtesy of Carl Pieper.)

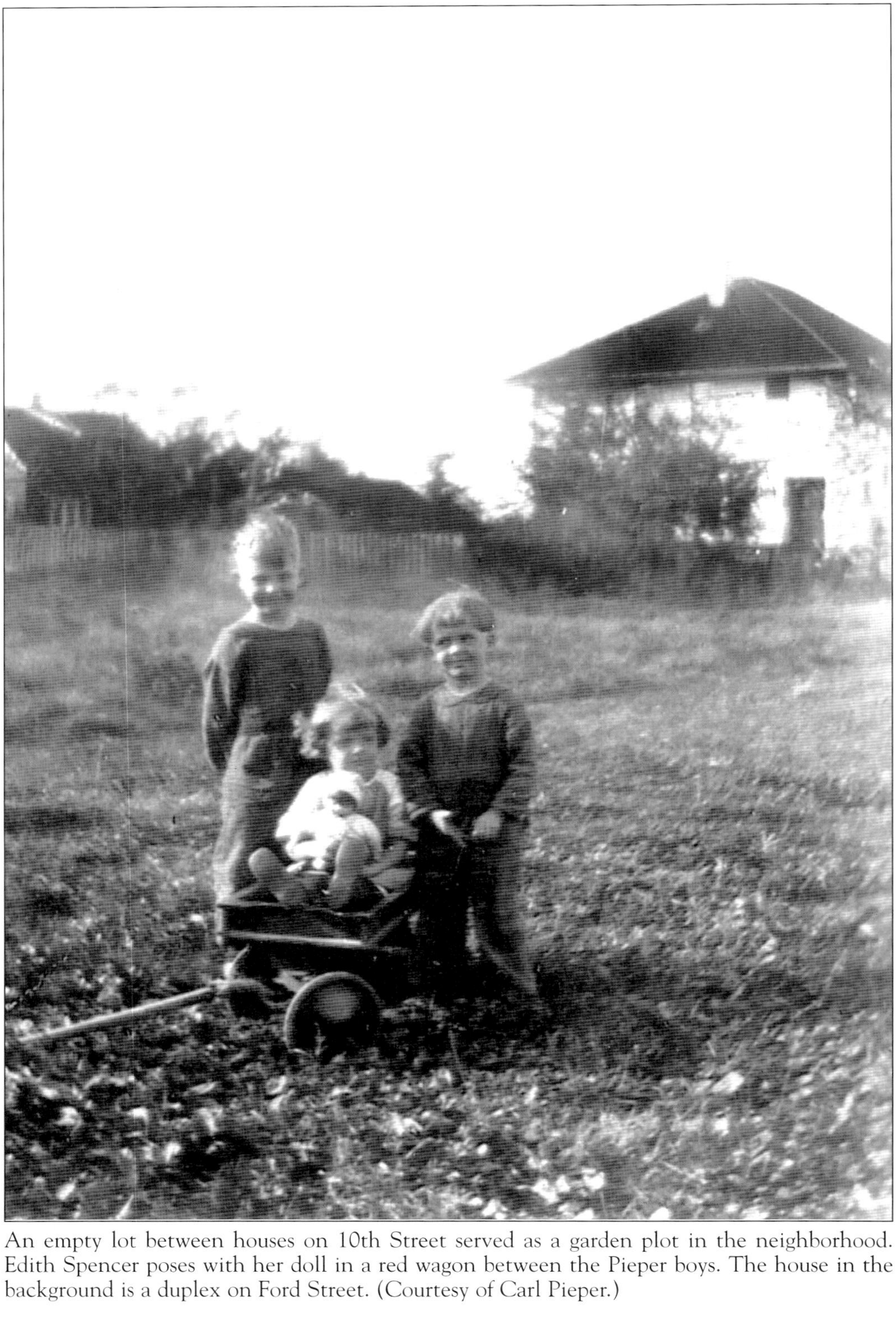

An empty lot between houses on 10th Street served as a garden plot in the neighborhood. Edith Spencer poses with her doll in a red wagon between the Pieper boys. The house in the background is a duplex on Ford Street. (Courtesy of Carl Pieper.)

Two unidentified girls pose on Ford Street looking east in the 1920s. (Courtesy of Carl Pieper.)

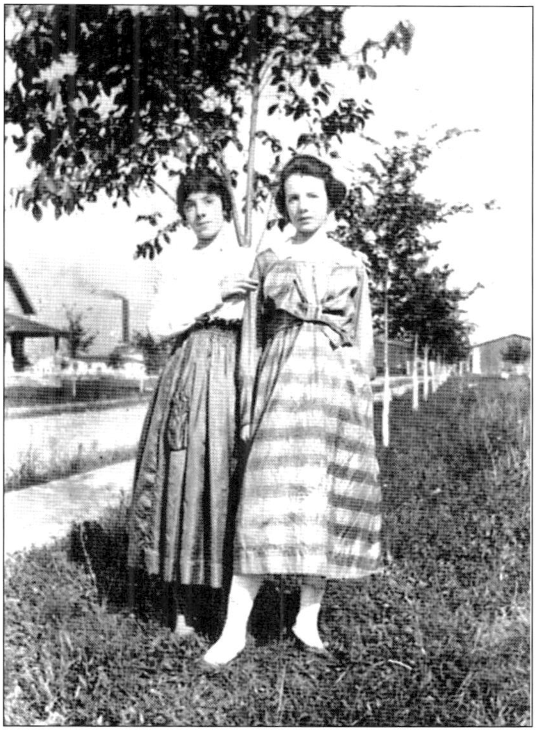

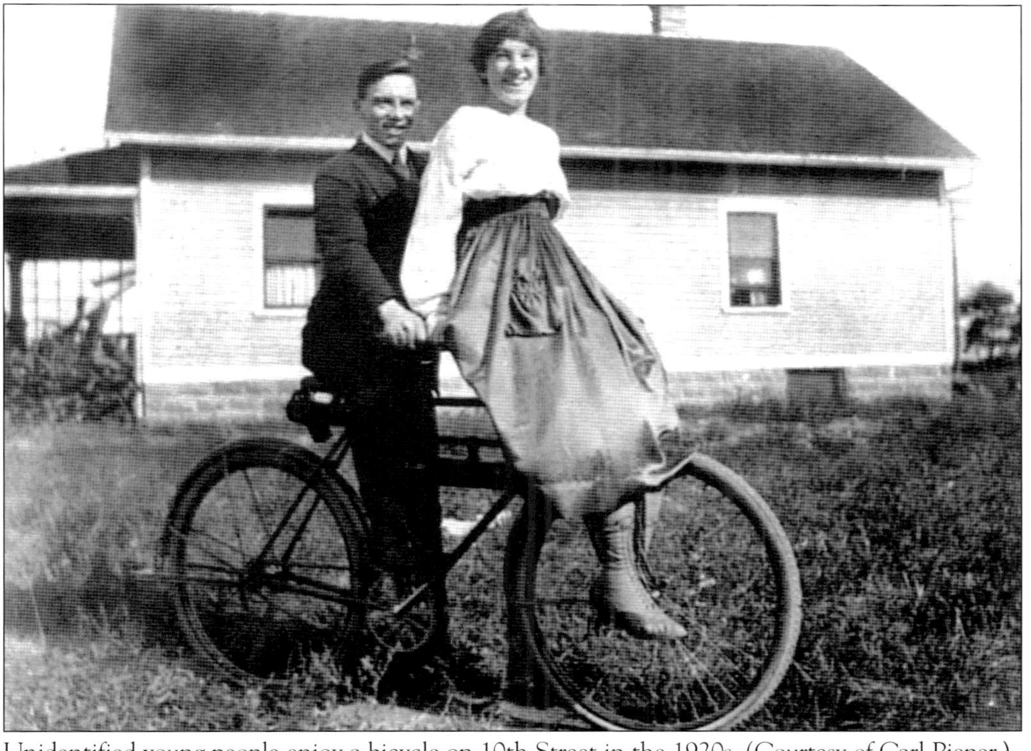

Unidentified young people enjoy a bicycle on 10th Street in the 1920s. (Courtesy of Carl Pieper.)

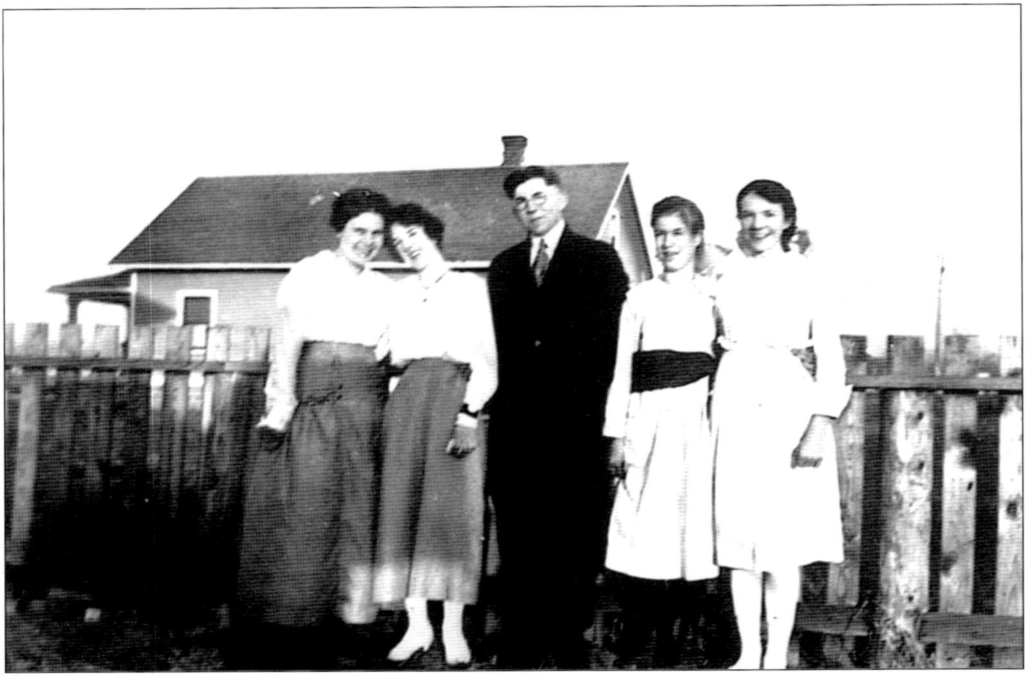

The Lacy family lived in the 4900 block of Ford Street. (Courtesy of Carl Pieper.)

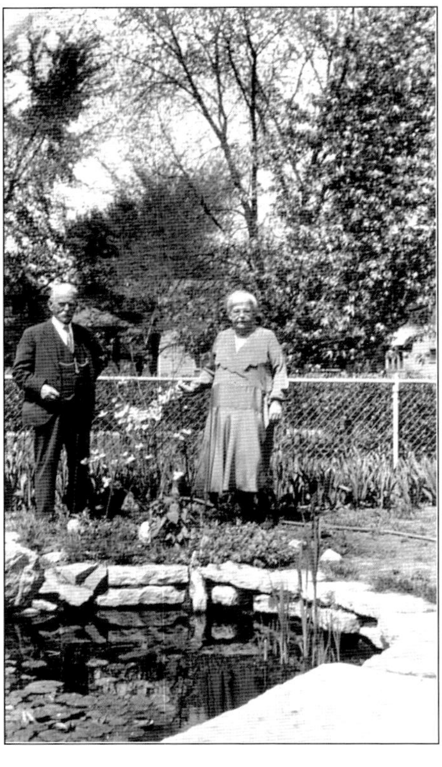

The rock garden that was in the yard of 4957 West 14th Street in the 1930s was built in the shape of Lost Lake, Wisconsin, a favorite vacation spot of the Spencer family. Here Emma Spencer and Robert McCord Adams (grandparents of Edith and Agnes Spencer) pose by the pond. (Courtesy of Edith Spencer.)

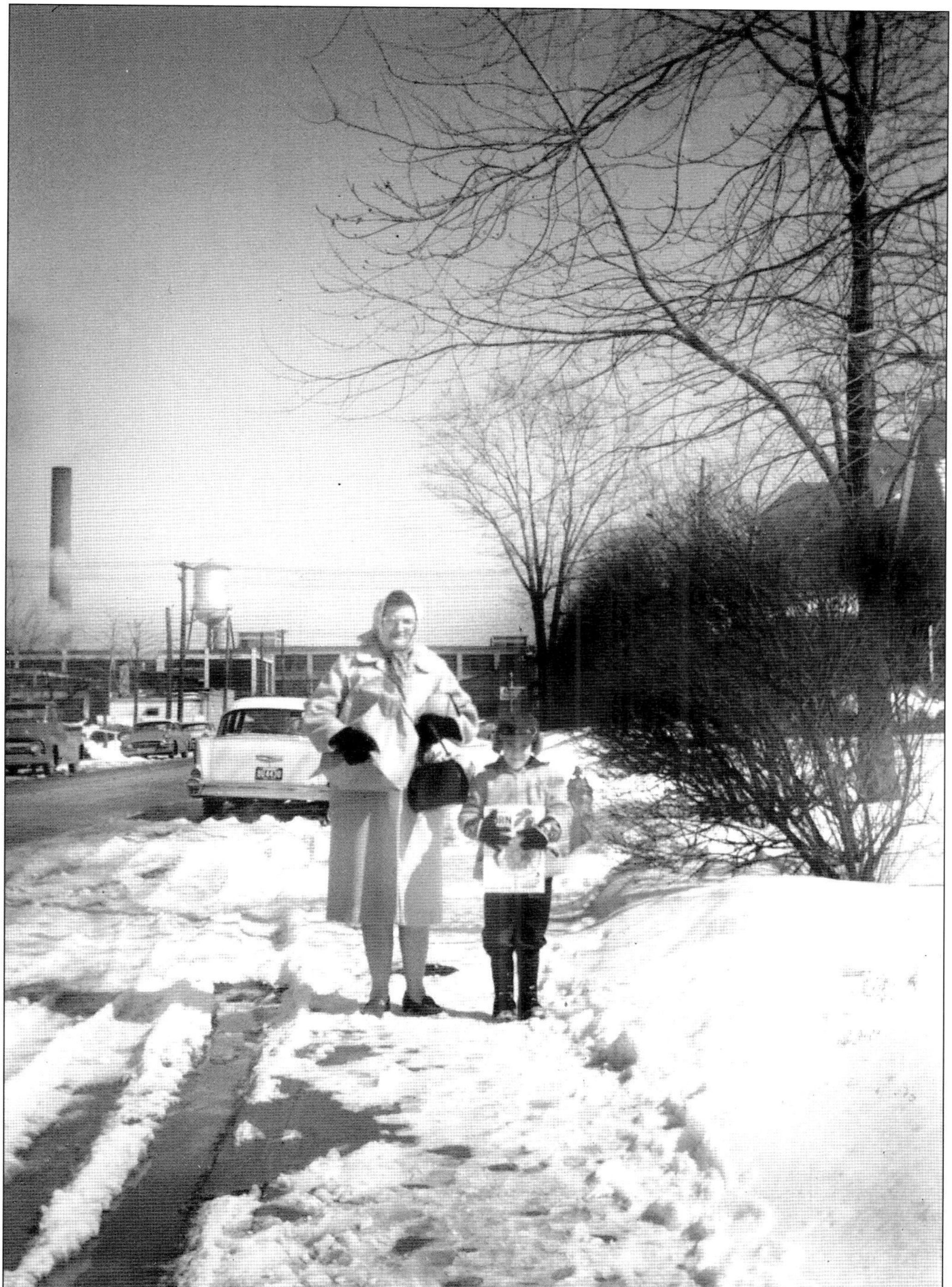

Jeanette Herring Spencer and a small helper walk home from the grocery store. This view looking east on 14th Street in 1960 shows a factory water tower and chimney still standing at the end of the street. (Courtesy of Edith Spencer.)

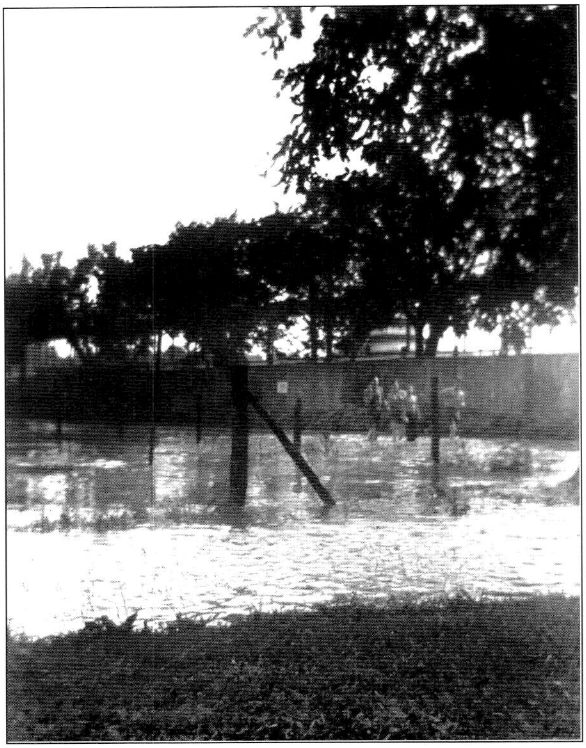

The "Hundred Year Flood" washed out Georgetown Road and many other streets in Speedway in the summer of 1937. (Courtesy of the Eppen Family.)

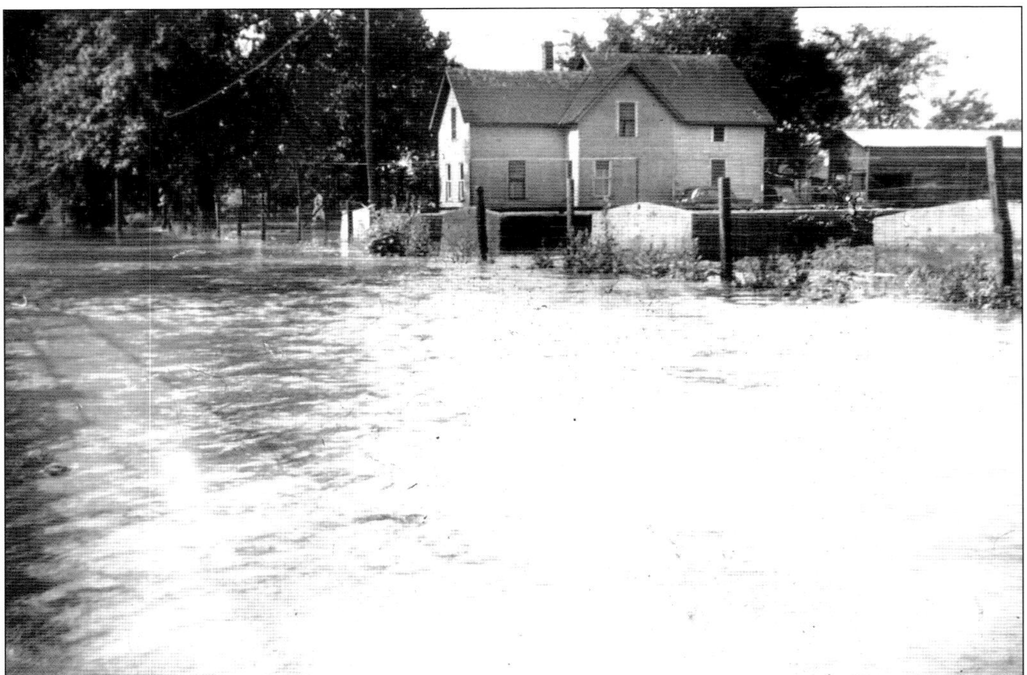

Here the worst flood in Speedway history covers Georgetown Road and the Eppen driveway. (Courtesy of the Eppen Family.)

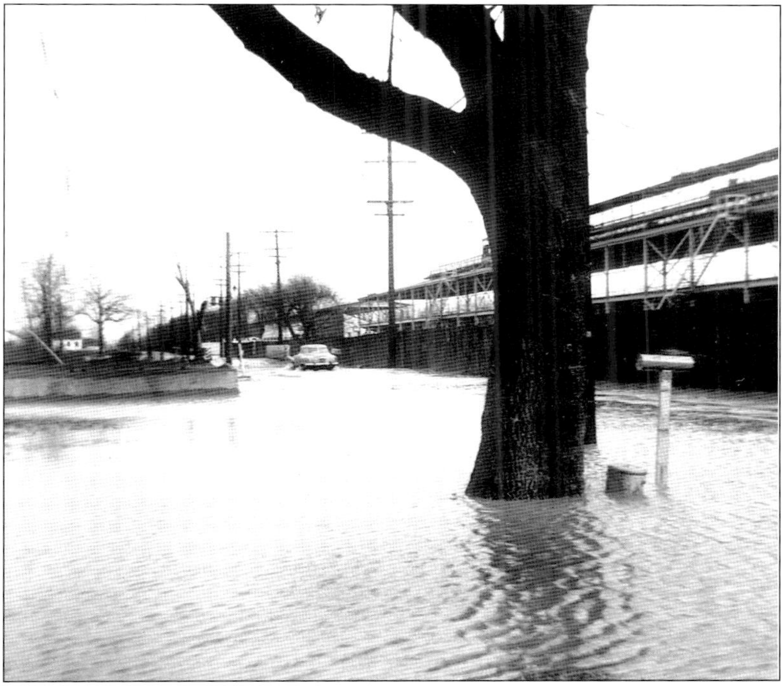

It did not take 100 years for a flood to strike again. In these two pictures, Georgetown Road is covered with water during the 1950s flood as cars struggle along outside of the Indianapolis Motor Speedway. (Courtesy of the Eppen Family.)

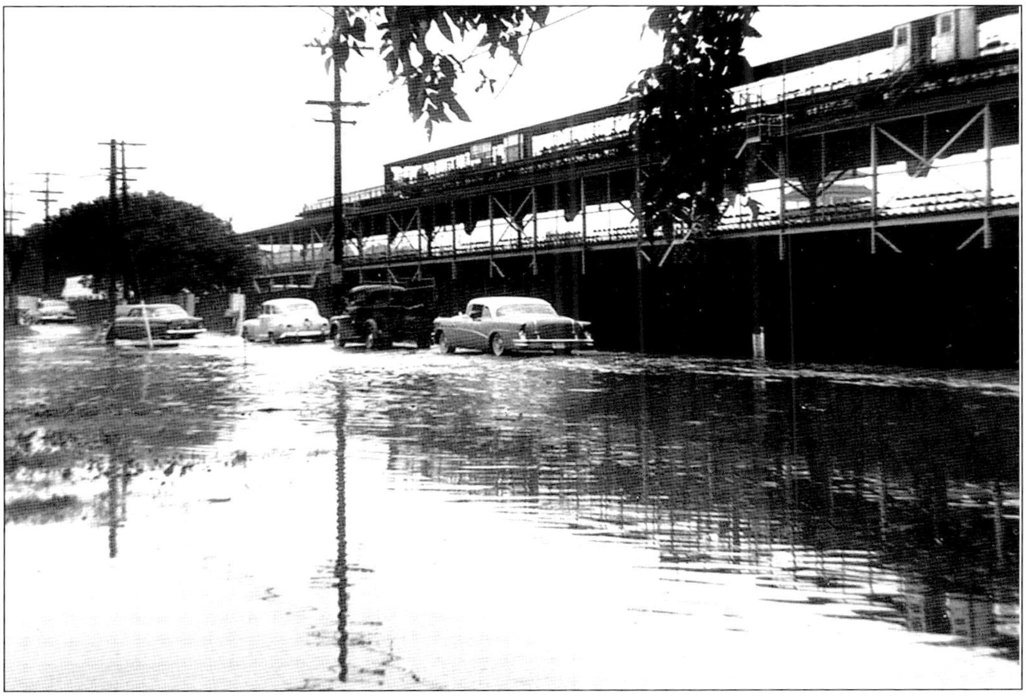

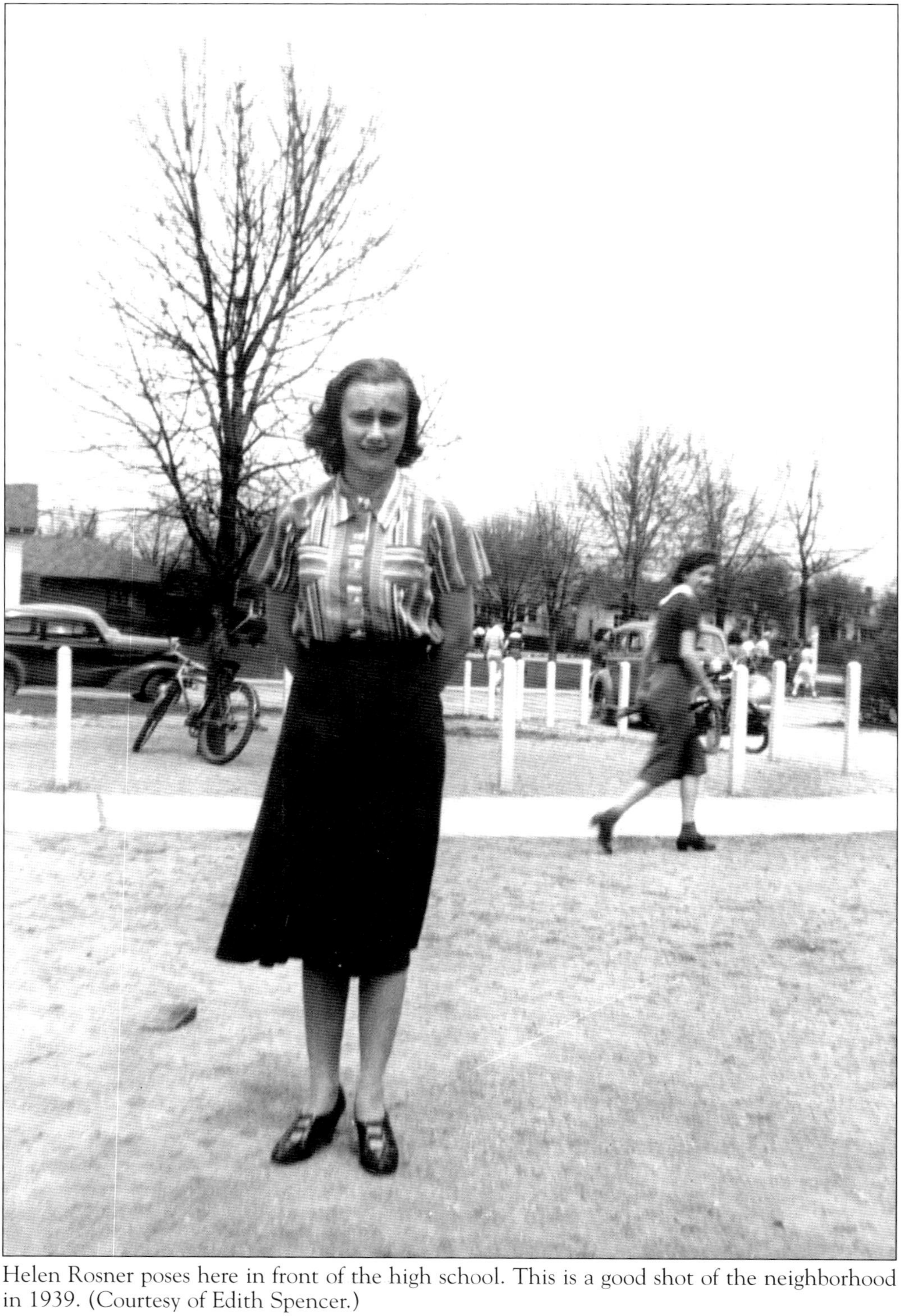

Helen Rosner poses here in front of the high school. This is a good shot of the neighborhood in 1939. (Courtesy of Edith Spencer.)

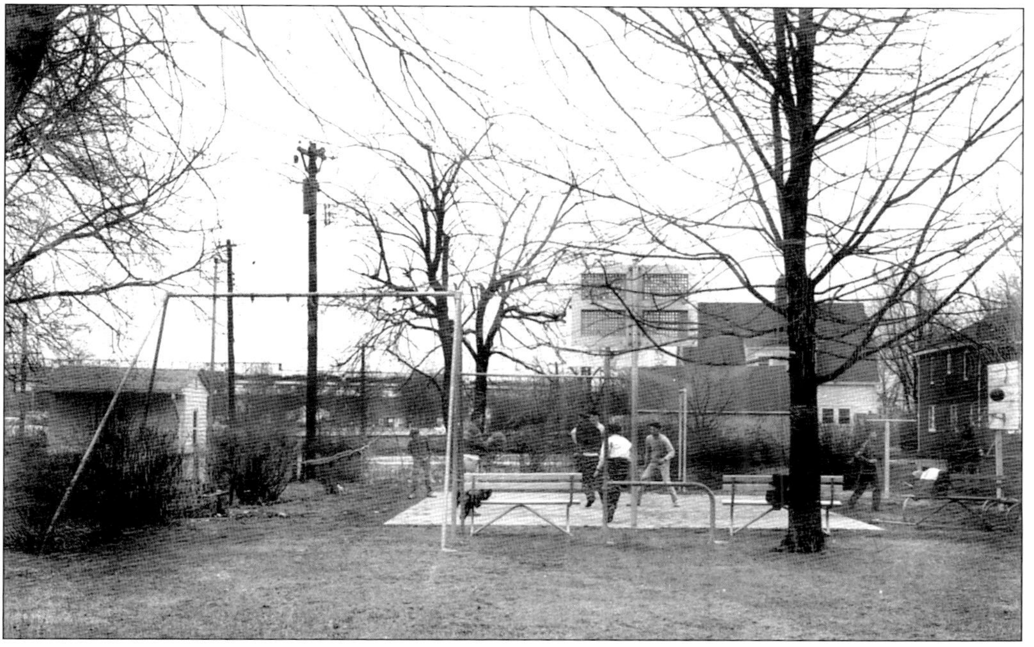

The only lighted basketball court in Speedway was in the backyard of 1639 Auburn Street at the O'Neal home. This basketball court was the practice ground for Indiana Pacer basketball champions such as Rick McGinnis and Billy Keller and Notre Dame's Bill O'Neal. (Courtesy of the O'Neal family.)

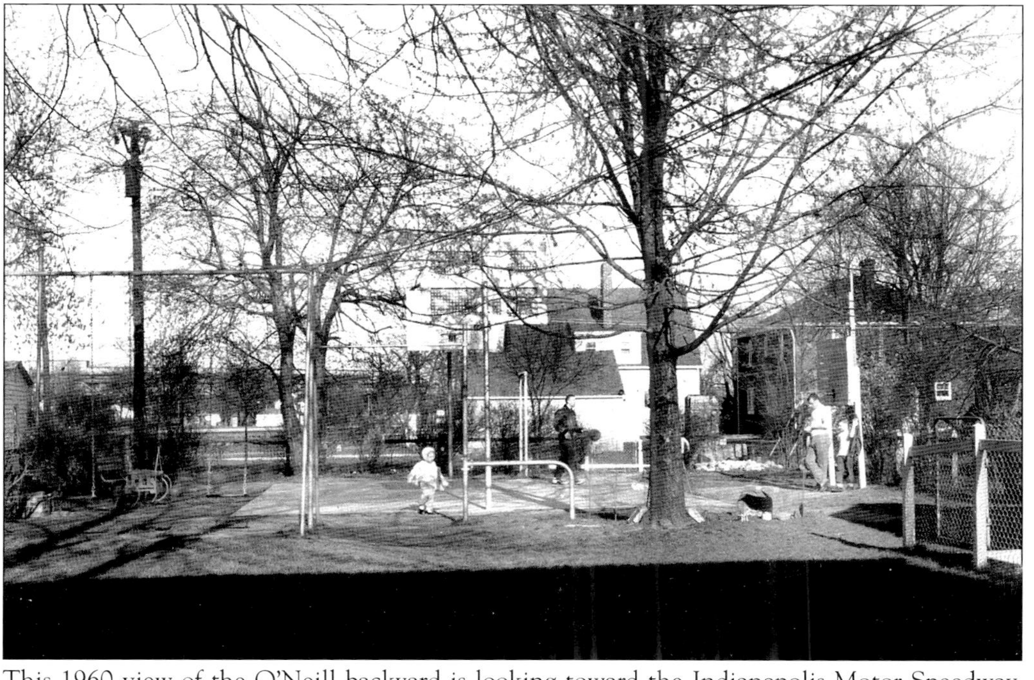

This 1960 view of the O'Neill backyard is looking toward the Indianapolis Motor Speedway, which is present in the background. (Courtesy of the O'Neal family.)

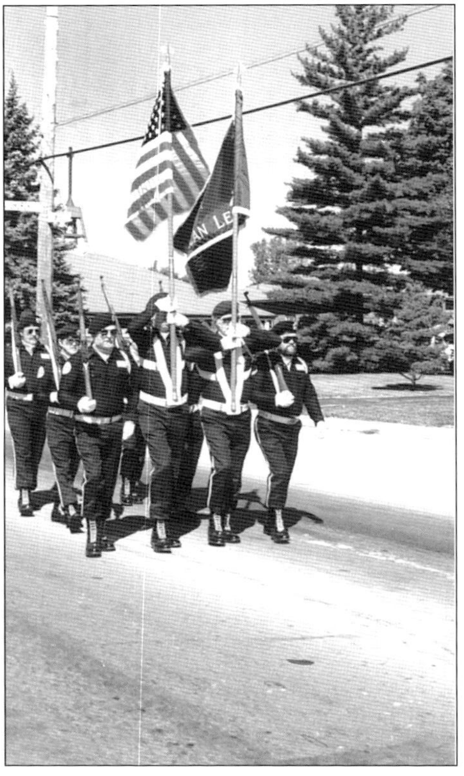

The American Legion Post 500 color guard came home with the national championship for many years in a row. (Courtesy of American Legion Post 500.)

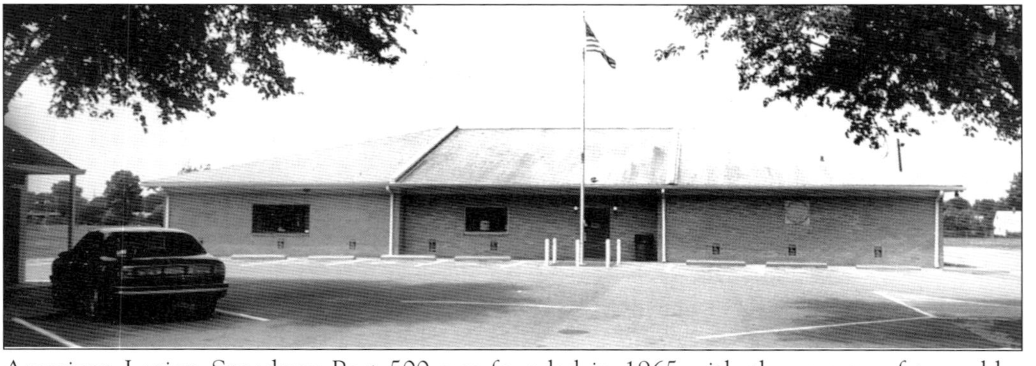

American Legion Speedway Post 500 was founded in 1965 with the merger of two older posts. The home of Post 500 was built across from the Indianapolis Motor Speedway in 1967. The post sponsors community activities and parks cars for the races. (Courtesy of American Legion Post 500.)

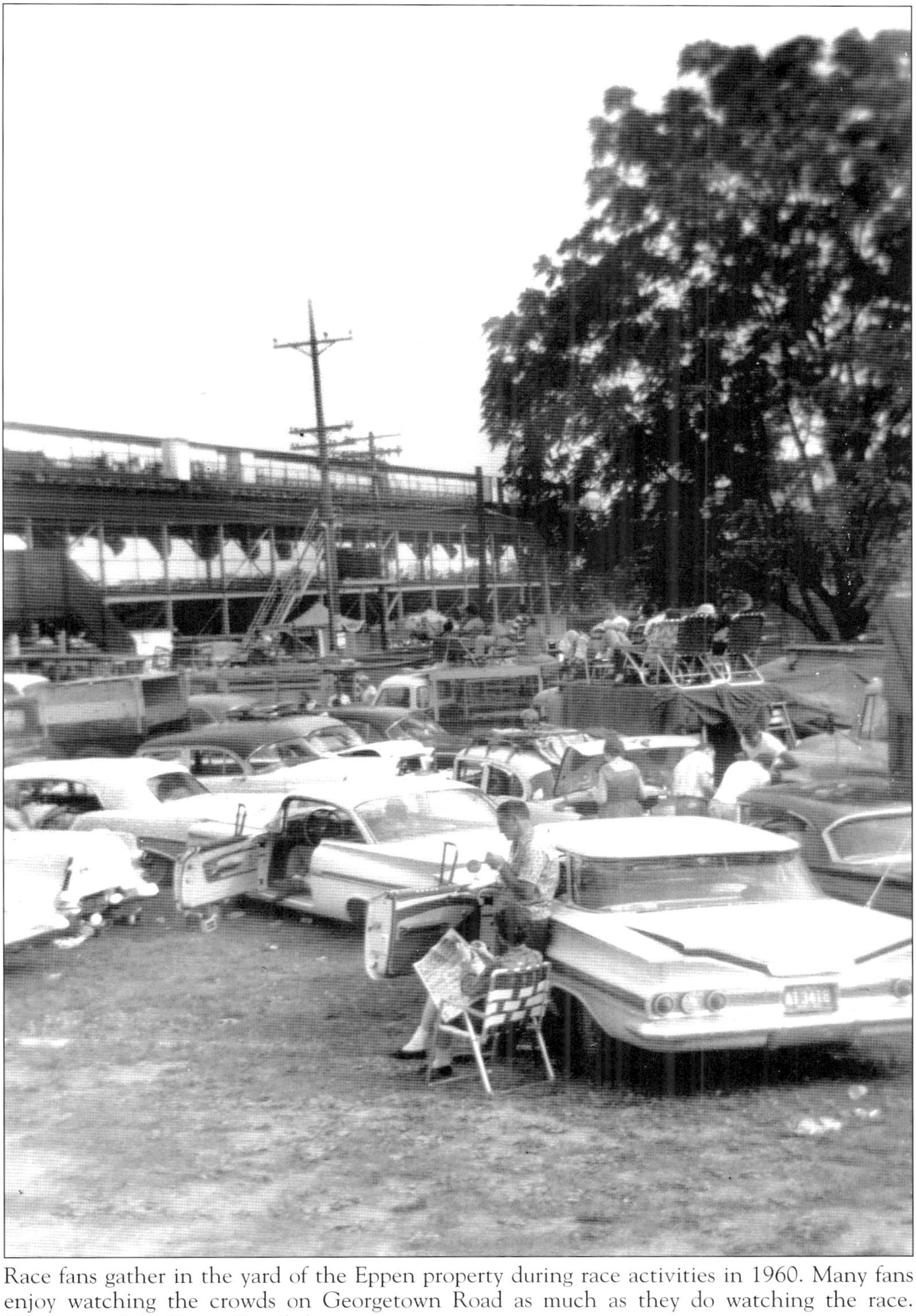

Race fans gather in the yard of the Eppen property during race activities in 1960. Many fans enjoy watching the crowds on Georgetown Road as much as they do watching the race. (Courtesy of the Eppen Family.)

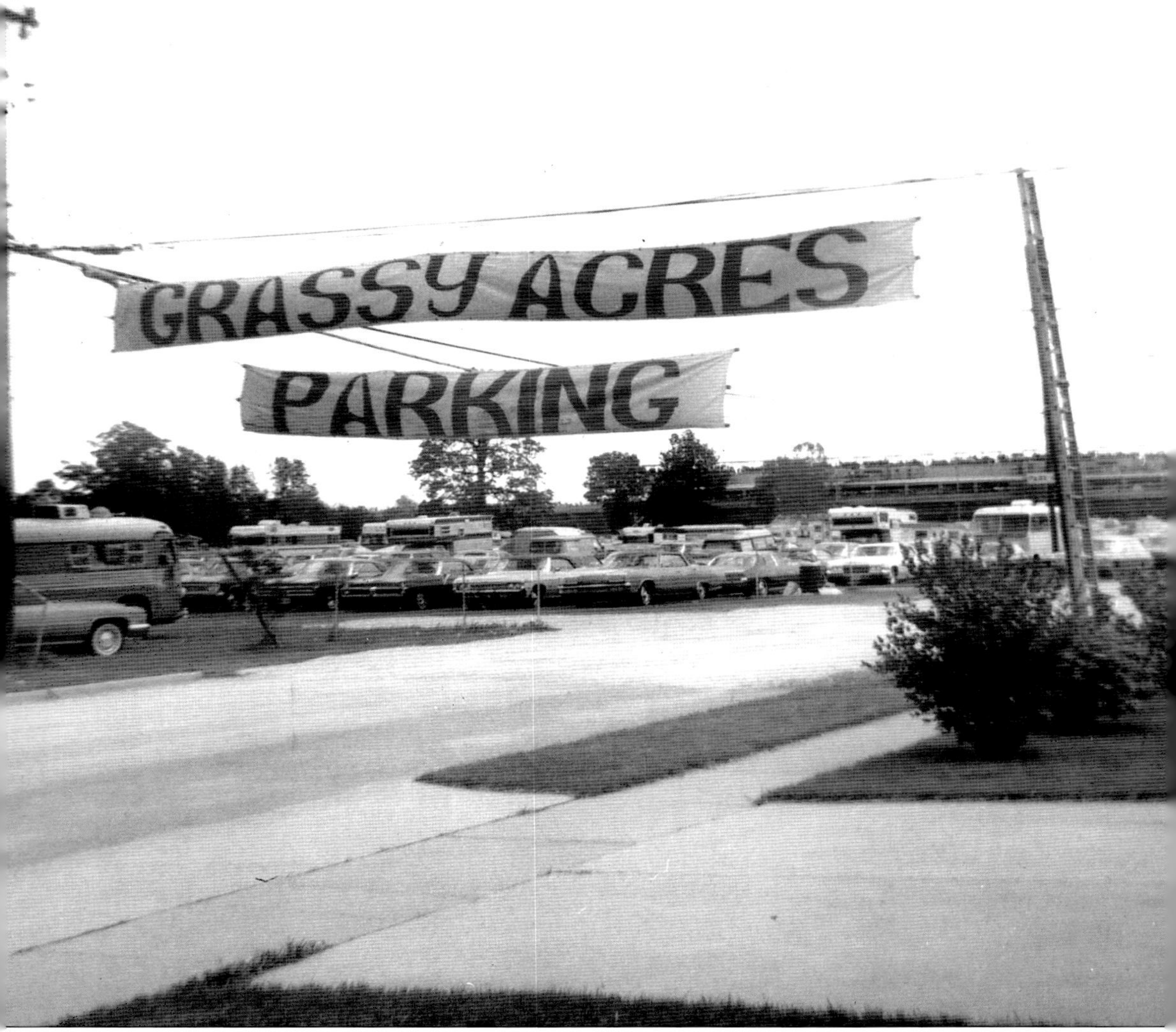

Parking for the race inspires interesting names for the family-operated lots around the Speedway area. (Courtesy of the Eppen Family.)

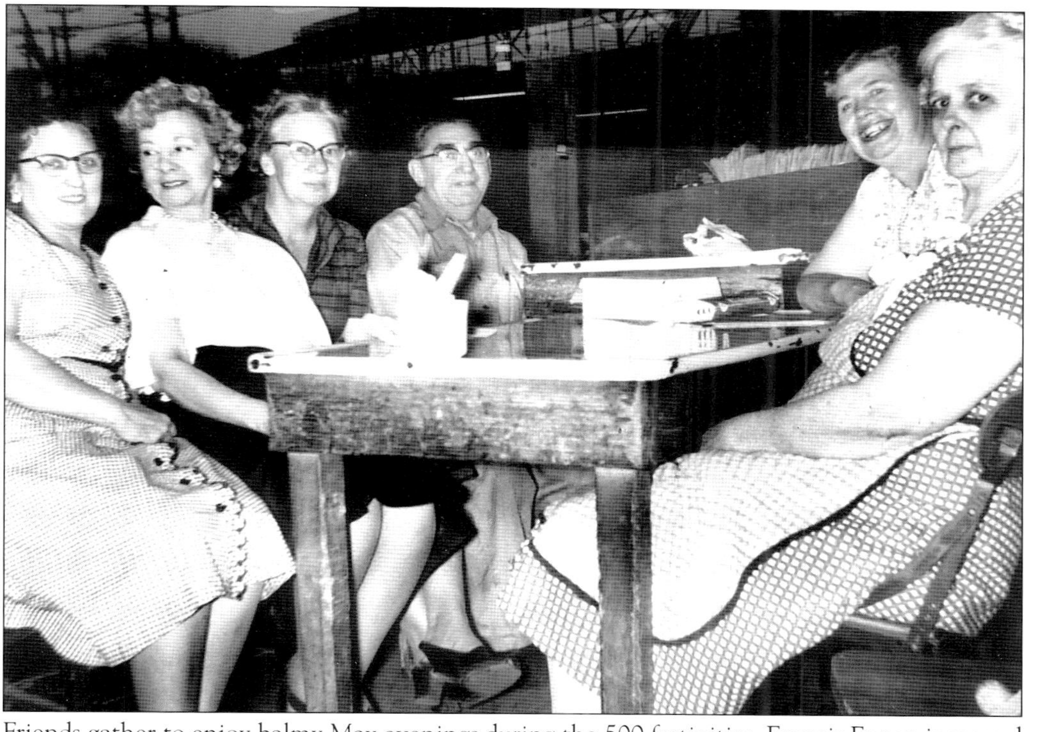

Friends gather to enjoy balmy May evenings during the 500 festivities. Francis Eppen is second from the right. (Courtesy of the Eppen Family.)

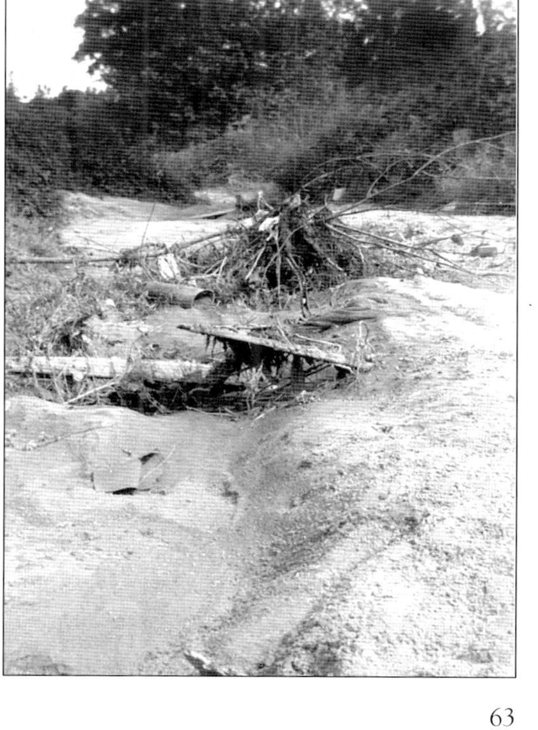

The old creek bed is seen here before the creek was relocated to accommodate new housing developments and changes in the neighborhood. (Courtesy of the Eppen Family.)

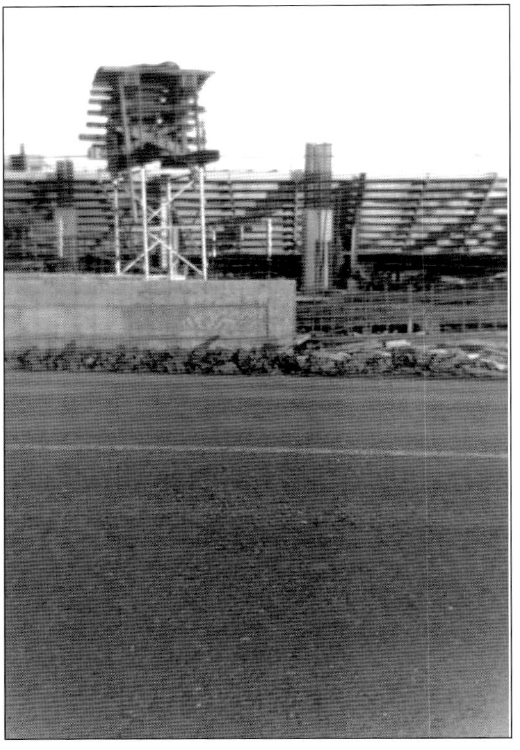

People who lived in Speedway watched as the track developed over the years. Many changes have taken place at the Indianapolis Motor Speedway since its founding in 1909. (Courtesy of the Eppen Family.)

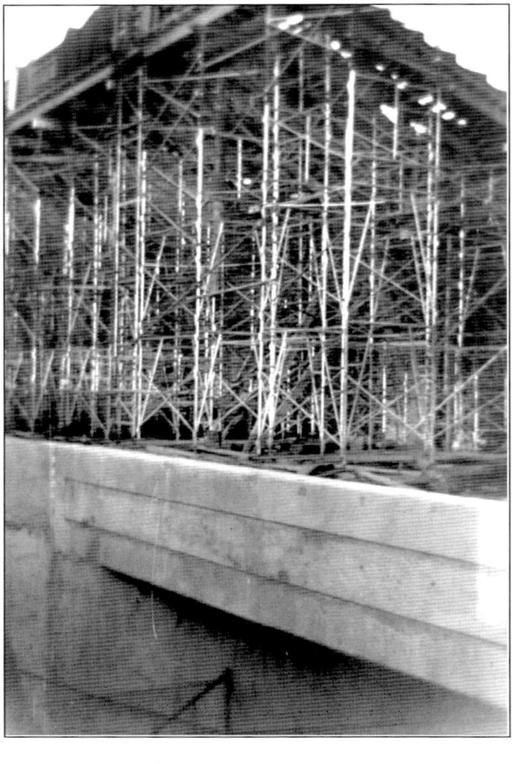

The changes in the IMS progressed through the years. This building project occurred in 1960 and included changes in the grandstand seating and tunnels. (Courtesy of the Eppen Family.)

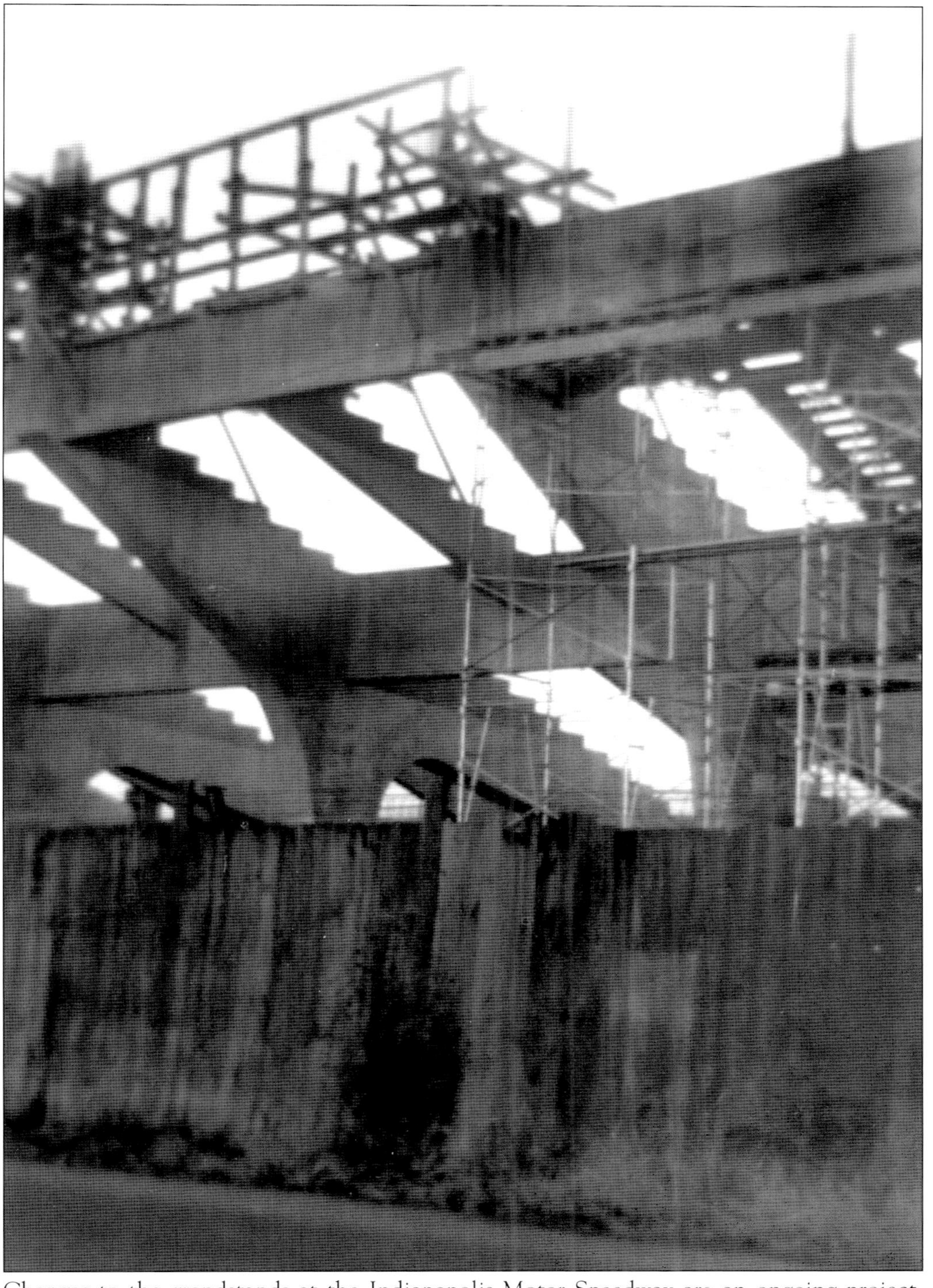

Changes to the grandstands at the Indianapolis Motor Speedway are an ongoing project. This shows how the stands were changed along Georgetown Road in 1960. (Courtesy of the Eppen Family.)

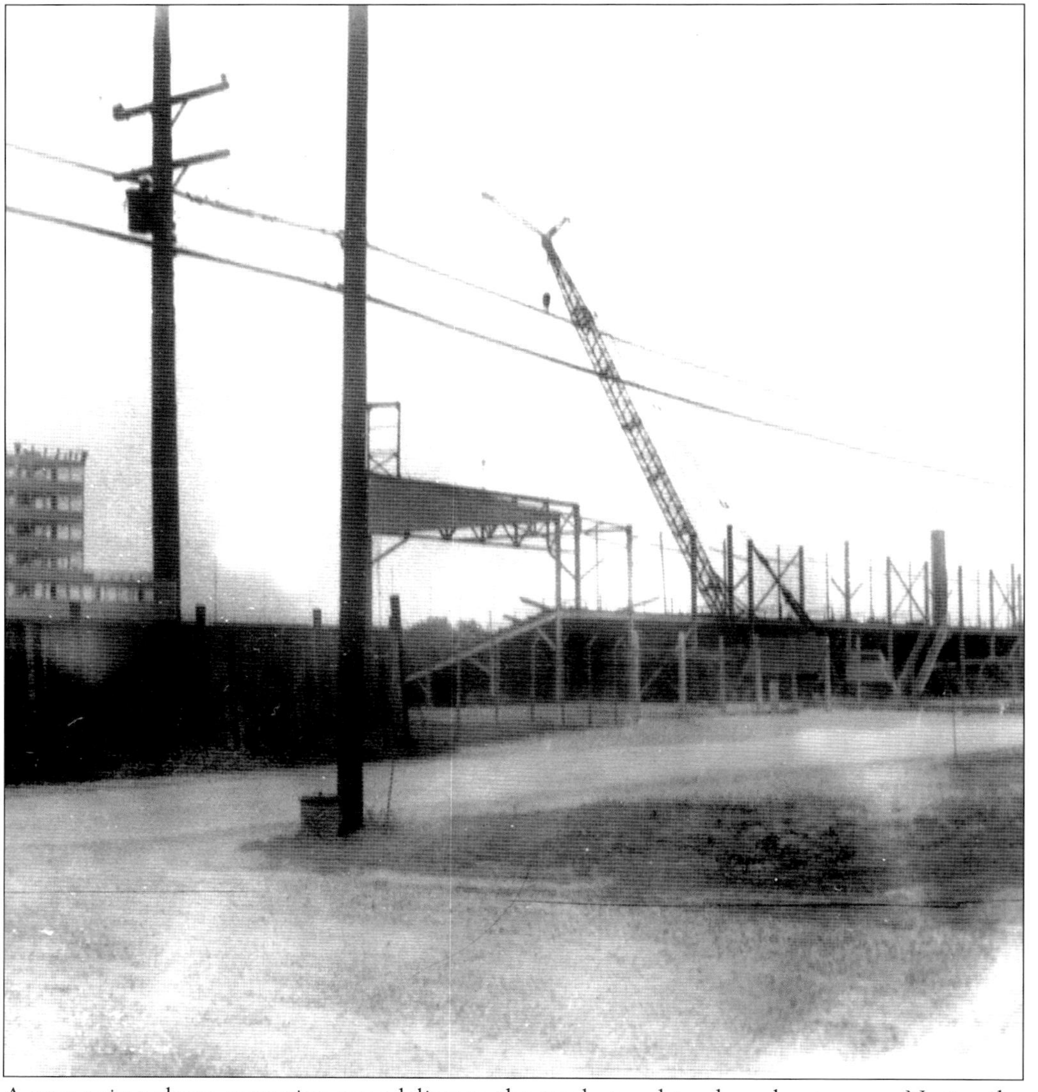

A crane rises above extensive remodeling to the track grandstands and entrances. Notice the tower in the far left of the picture. (Courtesy of the Eppen Family.)

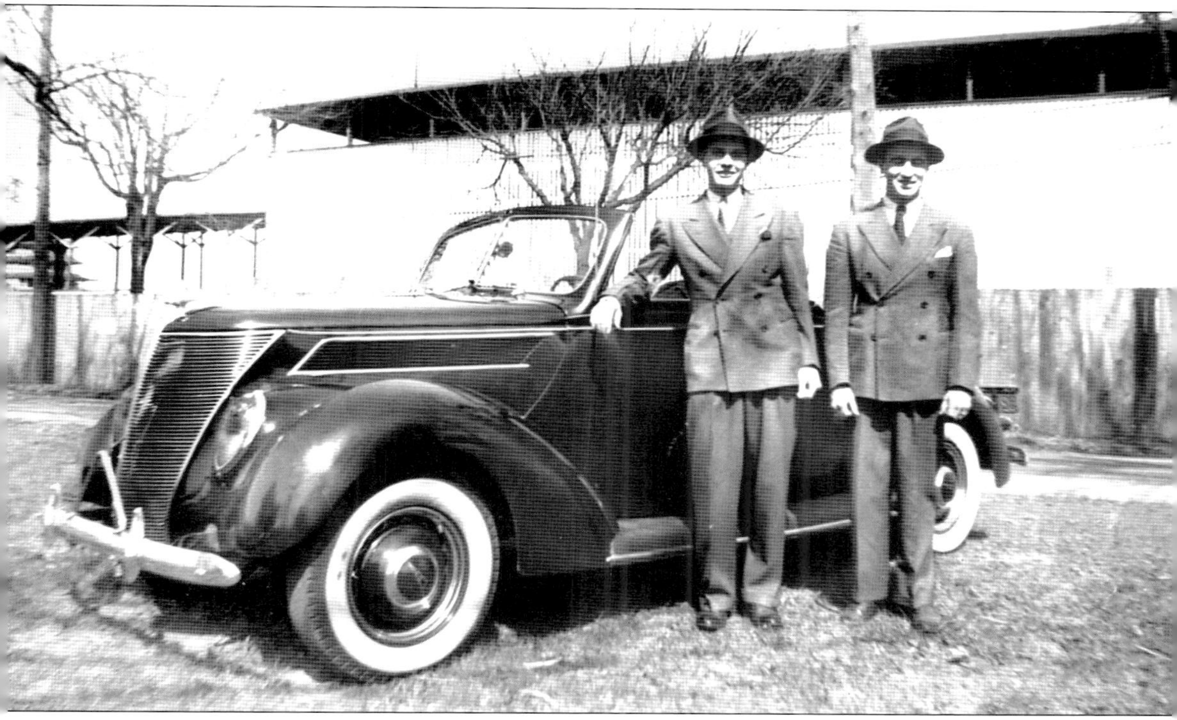

Earnest Eppen and Fred Myers pose in a sporty new car behind the Indianapolis Motor Speedway. (Courtesy of the Eppen Family.)

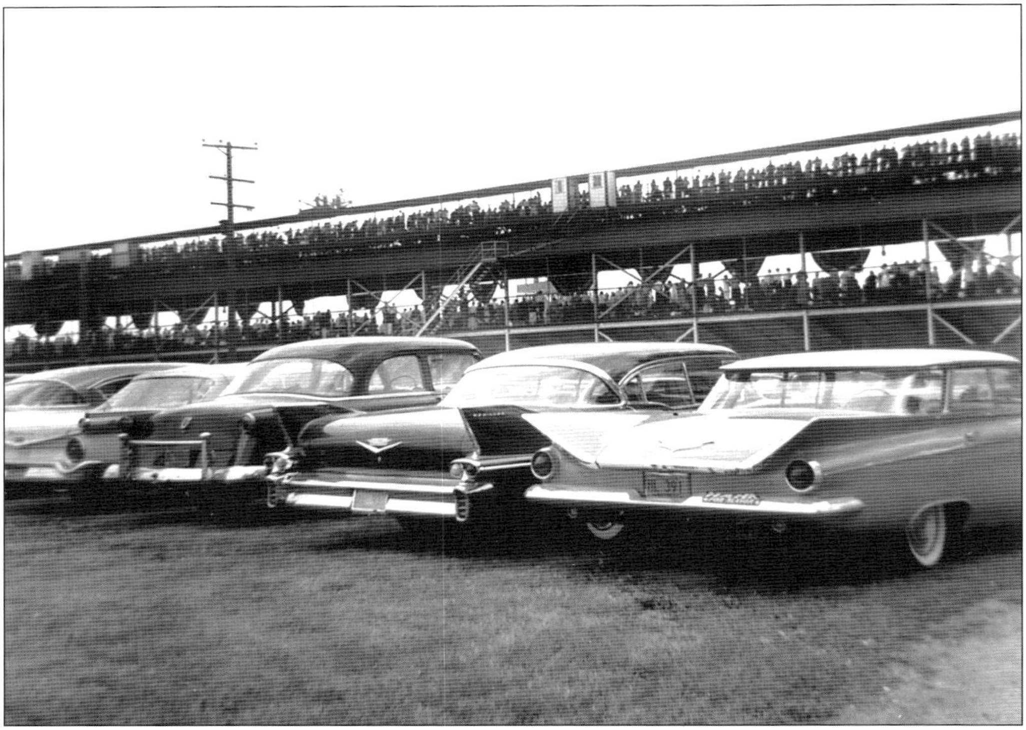

Race fans pack the stands for the Indianapolis 500 while their cars are parked safely across the street. Anyone who could park this close to the track on race day felt lucky. (Courtesy of the Eppen Family.)

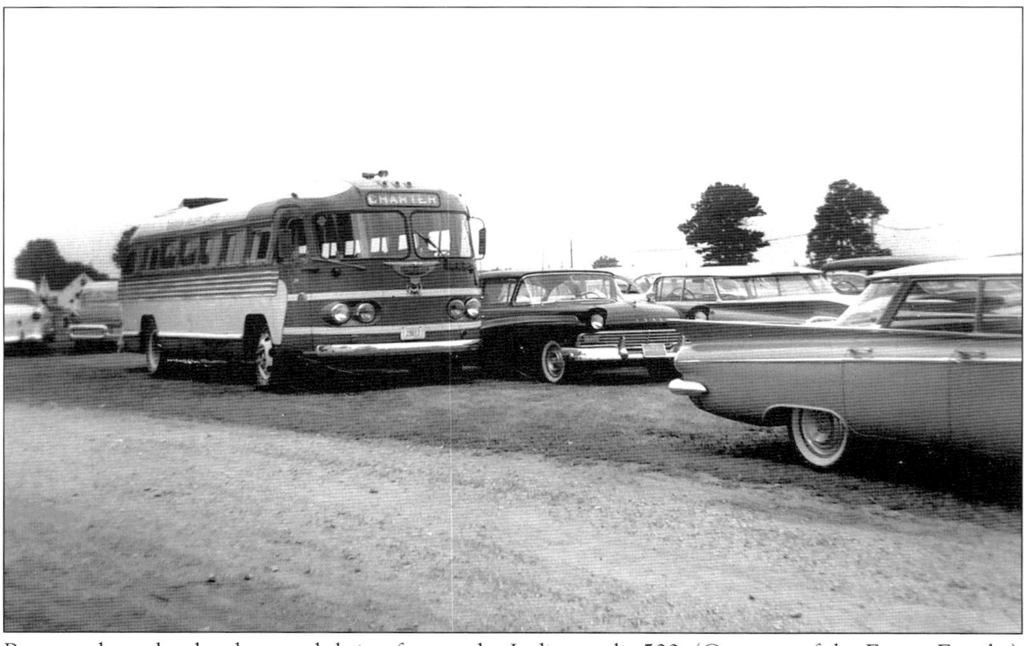

Buses and cars by the thousands bring fans to the Indianapolis 500. (Courtesy of the Eppen Family.)

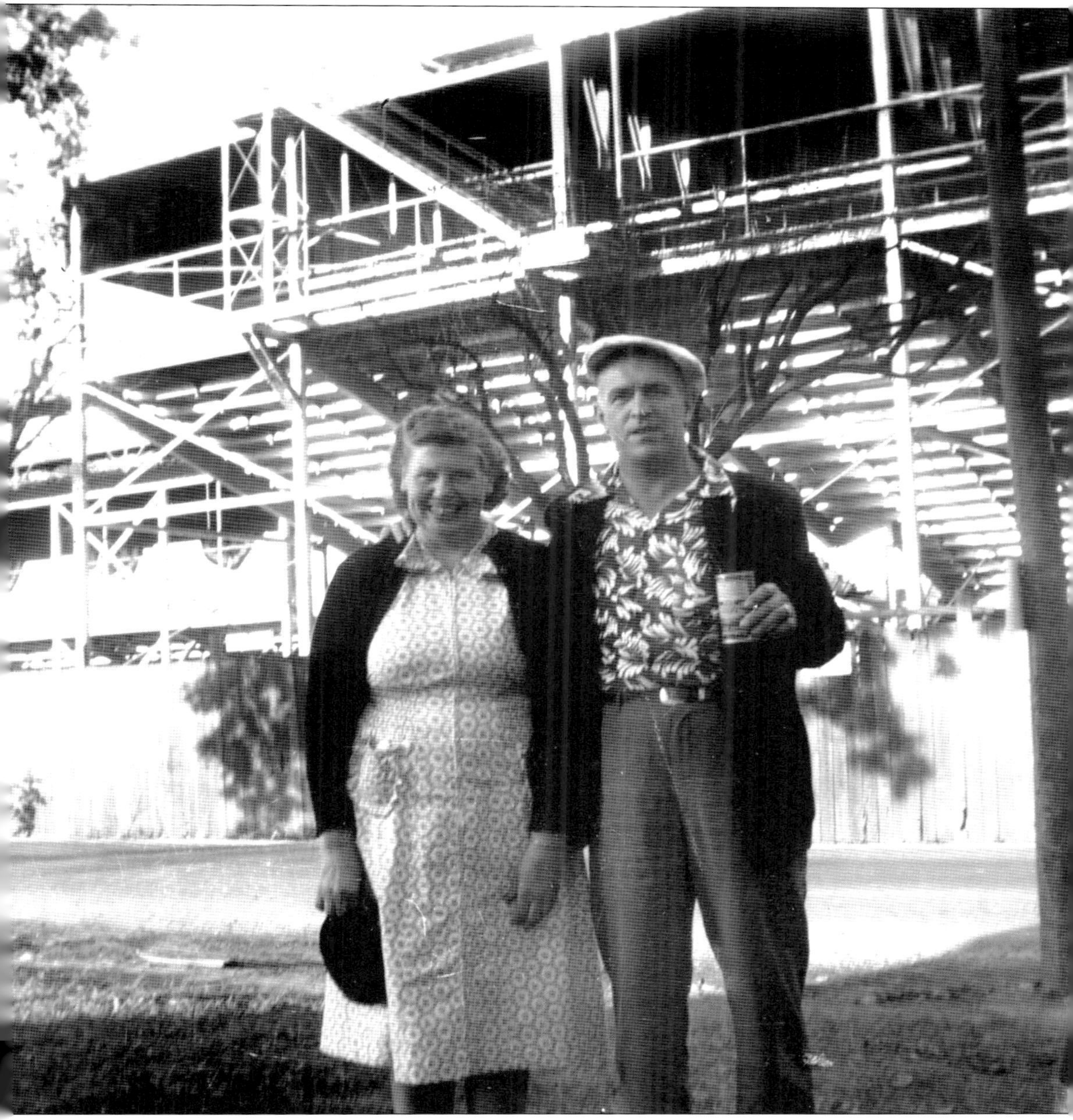

Ready for the race, Frances Eppen and a long-time racing fan friend pose together across from the track. (Courtesy of the Eppen Family.)

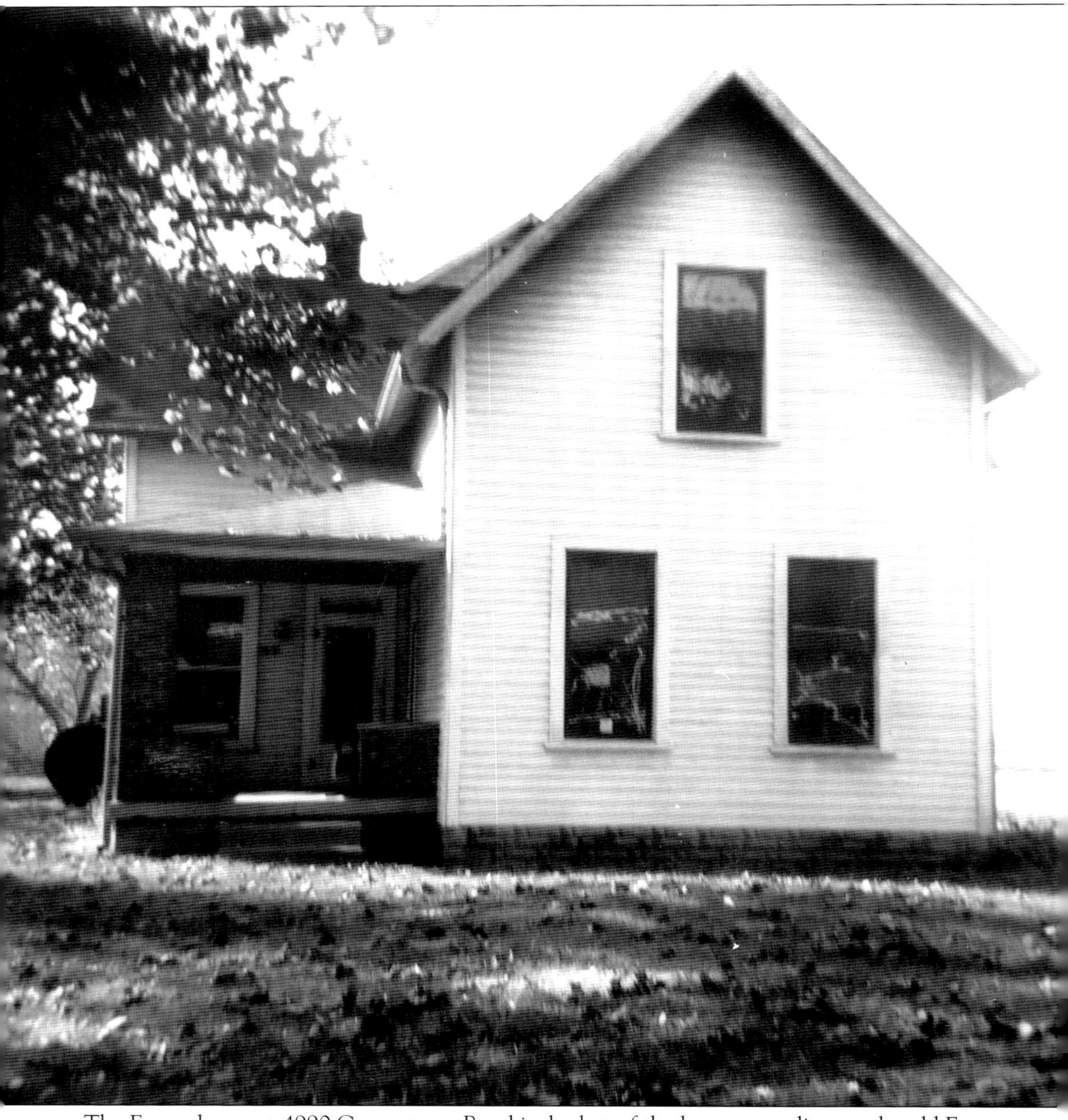

The Eppen home at 4990 Georgetown Road is the last of the houses standing on the old Eppen truck farm. (Courtesy of the Eppen Family.)

Four

Schools

Speedway High School's nickname is the Sparkplugs, and when the first annual was produced in 1941, it bore the title "The Speedette." Speed and racing are deeply integrated into the culture of Speedway, but the town also prides itself on excellent schools fostered by a supportive community.

The first school in the area was a Wayne township one-room brick schoolhouse on 10th Street. Speedway took over its own educational destiny in 1928, just two years after the organization of the civil town of Speedway, by taking over the operation of the school on Winton Avenue. The school was called simply Speedway School, and housed grades one through eight.

The growing town needed a high school, which was completed and opened in 1937. The location of the original school is now the location of Carl Fisher Elementary School, and the original high school has been absorbed into the junior high school. Since that time, the school system has grown to include four elementary schools named for the four founders of Speedway: James Allison, Carl Fisher, Frank Wheeler, and Arthur Newby. The Speedway Junior High School and the Howard J. Lacy II High School, in a newer location, make up the rest of the school system.

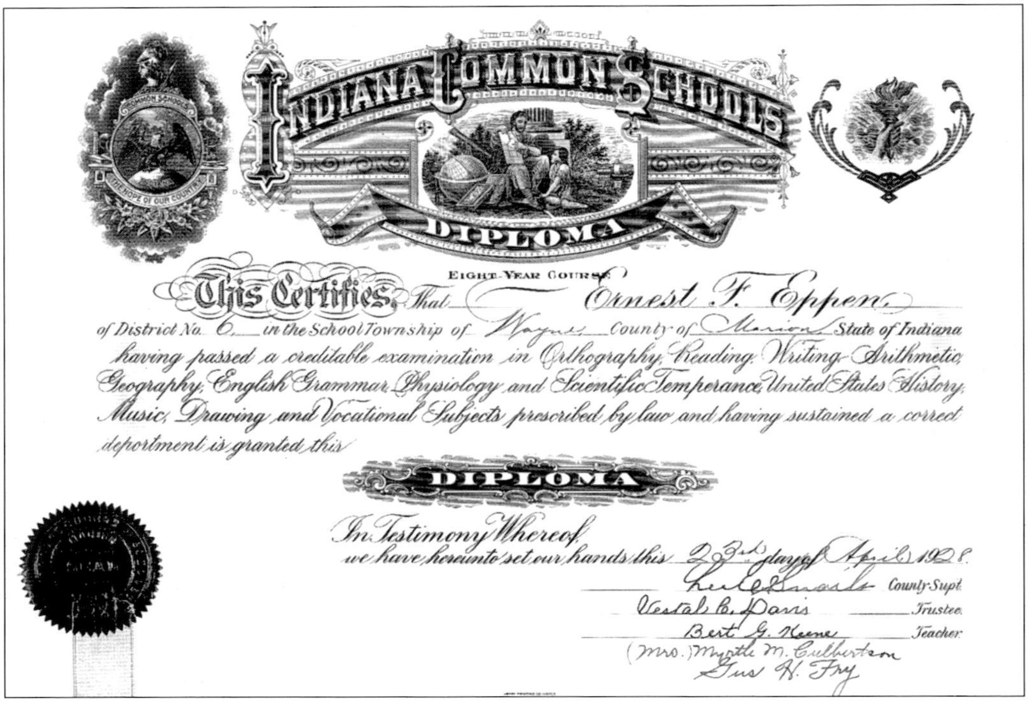

INDIANA COMMON SCHOOLS

DIPLOMA

EIGHT-YEAR COURSE

This Certifies, That Ernest F. Eppen of District No. 6 in the School Township of Wayne County of Marion State of Indiana having passed a creditable examination in Orthography, Reading, Writing, Arithmetic, Geography, English Grammar, Physiology and Scientific Temperance, United States History, Music, Drawing and Vocational Subjects prescribed by law and having sustained a correct deportment is granted this

DIPLOMA

In Testimony Whereof we have hereunto set our hands this 23rd day of April 1928.

County Supt.

Vestal C. Davis Trustee.

Bert G. Keene Teacher.

(Mrs.) Myrtle M. Culbertson

Gus H. Fry

When students completed the eighth grade in the Speedway schools, they received a diploma like this one. Speedway students then attended neighboring high schools until the town built its own. (Courtesy of the Eppen Family.)

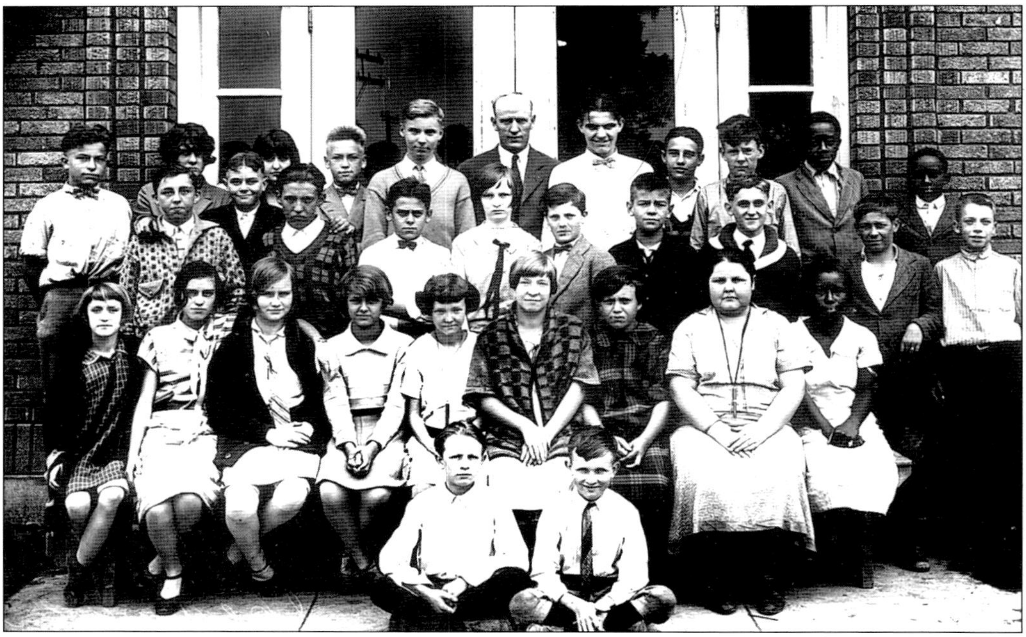

Ernest Eppen stands in the second row with his arms around two friends. This was the seventh and eighth grade class of 1927–1928. (Courtesy of the Eppen Family.)

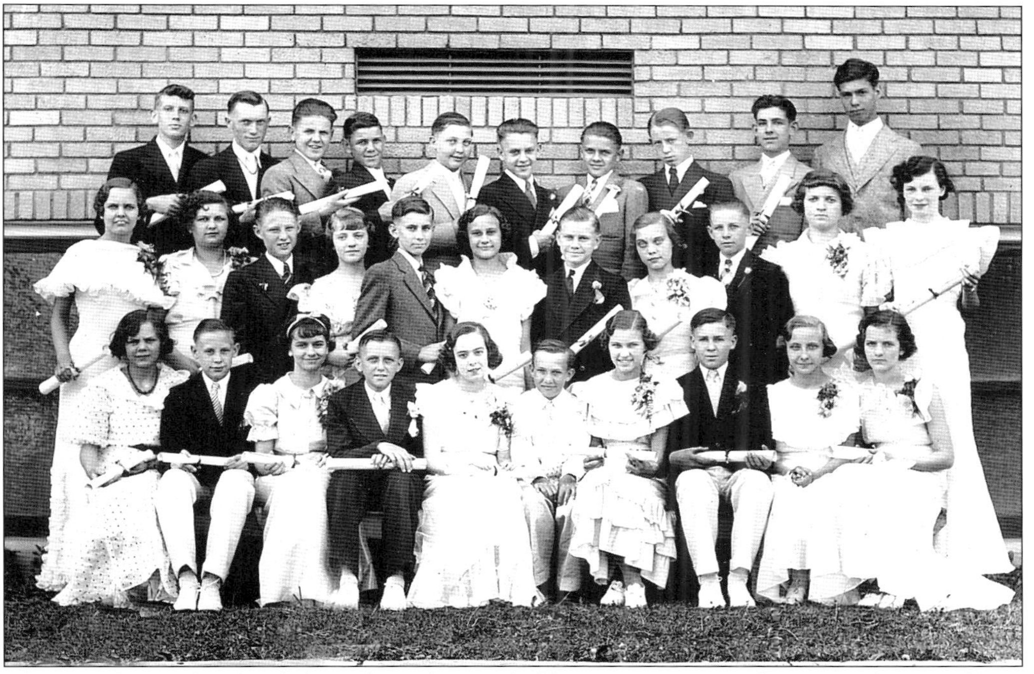

The Speedway School eighth grade graduation held in 1935 is pictured here. Carl Pieper (front row, third from right) poses with his classmates. (Courtesy of Carl Pieper.)

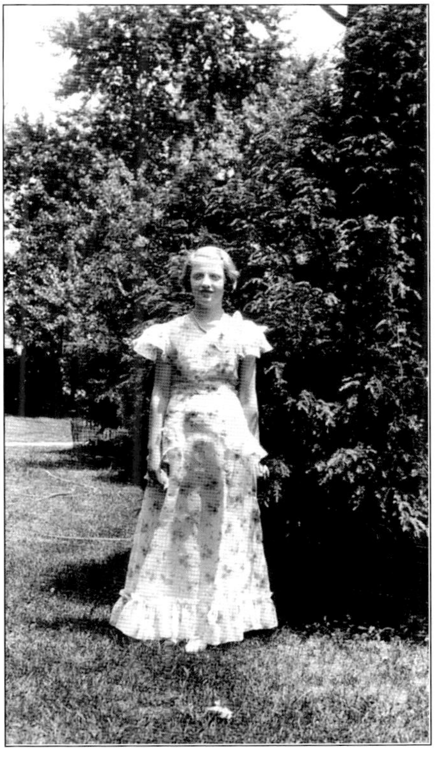

Edith Spencer wears her formal for the eighth grade graduation from Speedway School. (Courtesy of Edith Spencer.)

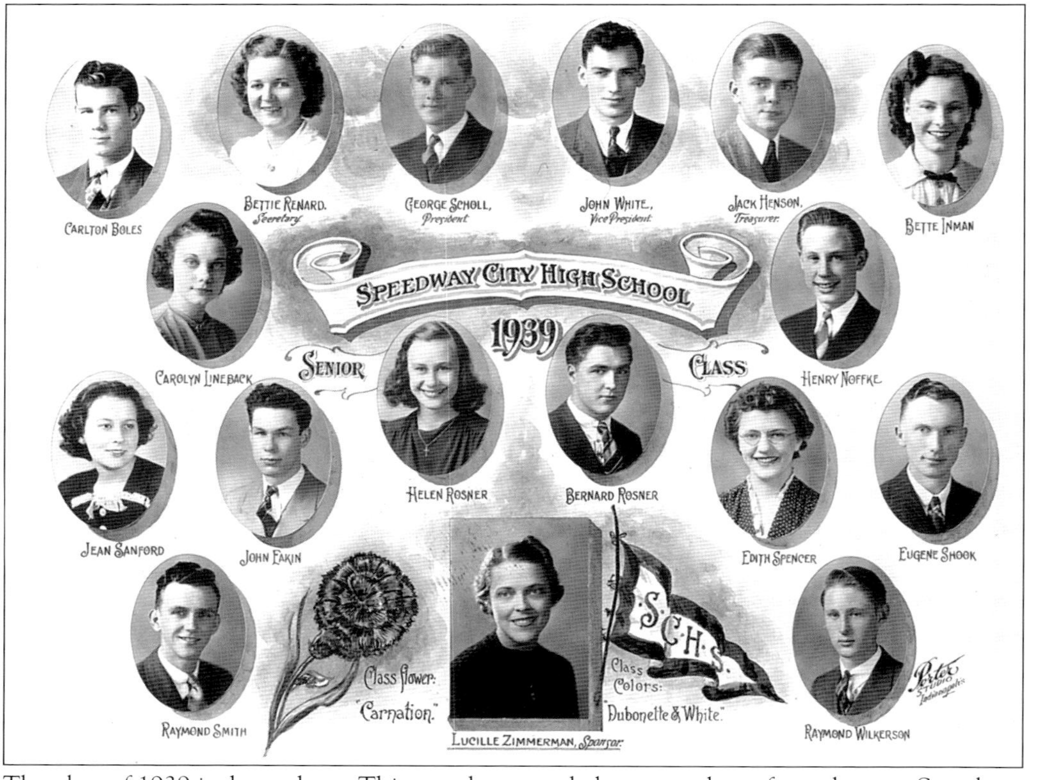

The class of 1939 is shown here. This was the second class to graduate from the new Speedway High School. (Courtesy of Edith Spencer.)

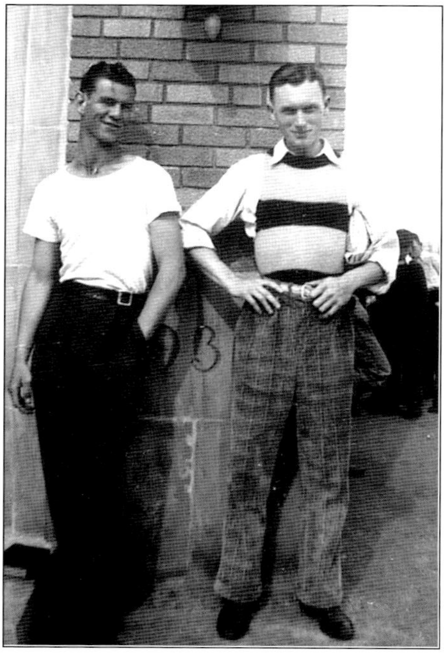

Seniors with the 1939 look pose outside of the school for casual shots. Here Carlton Boles and Eugene Shook pose. (Courtesy of Edith Spencer.)

These 1939 seniors were Barney Rosner and Raymond Smith. (Courtesy of Edith Spencer.)

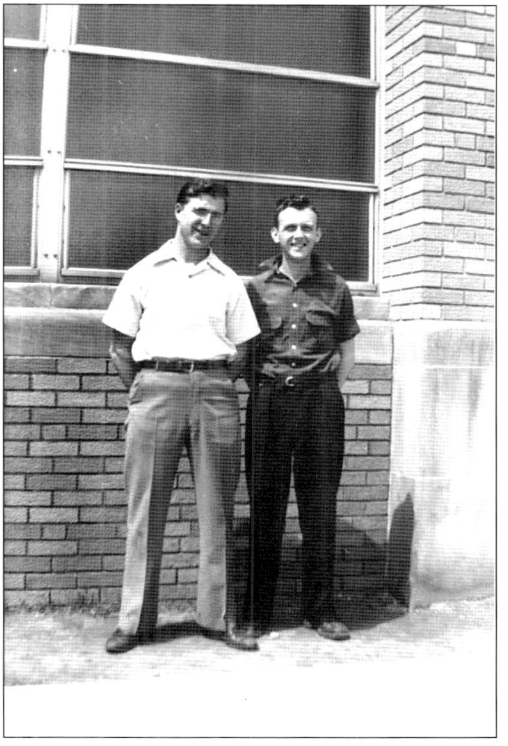

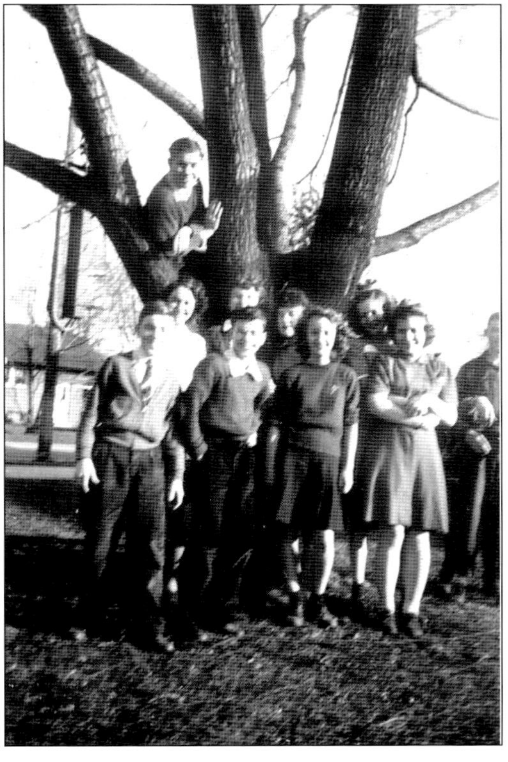

Members of the Speedway High School Latin Club pose for a casual shot in 1943. Their sponsor was Miss Agnes Spencer. (Courtesy of Edith Spencer.)

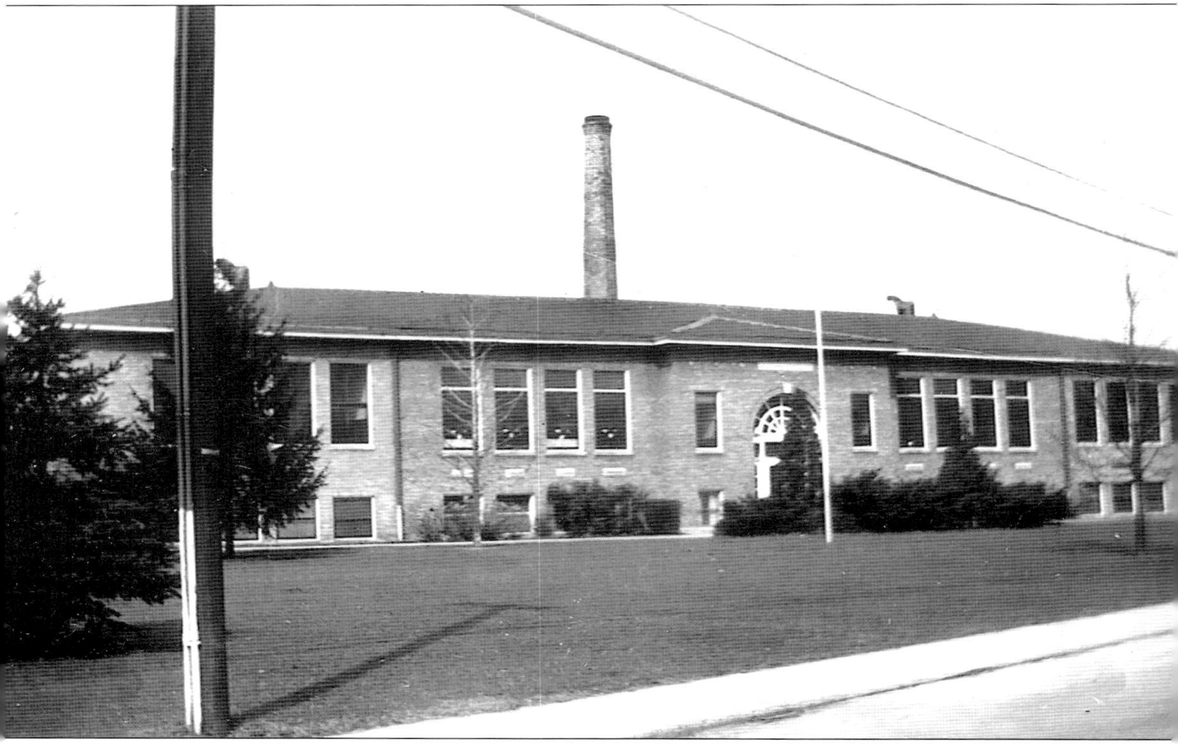

This Speedway School was built in 1918–1919. Speedway took control of its own schools in 1928. Prior to that date, the education of Speedway's children was the responsibility of Wayne Township Schools. Students were still sent to Ben Davis or Flackville schools to complete their high school work until Speedway High School opened in 1937. (Courtesy of Elizabeth Frazier.)

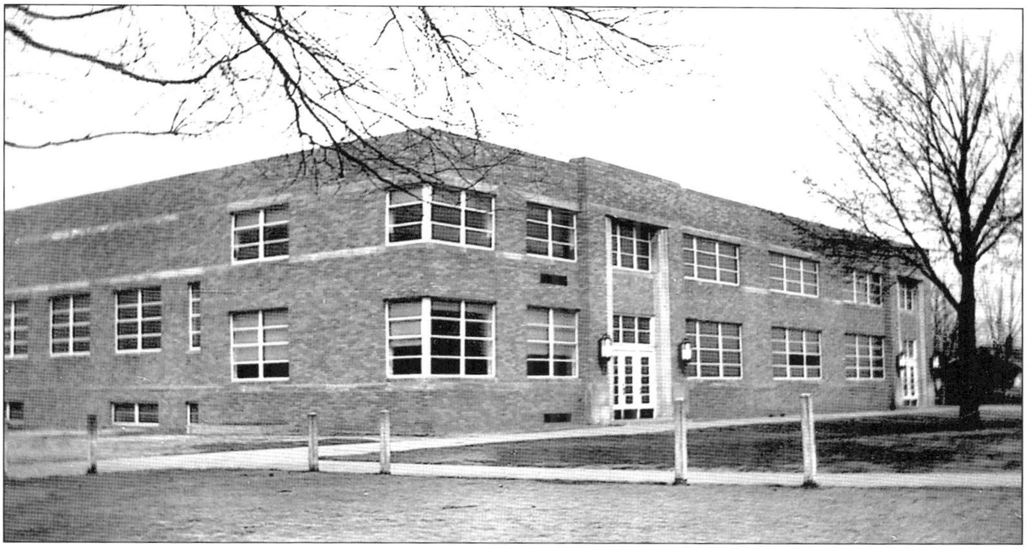

The cornerstone for the first Speedway High School was laid on January 6, 1937. The school consisted of a gym and seven classrooms. Today the old high school is incorporated into the Speedway Junior High School building. (Courtesy of Elizabeth Frazier.)

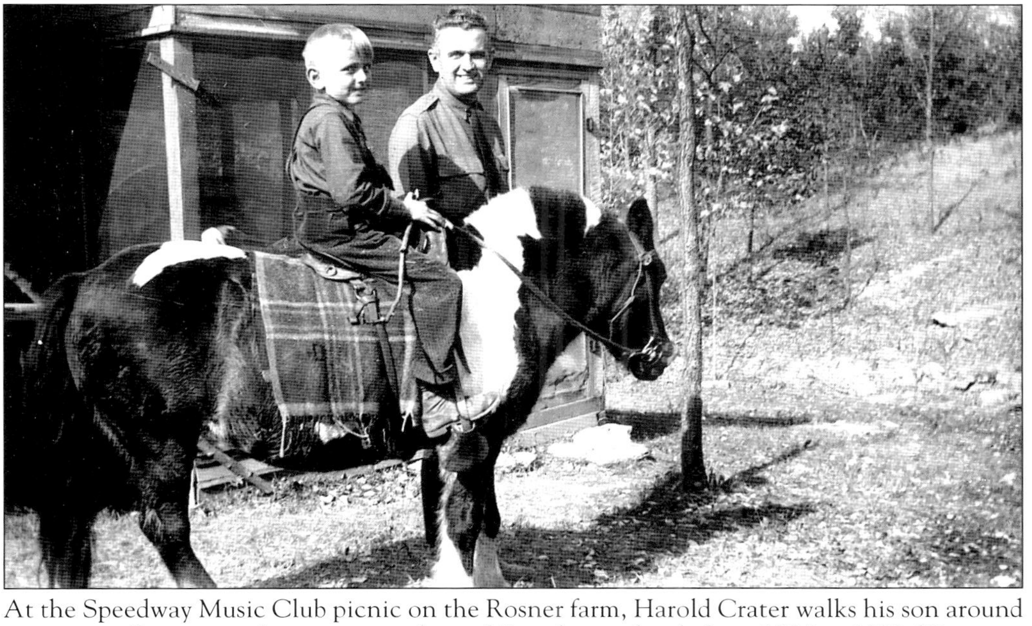

At the Speedway Music Club picnic on the Rosner farm, Harold Crater walks his son around on a pony. Crater was the superintendent of Speedway schools from 1936 to 1939 (Courtesy of Edith Spencer.)

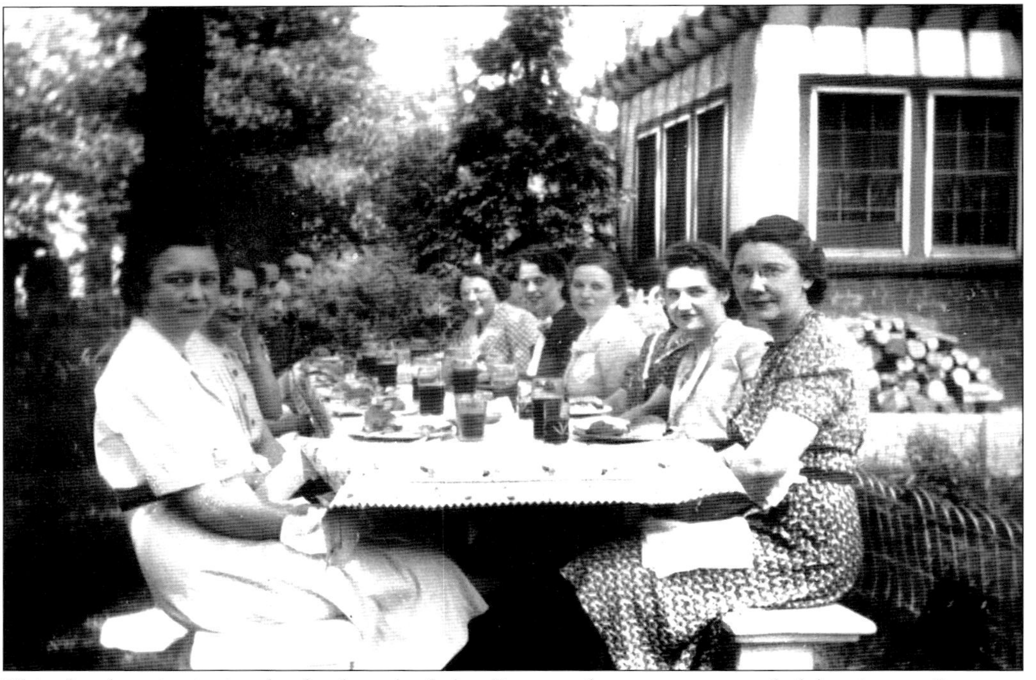

This faculty picnic in the backyard of the Spencer home was attended by Agnes Spencer, Virginia Updike, Lucille Zimmerman, Edna Baldauf, M. Bilby, and Muriel Thompson. (Courtesy of Edith Spencer.)

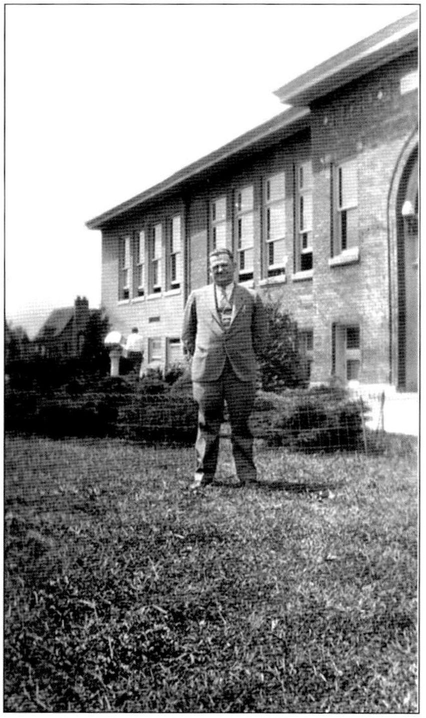

Roy Jay was the principal of the Speedway School from 1932 to 1936. Here he poses in front of the school. (Courtesy of Edith Spencer.)

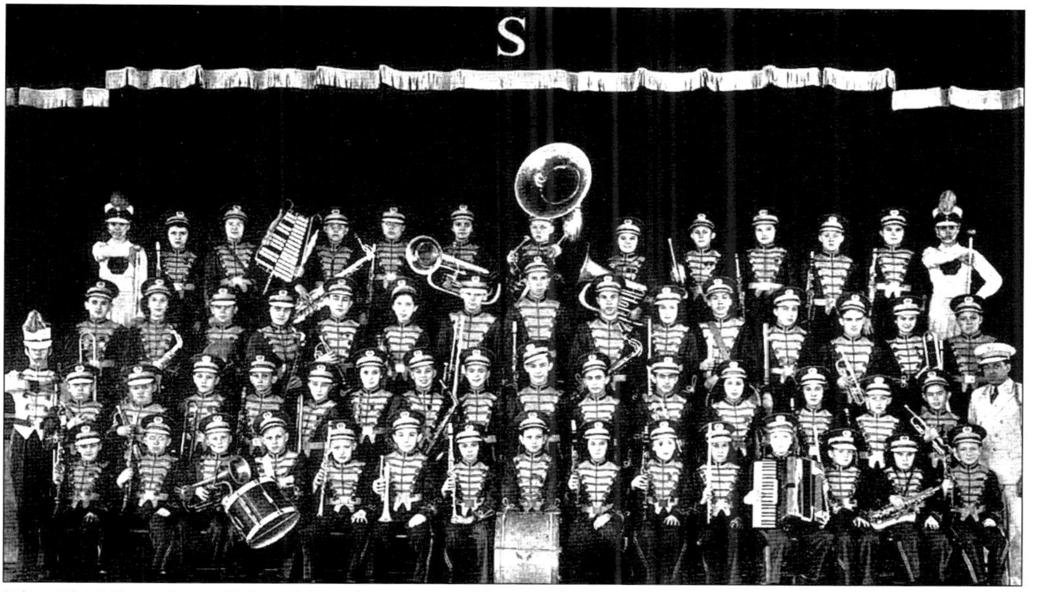

The 1941 Speedway School Band is pictured here. The band included children from elementary ages through high school. The band director, Mr. Lincoln Northcutt, stands in the front row, far right. (Courtesy of Speedway Schools.)

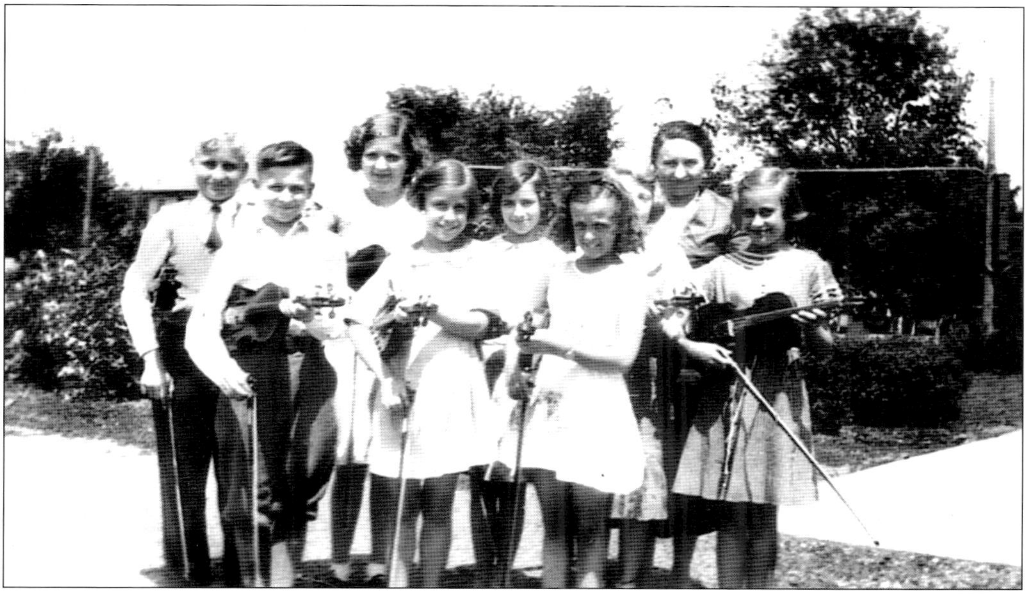

Violinists pose for a summer picture in the 1920s. Carl Pieper is the second student from the left. (Courtesy of Carl Pieper.)

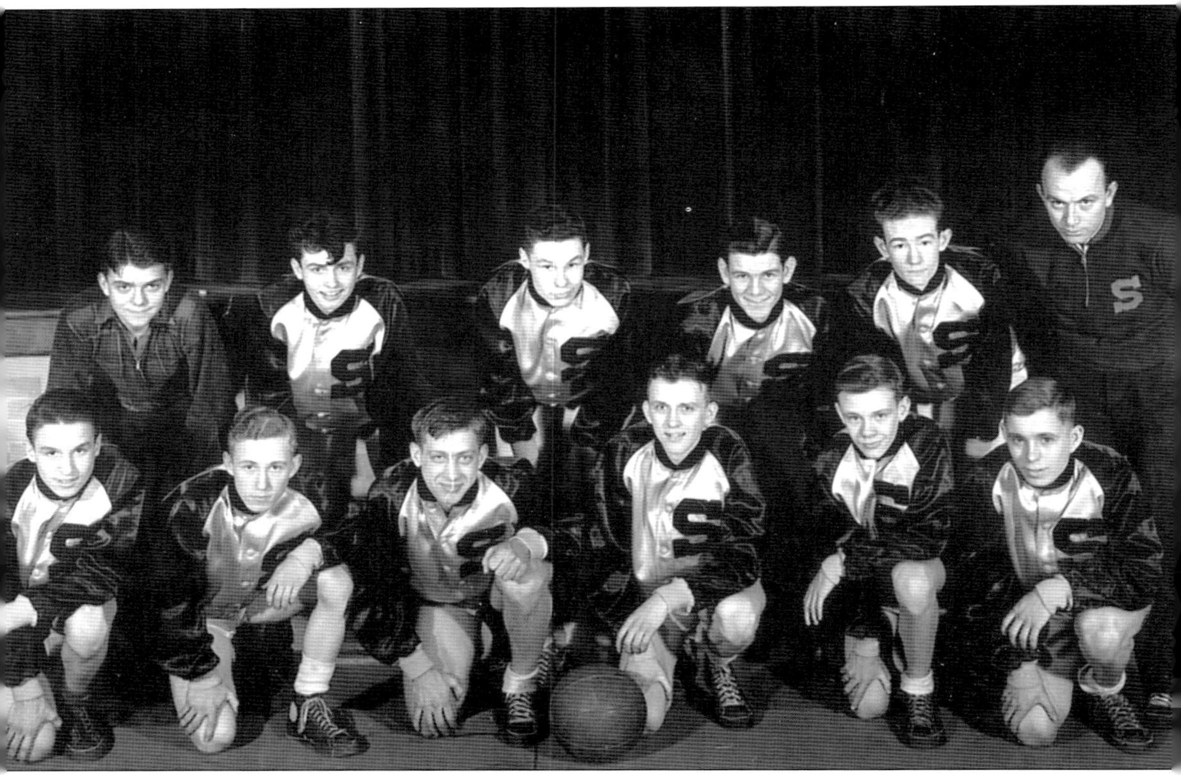

Many young men were coached by Ralph Johnson (back row, right). The 1937–1938 Speedway School basketball team included: (front row) John Ewing, Andy Downs, Burt Eversole, Raymond Smith, Paul Stamm, Art Higbee; (back row) Jack Henson, Harvey Phipps, John Eakin, Bus Boles, Joe Powderly, and Ralph Johnson, coach. (Courtesy of Charles Bennett.)

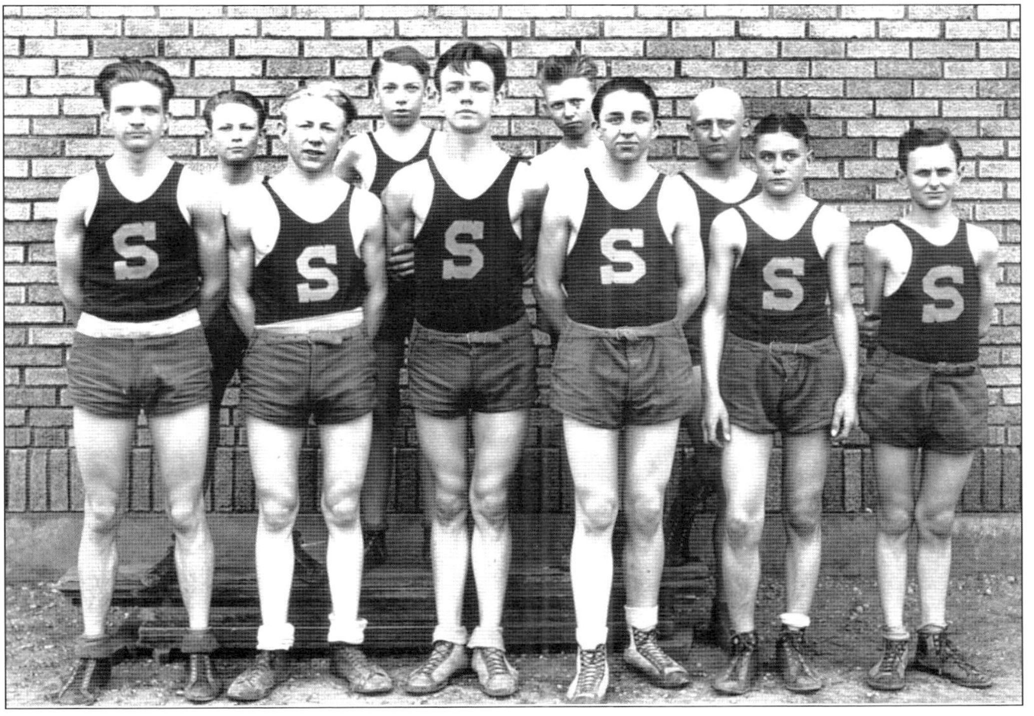

The basketball team of 1927 had a slightly different look. Ernie Eppen poses on the front row, second from the right. (Courtesy of the Eppen Family.)

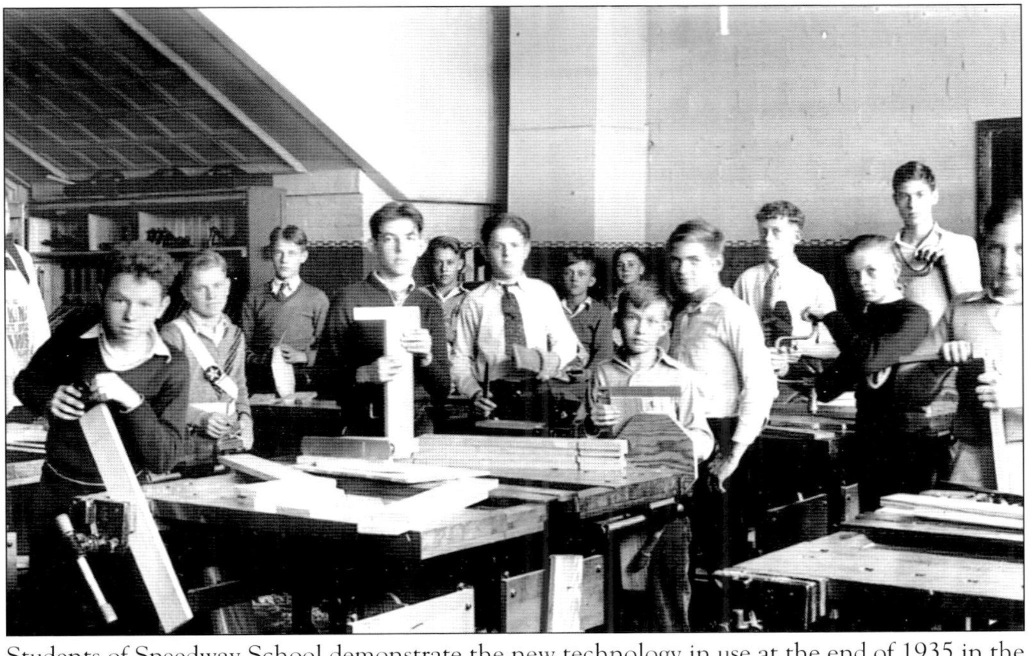

Students of Speedway School demonstrate the new technology in use at the end of 1935 in the industrial arts classes. Carl Pieper is in the very back, center. (Courtesy of Carl Pieper.)

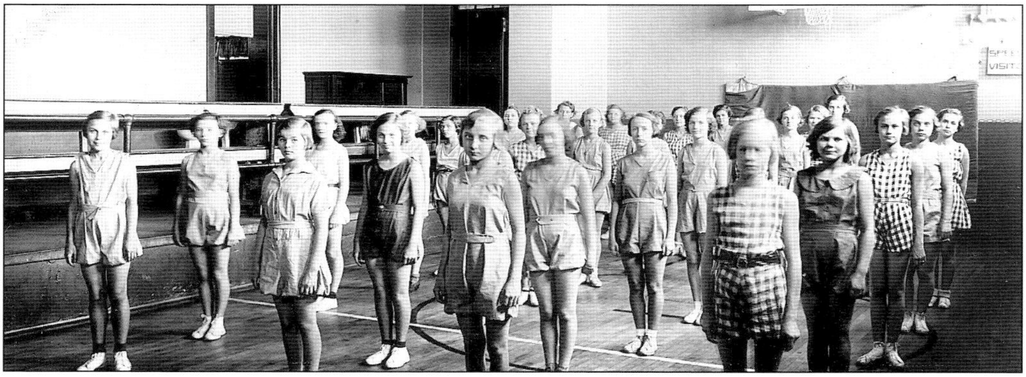

Here, girls line up for gym class in 1935. One-piece gym suits were standard wear for the day. (Courtesy of Edith Spencer.)

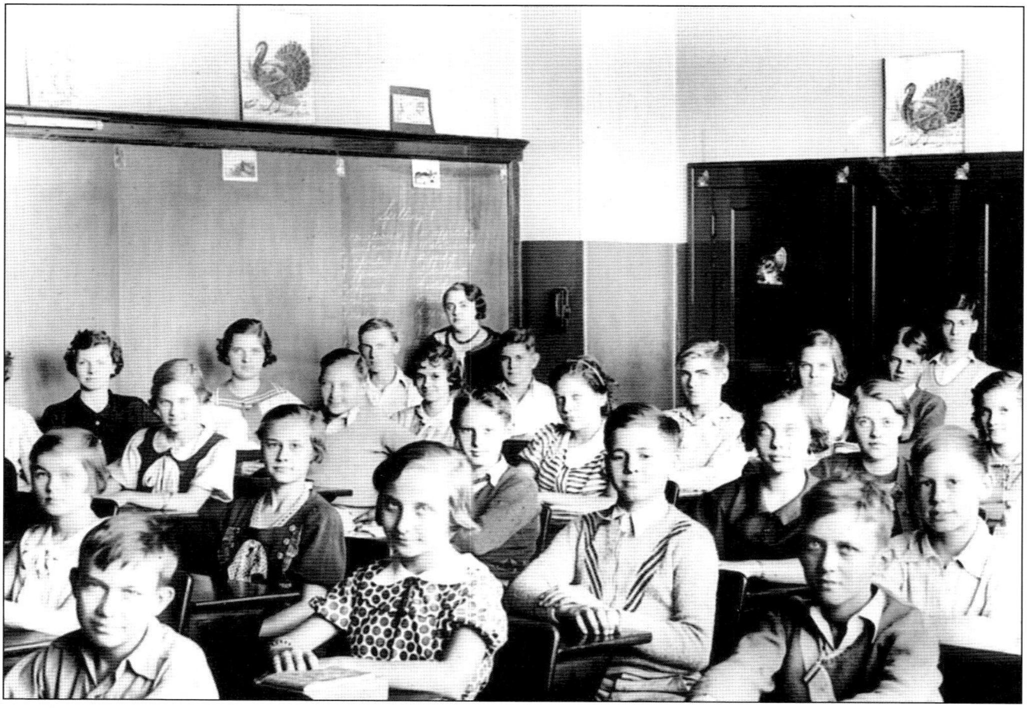

Students in the Speedway eighth grade class of 1935 pose in their English, spelling club, and homeroom classroom decorated for Thanksgiving. Carl Pieper poses in center front, third from left. Miss Agnes Spencer is in the back. (Courtesy of Carl Pieper and Edith Spencer.)

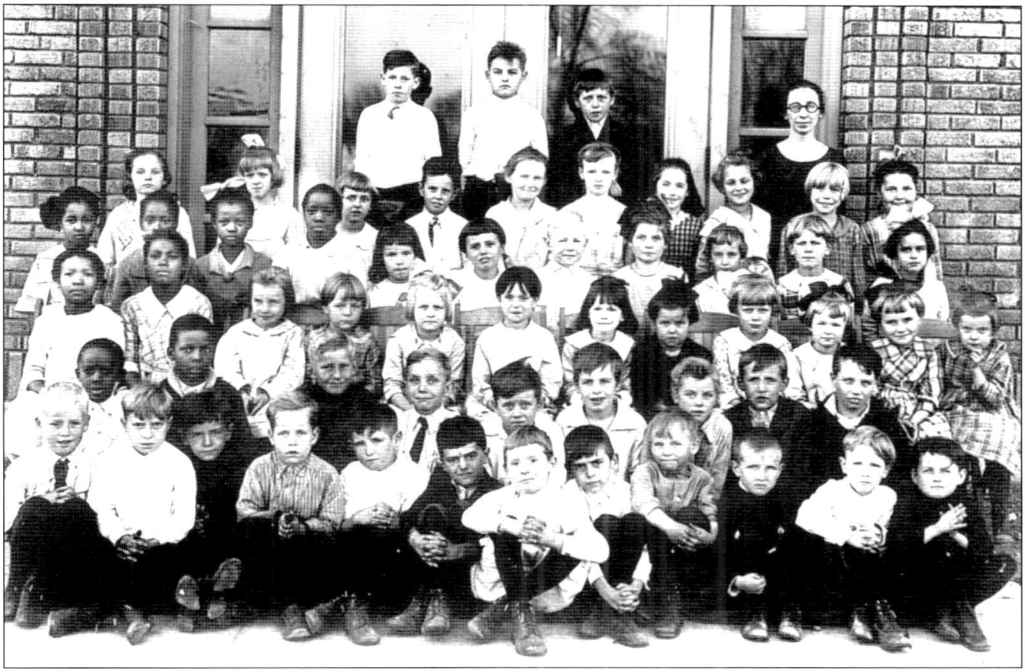

The first grade class of 1921 included Ernest Eppen in the second row, third from left. (Courtesy of the Eppen Family.)

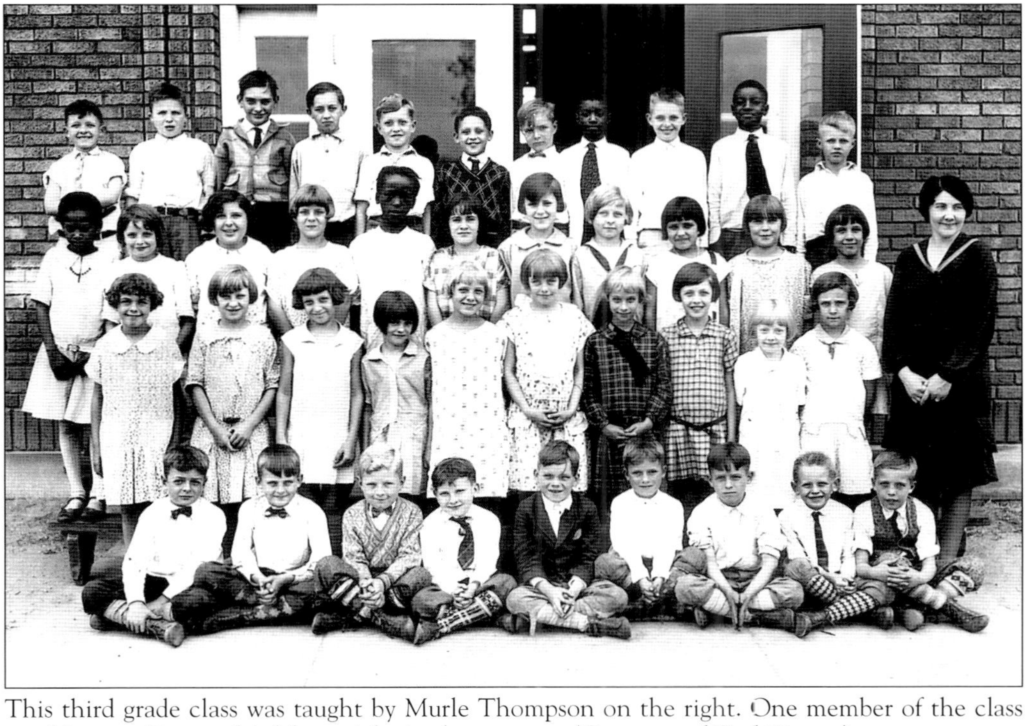

This third grade class was taught by Murle Thompson on the right. One member of the class was Herman Pieper, third from right in the top row. (Courtesy of Carl Pieper.)

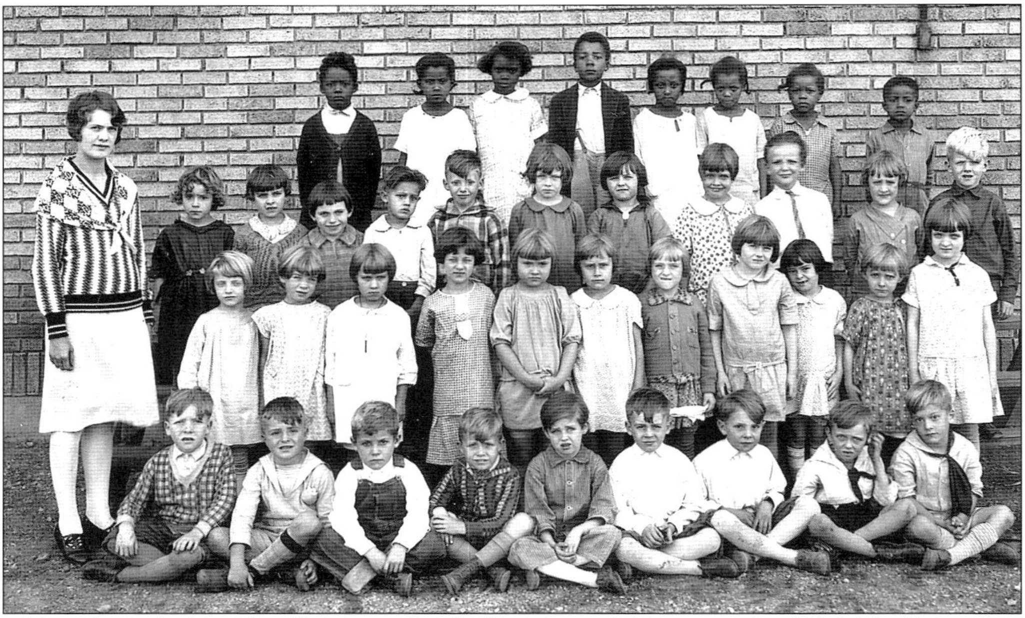

Miss Irene Robey was the teacher of this first grade class in 1927–1928. The class included Carl Pieper, fourth from the right in the front row. (Courtesy of Carl Pieper.)

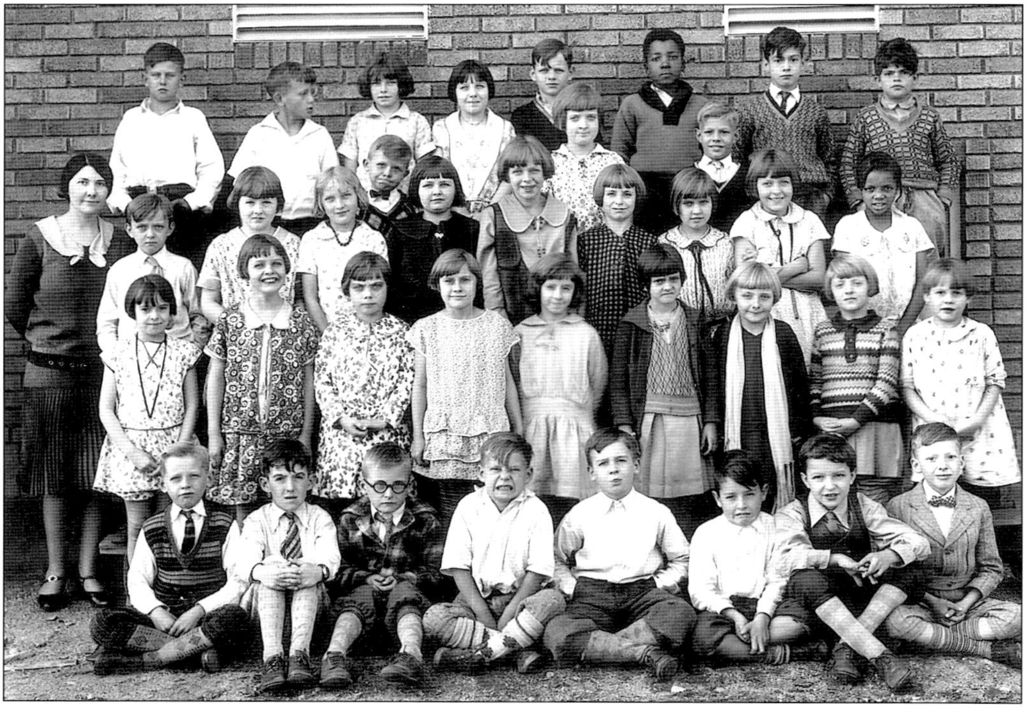

Murle Thompson was the teacher in charge of this third grade class in 1929-1930. Carl Pieper (first row, fourth from right) is surrounded by his classmates in knickers. Little boys who like to make faces at the camera have not changed much over the years. (Courtesy of Carl Pieper.)

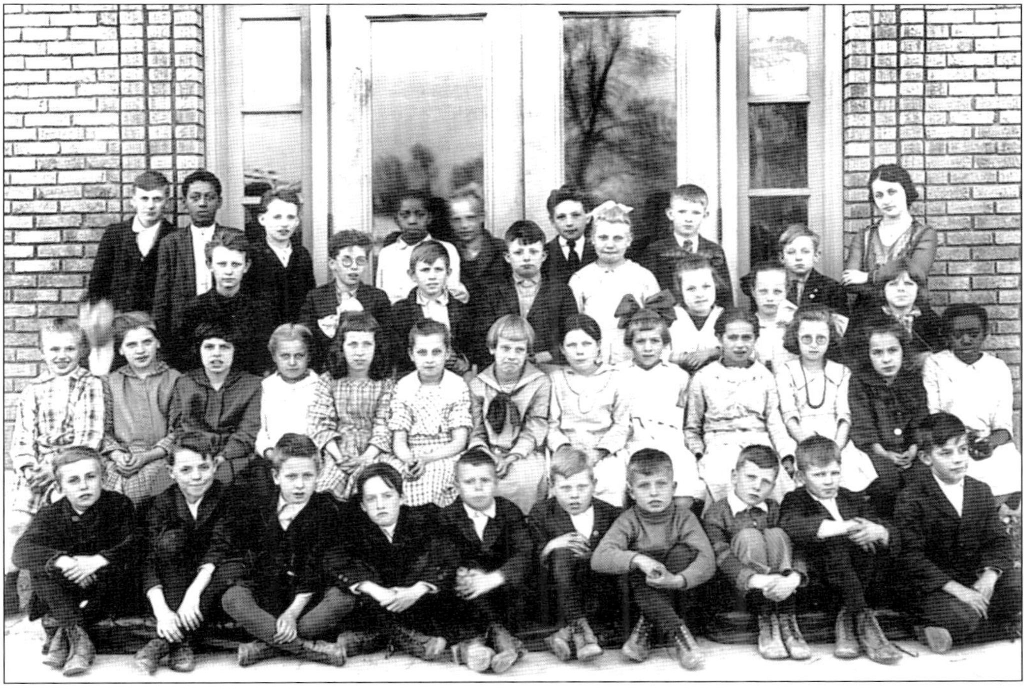

Around 1920, the fourth grade at Speedway school was taught by Mrs. (Fogelman) Ramsay. Francis and Louise Eppen are in this class. (Courtesy of the Eppen Family.)

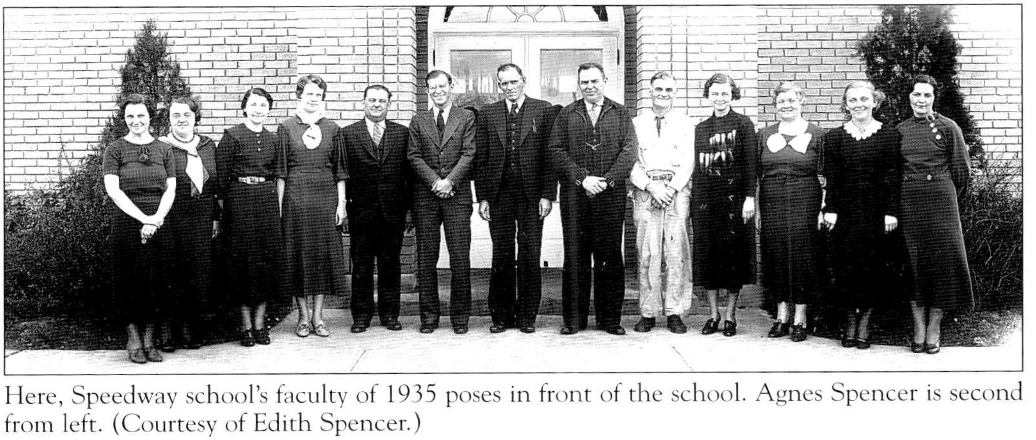

Here, Speedway school's faculty of 1935 poses in front of the school. Agnes Spencer is second from left. (Courtesy of Edith Spencer.)

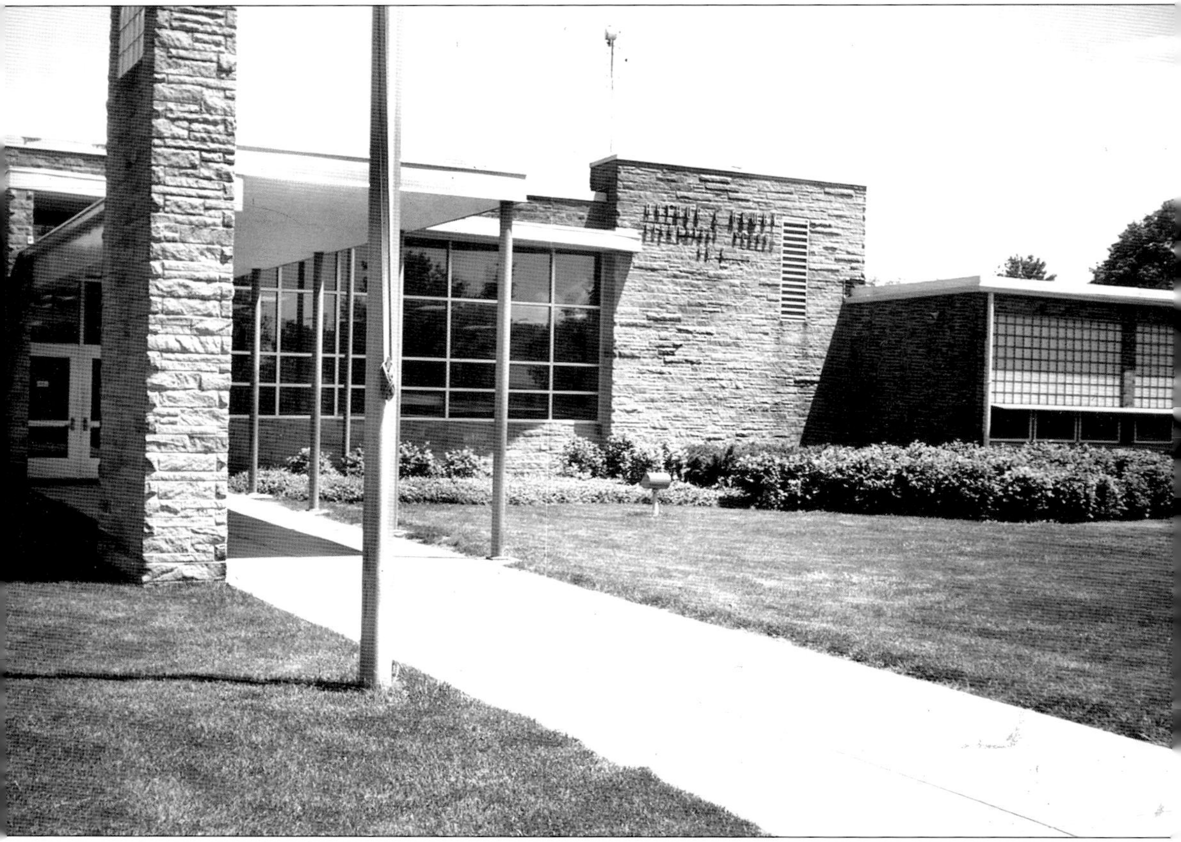

Arthur C. Newby Elementary School was built in 1951. It is one of the four elementary schools in Speedway named for the founders of the Indianapolis Motor Speedway.

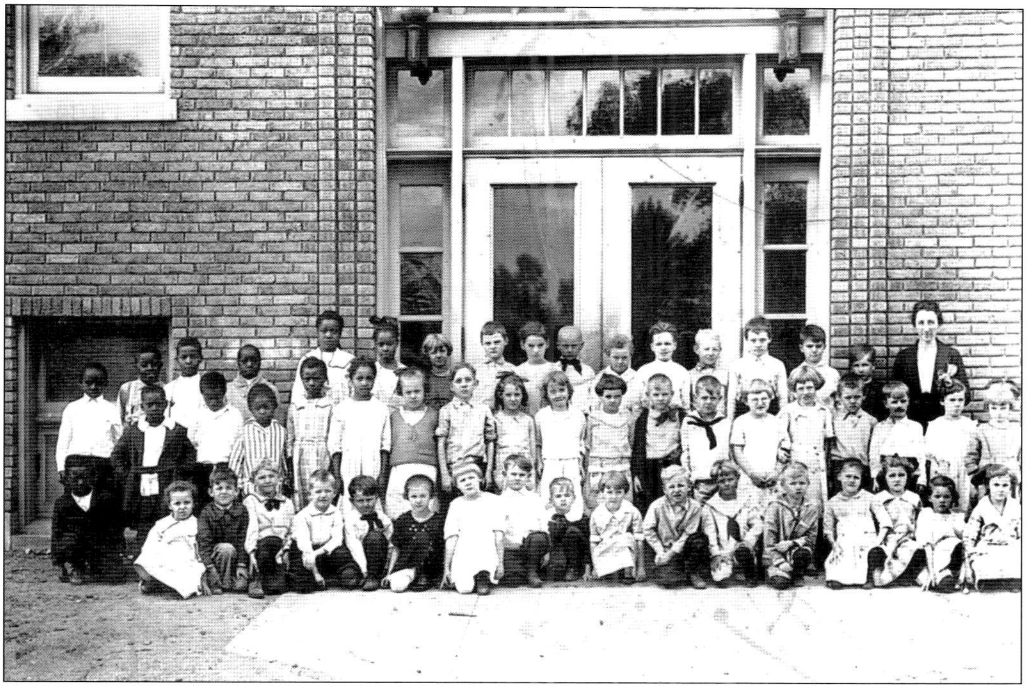

In front of Speedway School in 1921, a group of second graders pose for their class picture. Ernest Eppen is in the back row, eighth from the right. (Courtesy of the Eppen Family.)

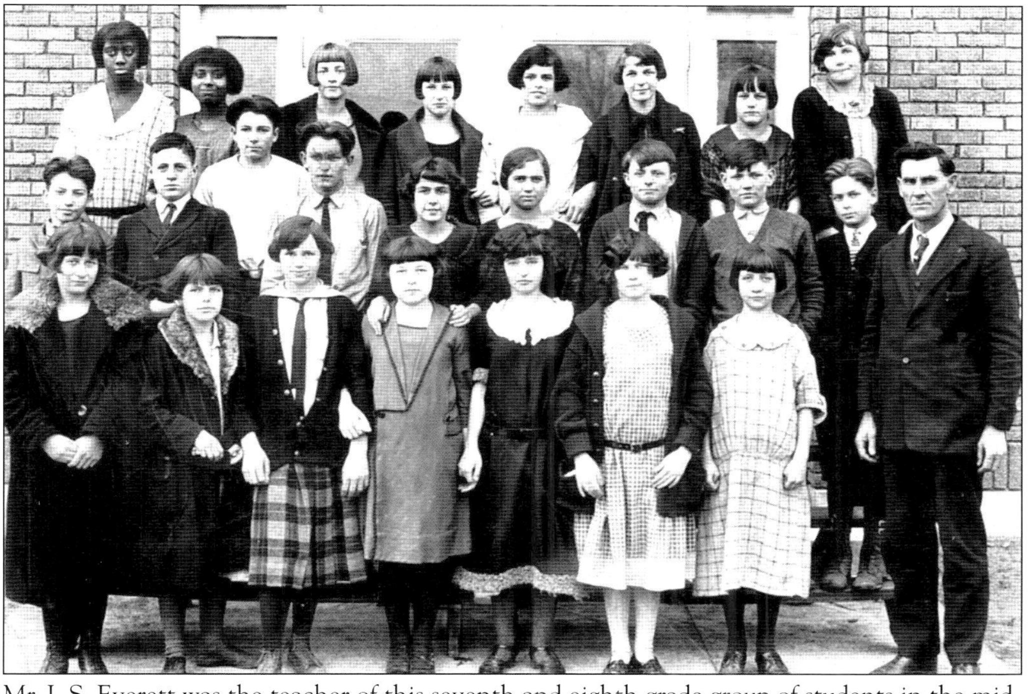

Mr. L.S. Everett was the teacher of this seventh and eighth grade group of students in the mid-1920s. Frances and Louise Eppen are among the students. (Courtesy of the Eppen Family.)

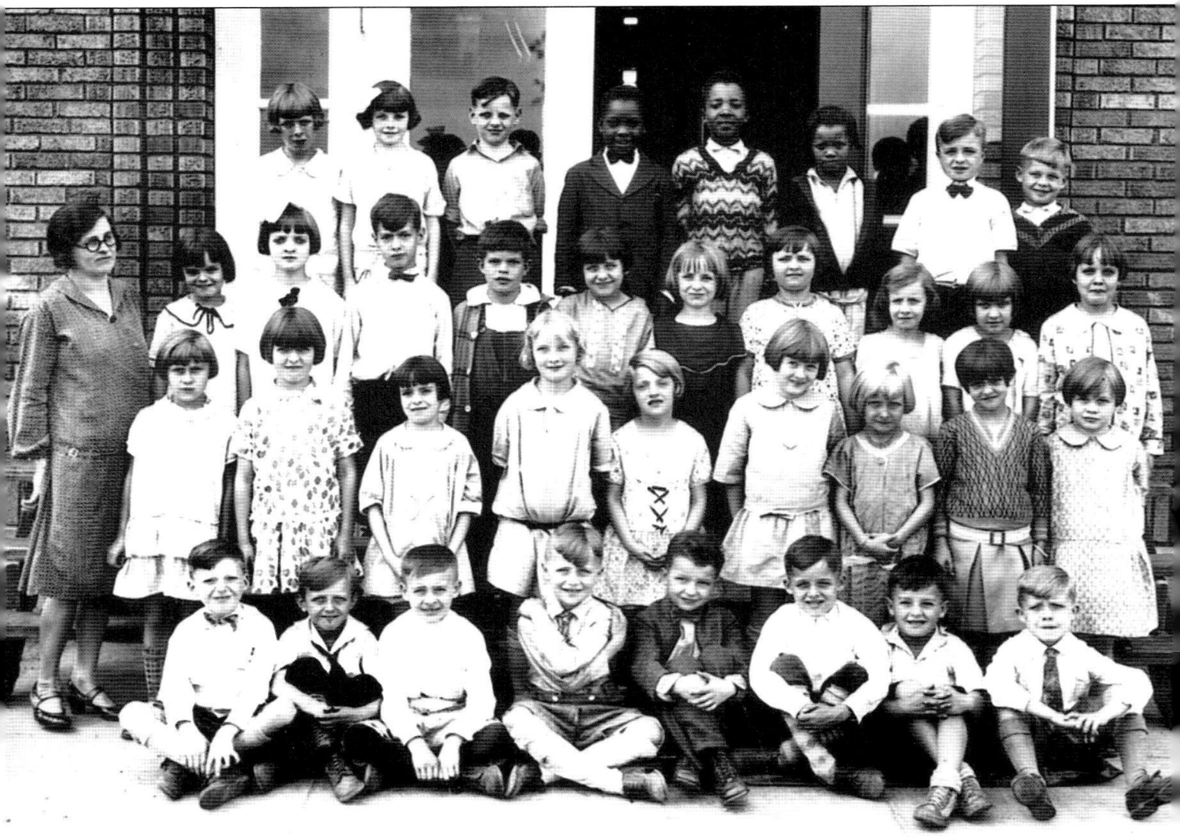

Rose Kreutzinger was the teacher with this class of second graders in 1928–1929. Carl Pieper is third from the left on the ground. (Courtesy of Carl Pieper.)

Five

Places Remembered

The town of Speedway did not remain outside of the encroaching city of Indianapolis for long. The fields and farms of the outlying area gave way to the building boom that followed WW II and continue to do so today. The farmlands became shopping plazas and housing additions. The sights and sounds of the small town six miles from Indianapolis changed dramatically with the times. Even today, landmarks disappear and change as the town grows and develops.

But pictures and memories of the days gone by still exist. Ernie Eppen remembers the soldiers who were German prisoners of war during WW I being held in the military facility on the corner of Main and 10th Streets. He remembers the soldiers coming to the farm to get soil for planting their own crops, and he also remembers that the German soldiers liked the United States very well. Perhaps they were lucky to have ended up in Speedway.

The reflections of days gone by are quickly disappearing. But we can still peek into the past through the pictures that remain.

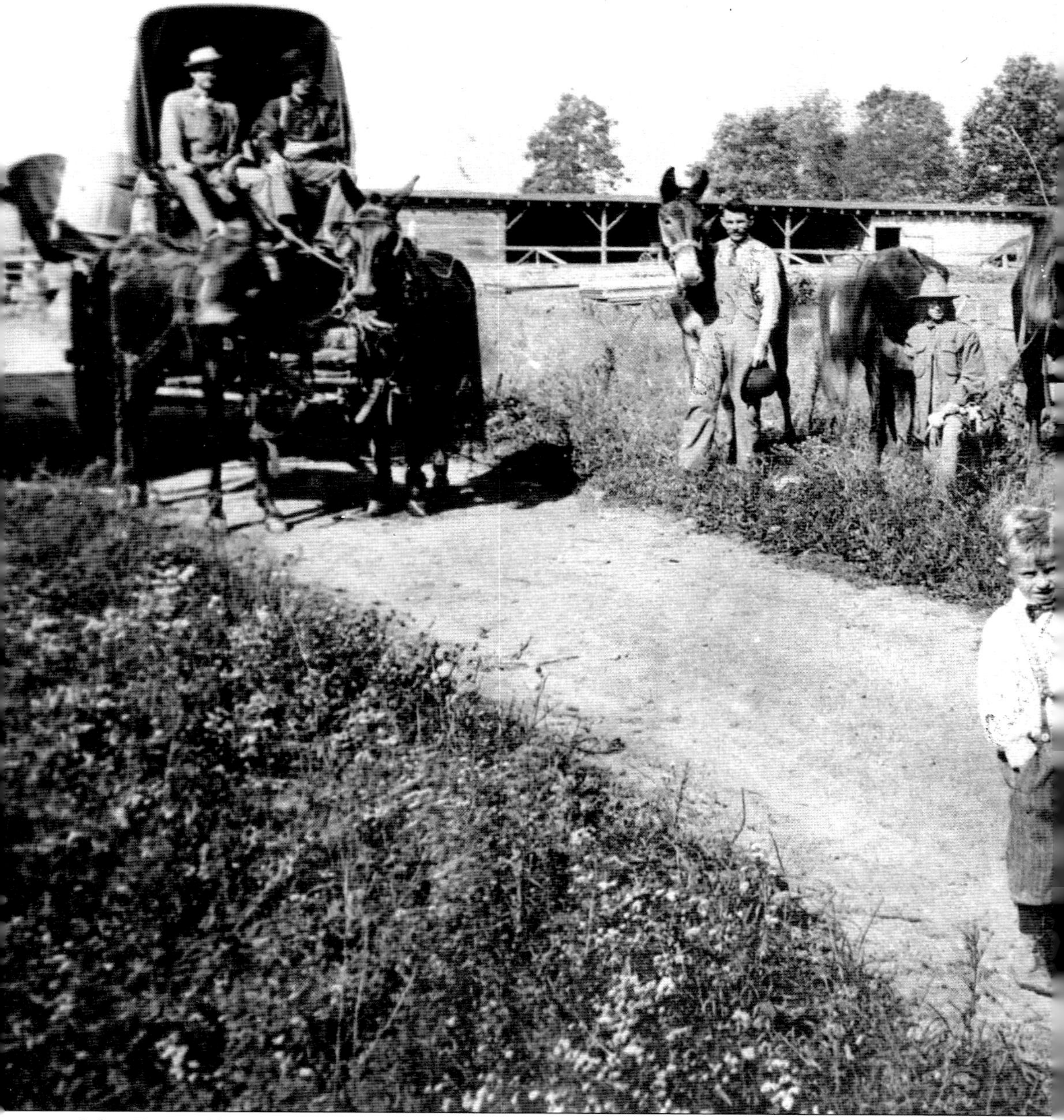

John Eppen (first man standing on left) bought his farm on Georgetown Road in 1908. Here the family and workers pose for a picture in 1910. Herman and Reinhart Eppen are in front with the basket. John Adams and Curt Manner are on the wagon, then John Eppen, unidentified,

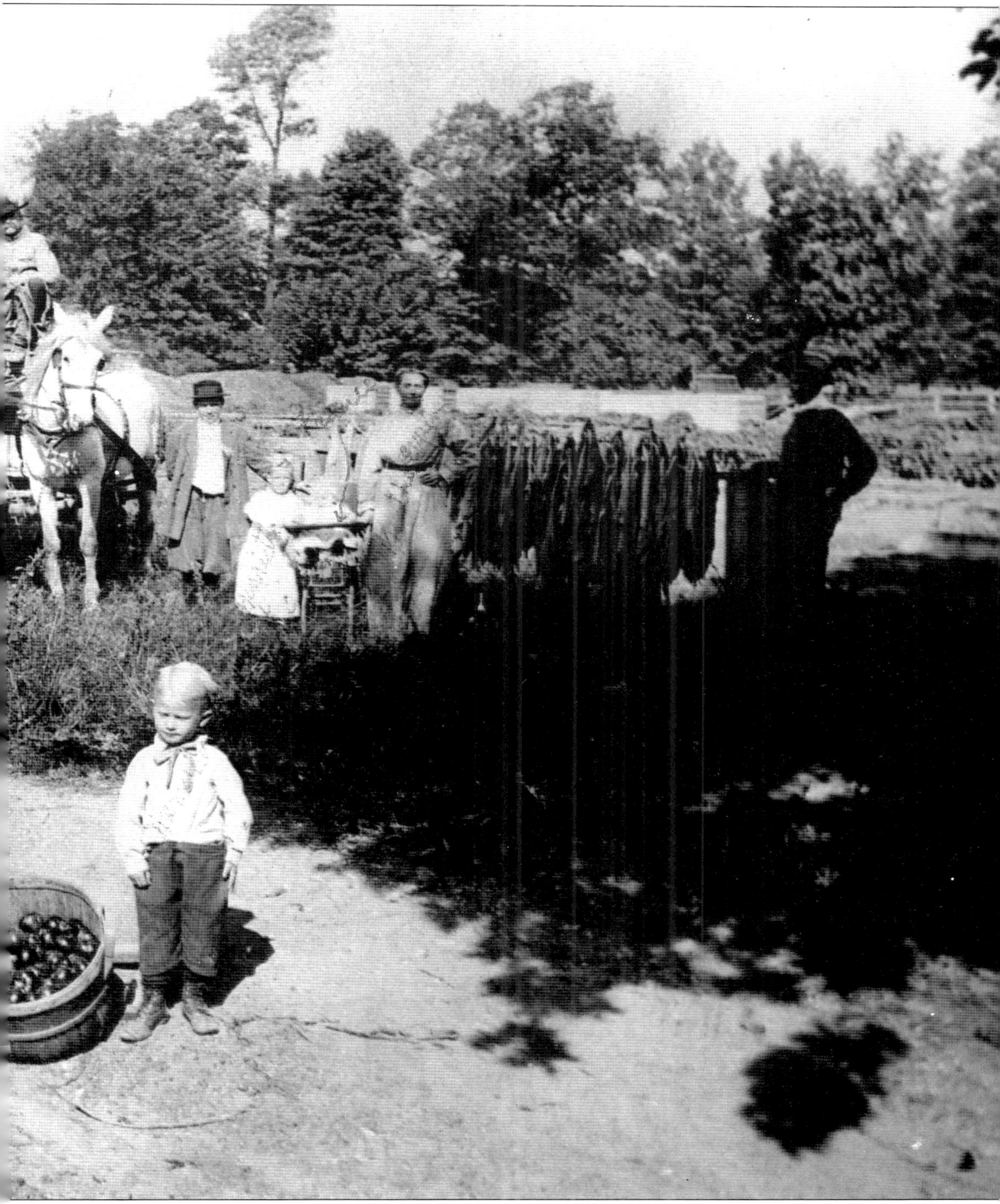

Frank Ziegelmueller, Harry Adams, Bertha Eppen, Harry Adams, Henrietta and Frances Eppen, Bertha Eppen (John's wife), and Jim County. (Courtesy of the Eppen Family.)

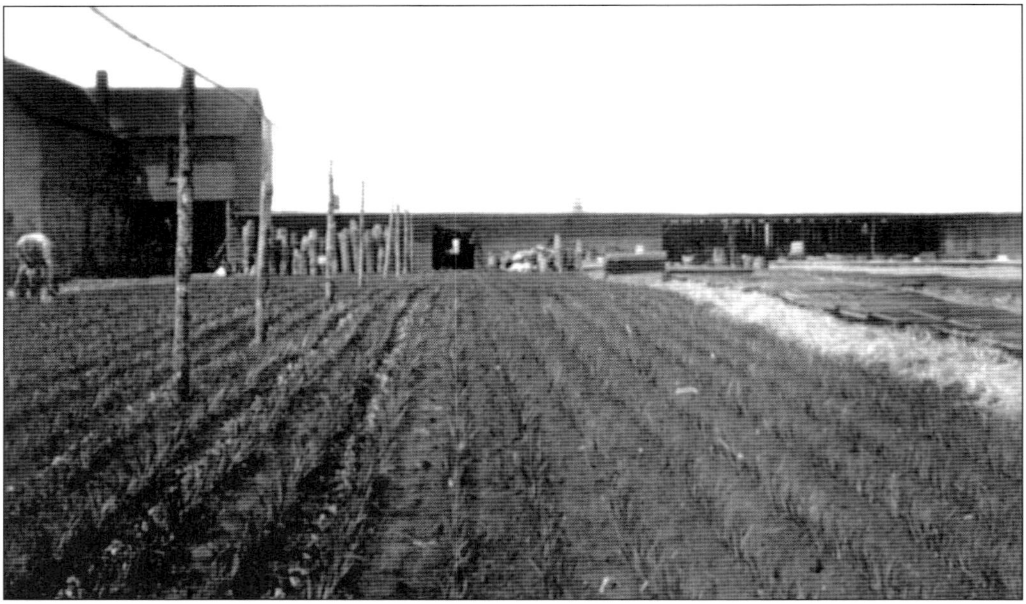

These onion fields and sheds stretched out behind the house on Georgetown Road. During spring break, many students from the area would earn money working in the onion fields. (Courtesy of the Eppen Family.)

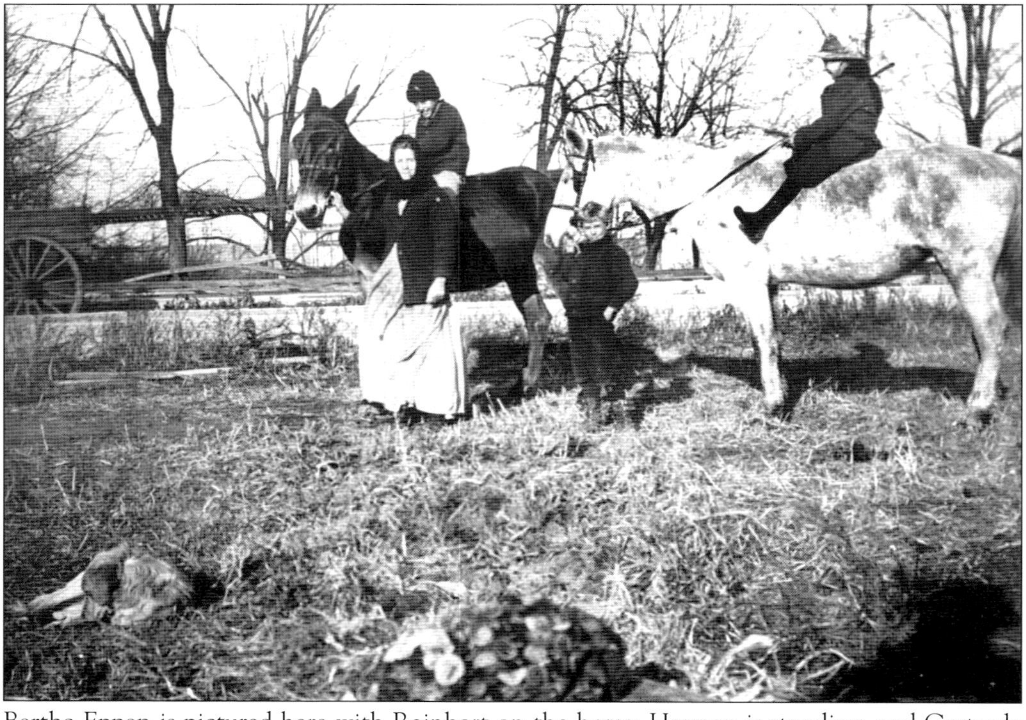

Bertha Eppen is pictured here with Reinhart on the horse; Herman is standing, and Gertrude Wenzler is on the light-colored horse in the field along Georgetown Road. (Courtesy of the Eppen Family.)

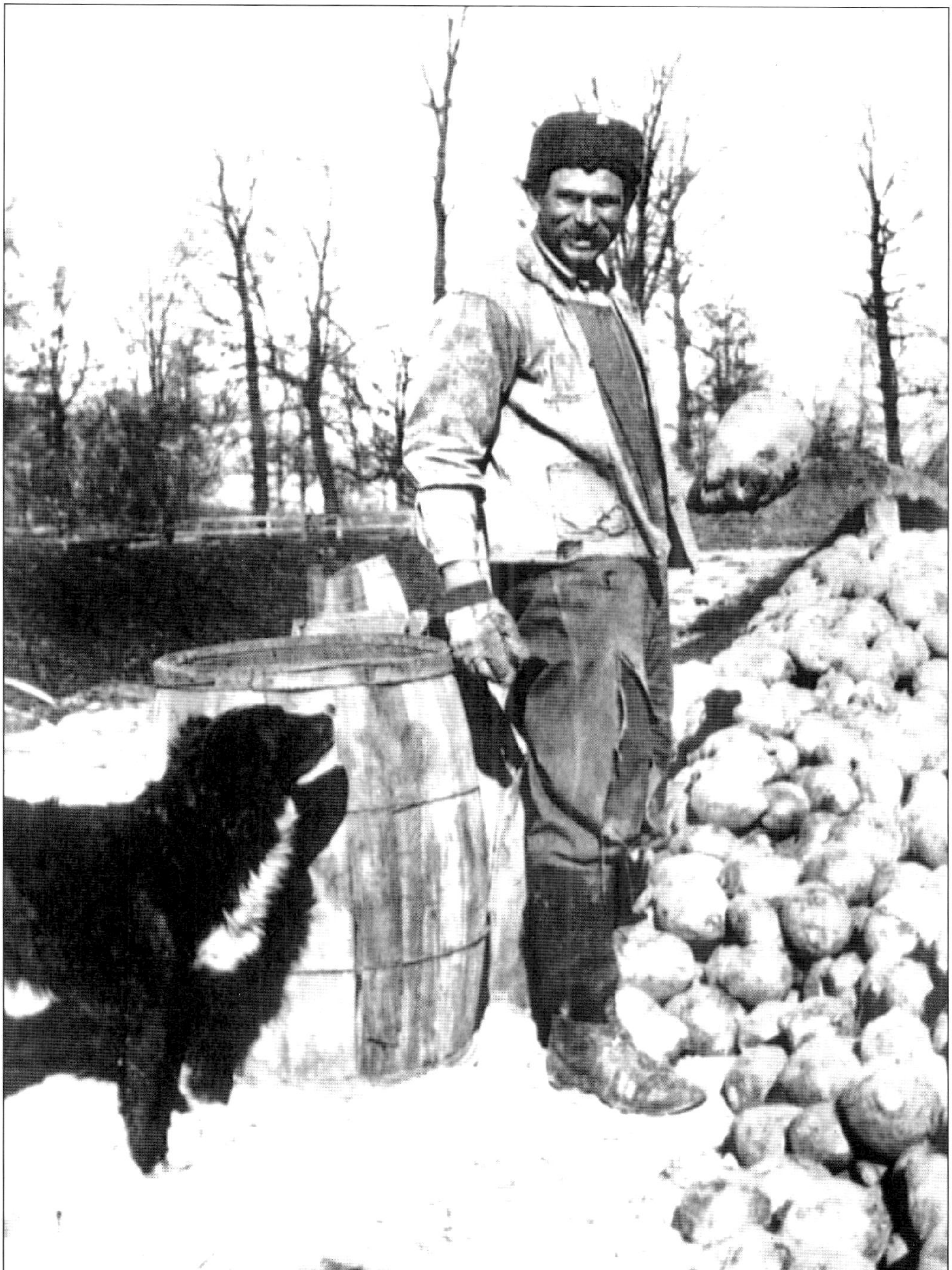

John Eppen is shown here with a rutabaga crop. On his 45-acre truck farm he also raised winter and spring onions, beets, carrots, dill, sage, and other crops to sell around the courthouse in downtown Indianapolis. Later, the truck market moved to the area where Eli Lily is located today. (Courtesy of the Eppen Family.)

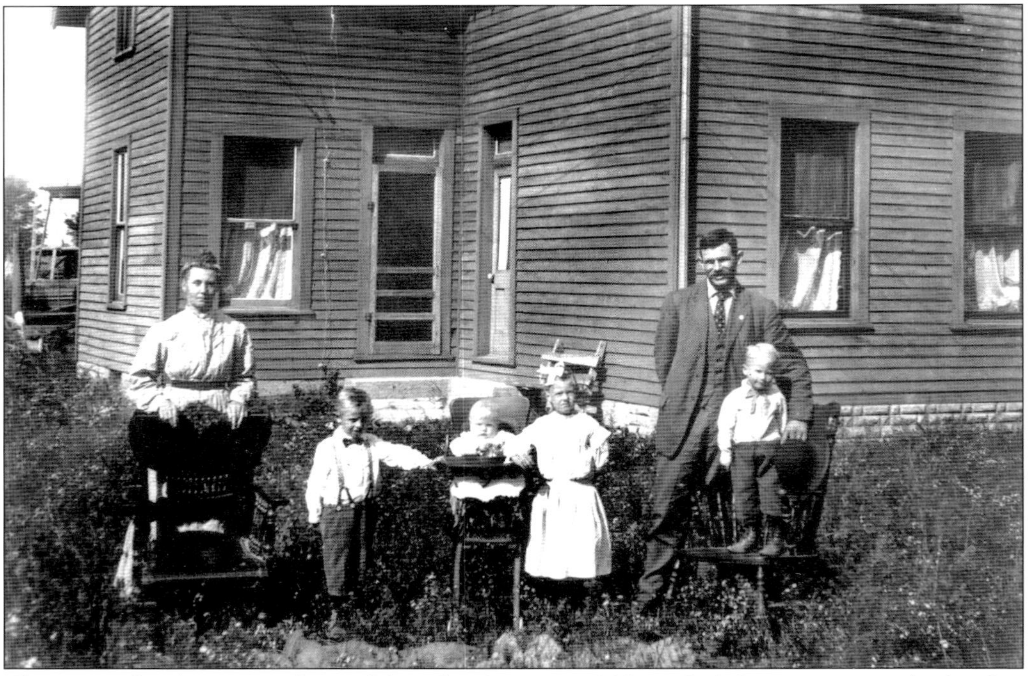

The Eppen family poses in front of their farmhouse in 1909 or 1910. It was common for families of that time to pose with prized possessions, which may be why Mrs. Eppen is holding the chair. Pictured are Bertha Eppen, Reinhart, Frances, Henrietta, John, and Herman. (Courtesy of the Eppen Family.)

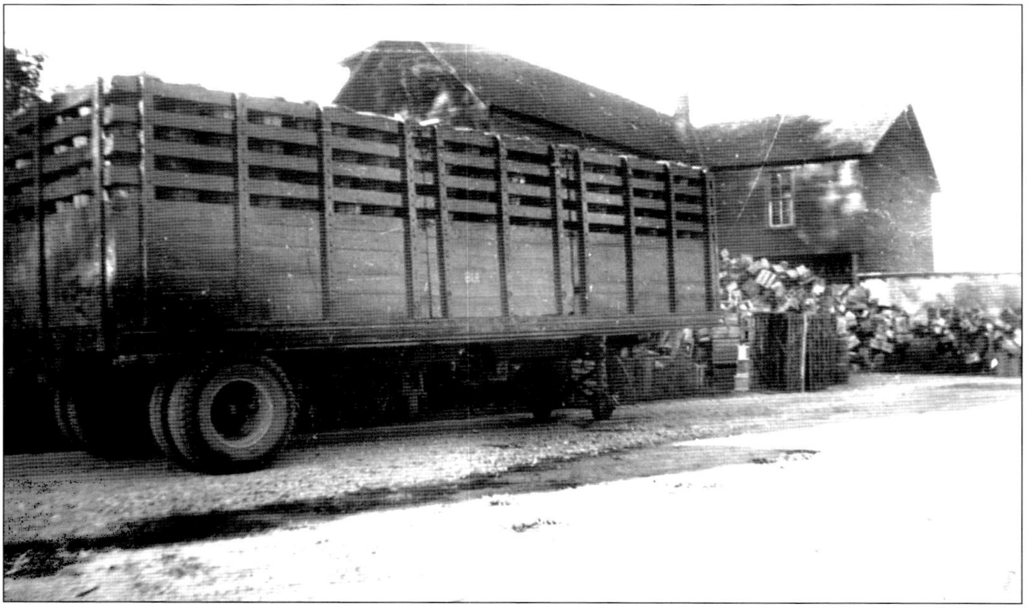

A large truck filled with market produce waits outside of the old Eppen home. (Courtesy of the Eppen Family.)

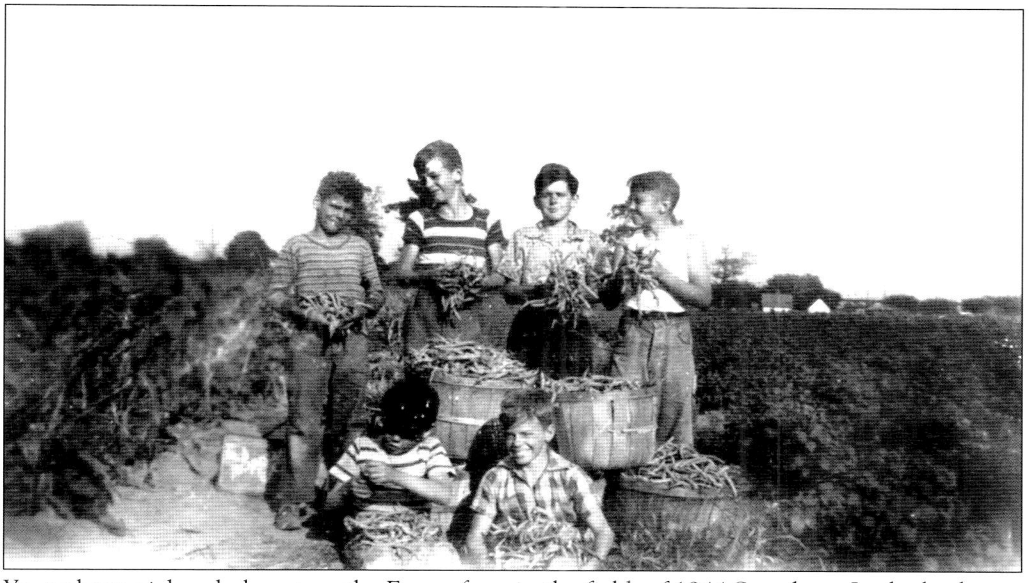

Young bean pickers help out on the Eppen farm in the fields of 1944 Speedway. In the back row, Bill Munshower, second from left, stands with three unidentified friends. In the front row, Ernie Eppen and Mike Walker hold piles of beans. (Courtesy of the Eppen Family.)

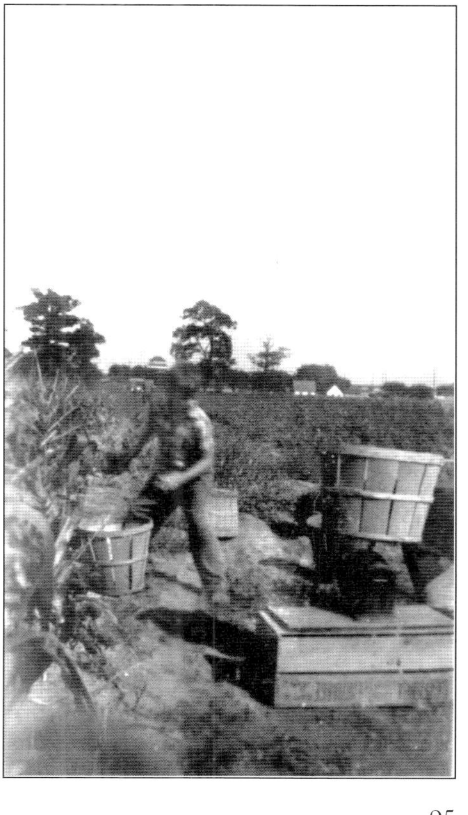

Mike Walker works hard to harvest beans on the Eppen farm in 1944. (Courtesy of the Eppen Family.)

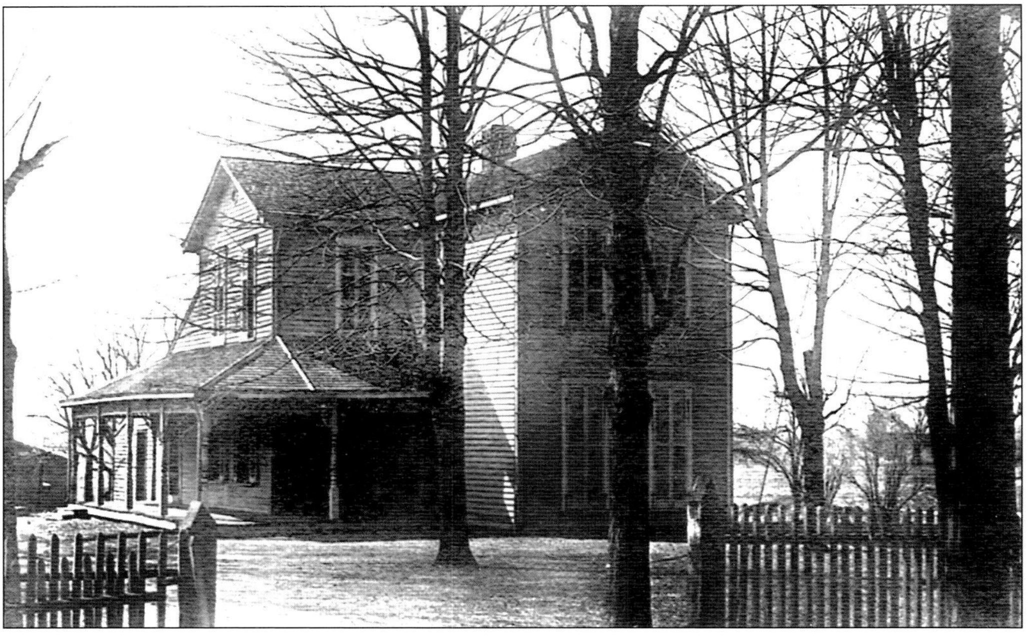

The Wenzler farmhouse stood in the 4900 block of West 10th Street where Allison Plants 3 and 4 are located today. (Courtesy of Carl Pieper.)

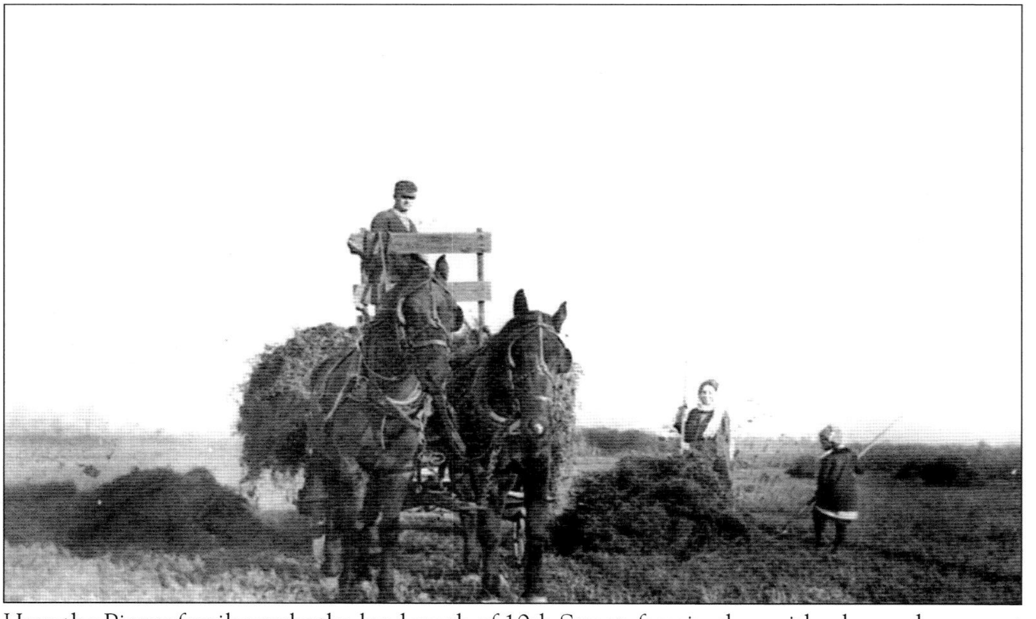

Here the Pieper family works the land south of 10th Street, farming hay with a horse-drawn cart in the same place where jet engines were later made by Allison. (Courtesy of Carl Pieper.)

The cornfield of the Wenzler farm was the site for Halloween frivolity. Notice the costumes. (Courtesy of Carl Pieper.)

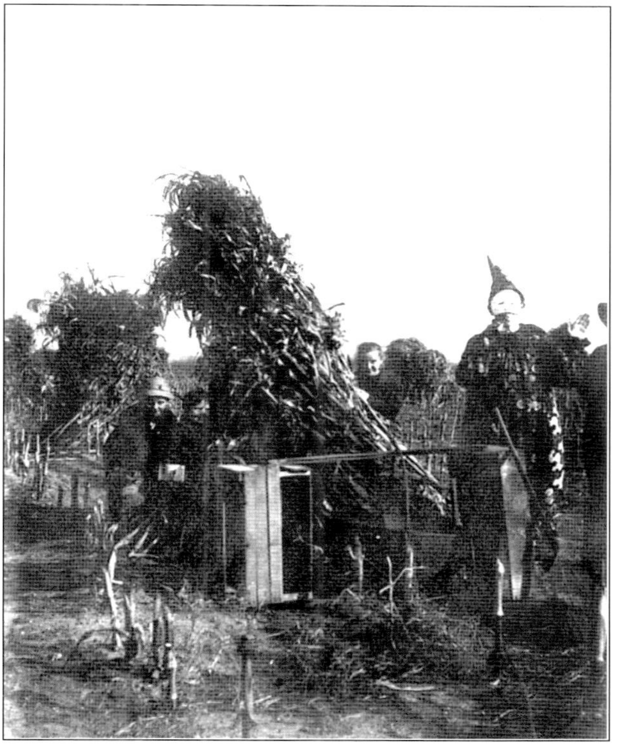

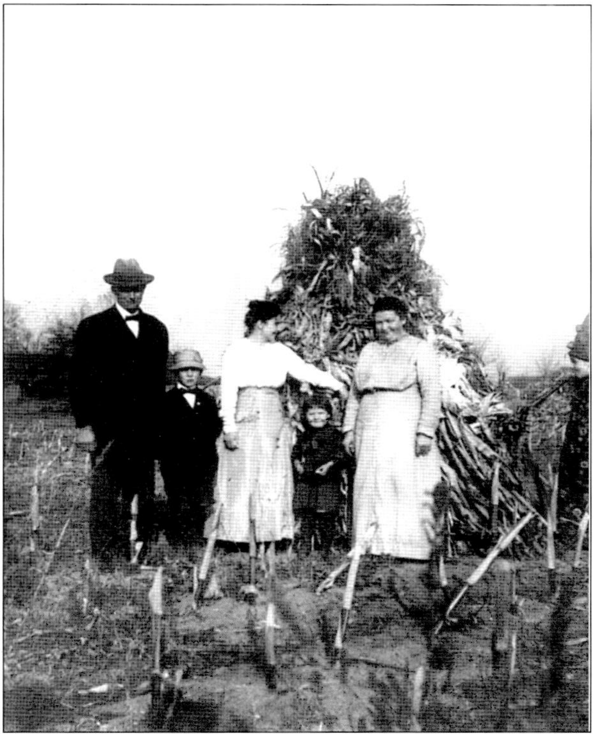

A child dressed for Halloween can be seen on the right side of this picture. Caroline Pieper reaches out to her neighbor as the family poses in front of an old corn shock on the old Wenzler farm. (Courtesy of Carl Pieper.)

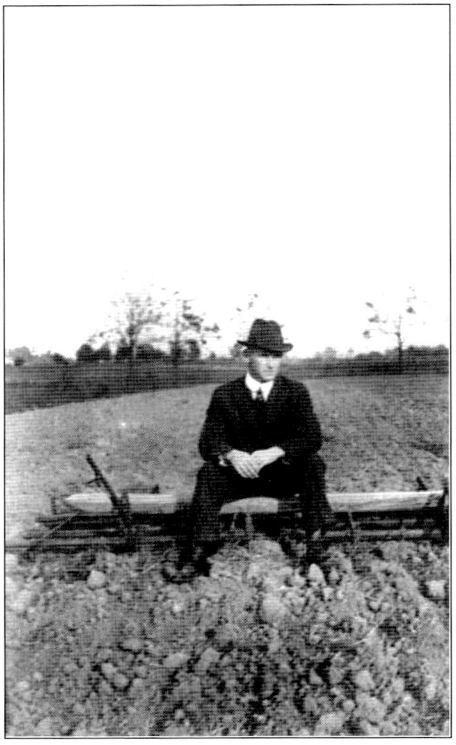

Herman F. Pieper sits looking out over the farmland south of West 10th Street. (Courtesy of Carl Pieper.)

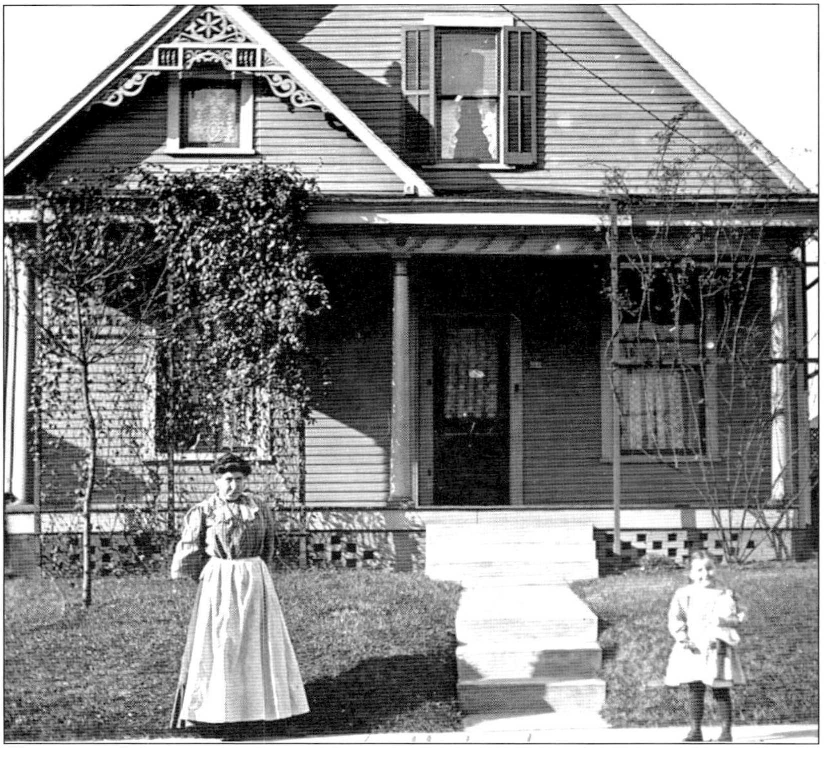

Mrs. Wenzler and daughter Gertrude pose in front of their home. (Courtesy of the Eppen Family.)

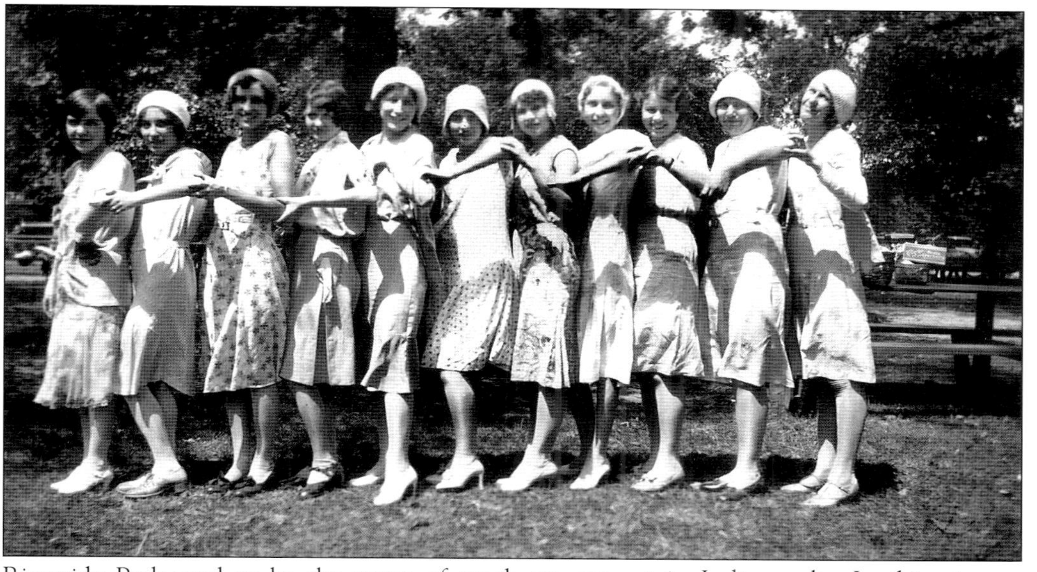

Riverside Park used to be the scene of much amusement in Indianapolis. In this picture, Margaret ?, Dorothy ?, Margaret ?, Flora ?, Treva ?, Gertrude ?, Vivian ?, Henrietta Eppen, Louise Eppen, Francis Eppen, and Henrietta ? enjoy themselves on a picnic. (Courtesy of the Eppen Family.)

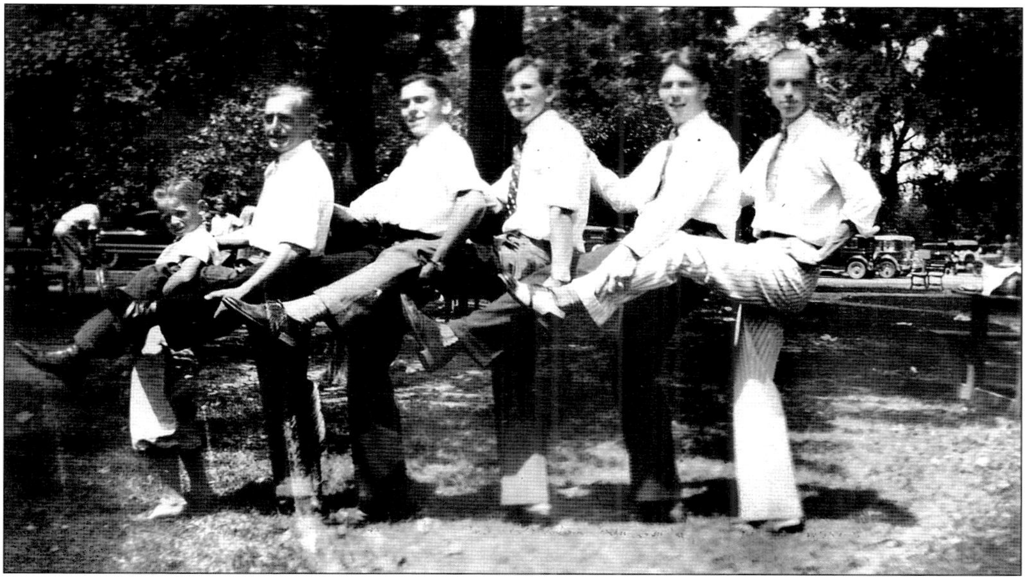

Here, ? Grayson Jr. and Sr., Lawrence ?, Louis Howard, and John Howard kick up their heels at Riverside Park. (Courtesy of the Eppen Family.)

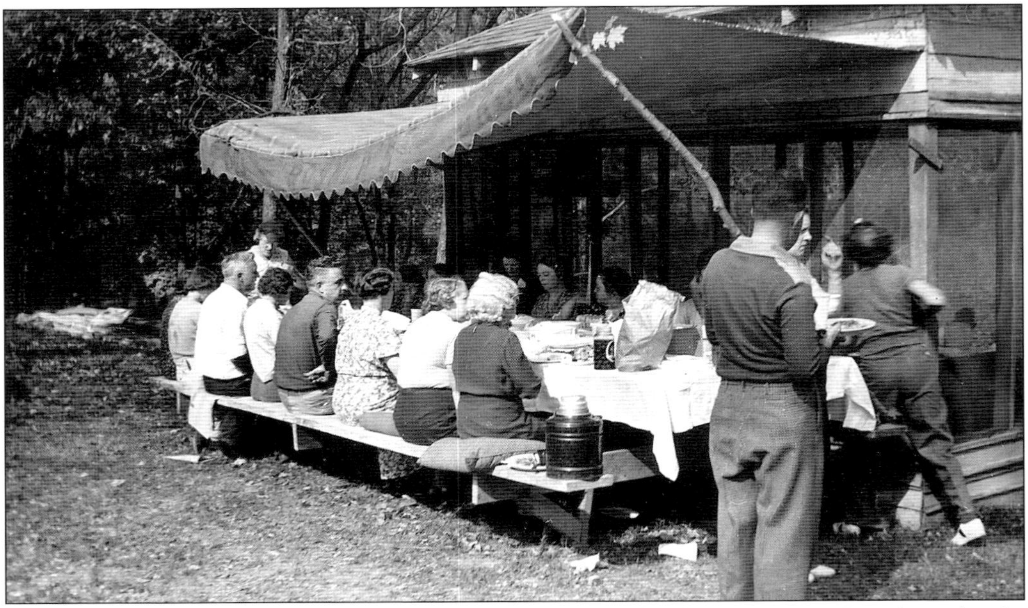

The Rosner farm was not in Speedway, but it was owned by the prominent Speedway family, and was often used for Speedway functions. Here the Speedway Music Club holds their picnic at the farm around 1938. (Courtesy of Edith Spencer.)

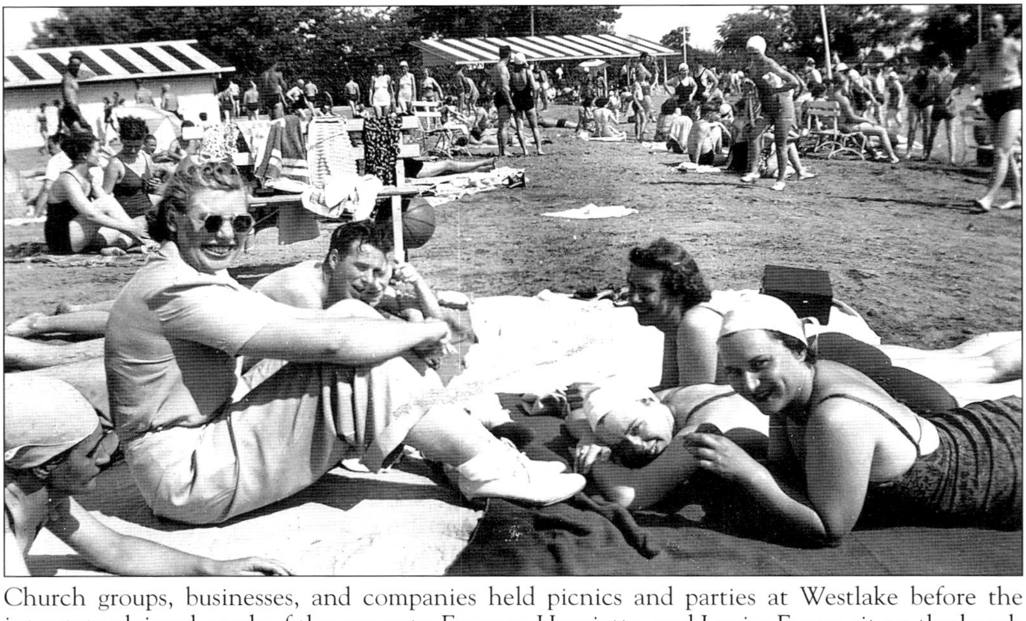

Church groups, businesses, and companies held picnics and parties at Westlake before the interstate claimed much of the property. Frances, Henrietta, and Louise Eppen sit on the beach with Lolita ?. (Courtesy of the Eppen Family.)

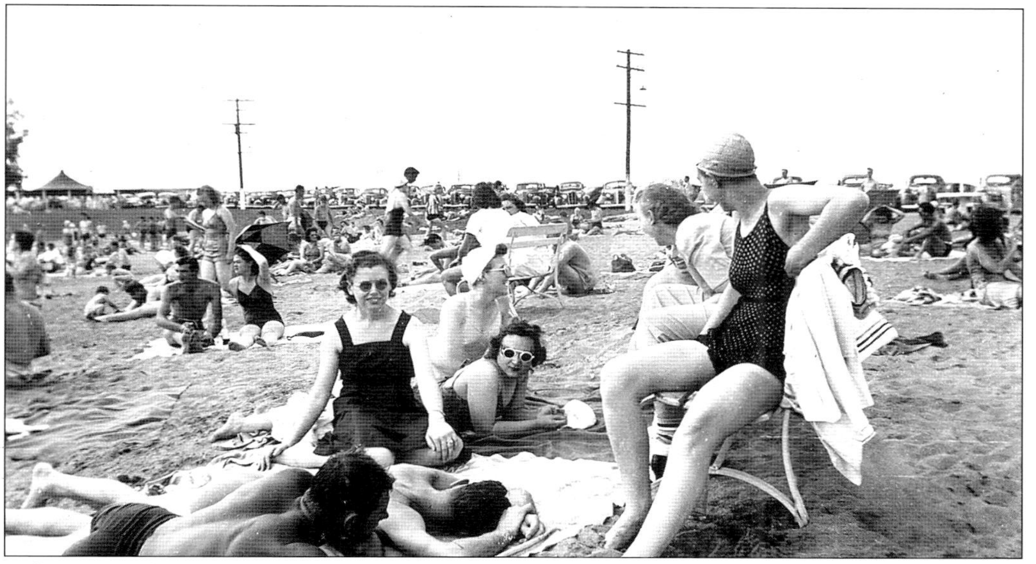

Relaxing on the beach of Westlake are Vernice ?, a friend, Louise Eppen, Lolita ?, Frances Eppen, and Mary ?. Notice the cars parked in the background. (Courtesy of the Eppen Family.)

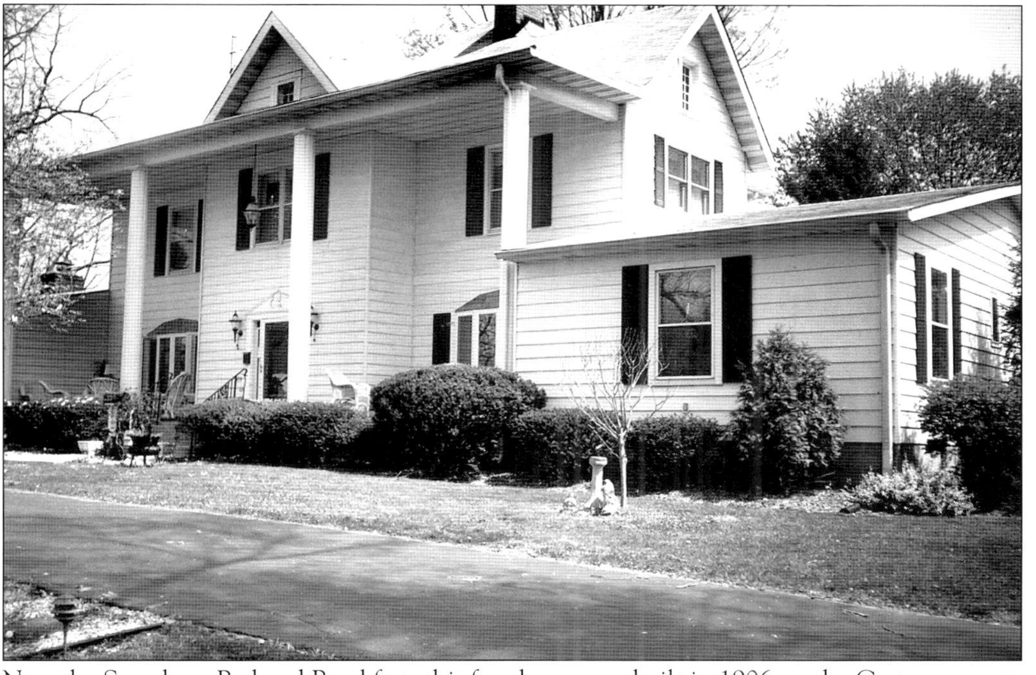

Now the Speedway Bed and Breakfast, this farmhouse was built in 1906 on the Carter property known as Bakers Walnut Grove. The wood in the house was milled from the walnut trees that stood on the property.

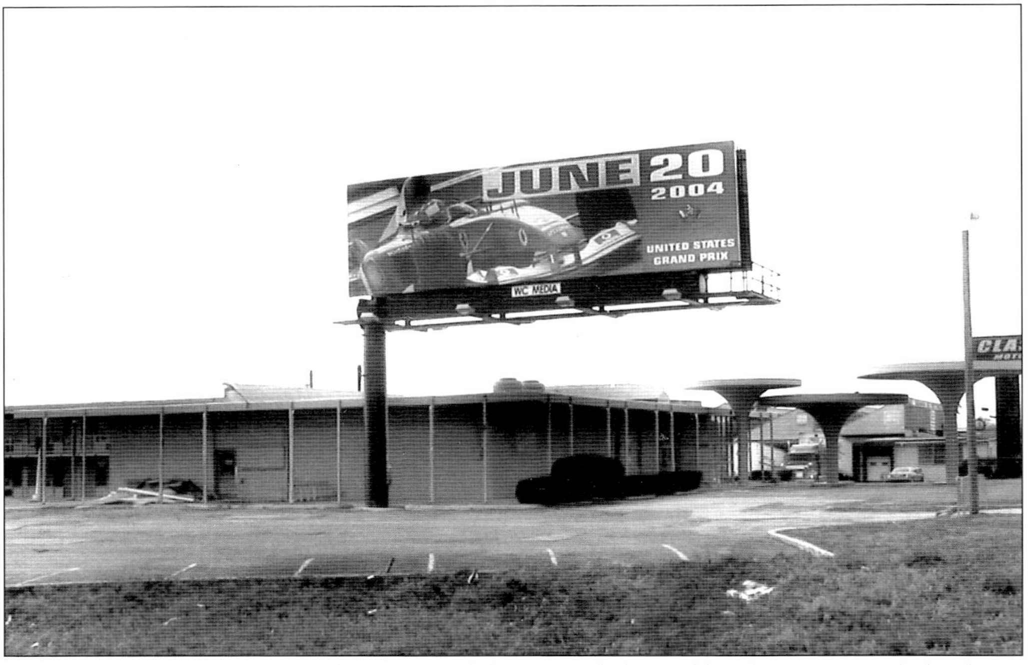

The Classic Motor Lodge started out as a Holiday Inn and changed hands many times before being demolished in 2004 to make way for Indianapolis Motor Speedway expansion projects of the future.

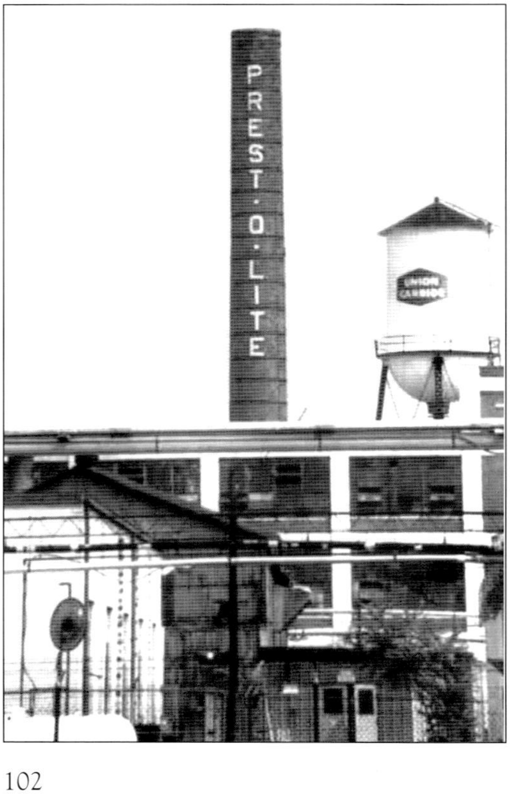

Prest-O-Lite Corporation was the cornerstone for the beginnings of Speedway's automotive industries. Founded by Carl Fisher and James Allison, the company originally made acetylene cylinders used in the early days of automobile headlights. These old landmarks showed the merger of Prest-O-Lite and Union Carbide. (Courtesy of Don Ketterhenry.)

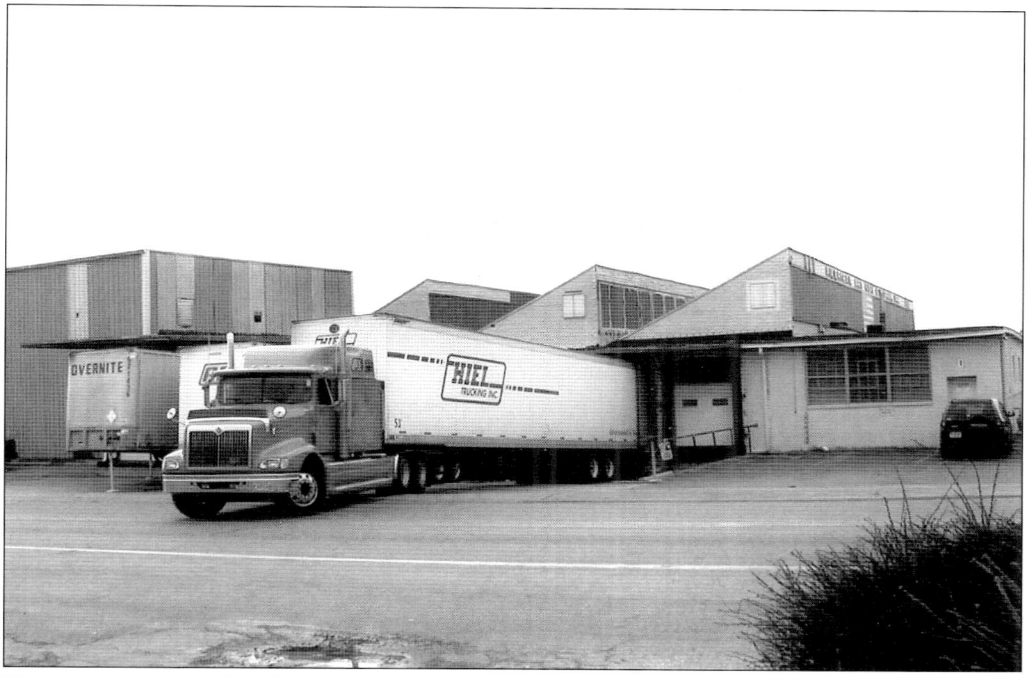

The American Art Clay Company made its home across the street from the Indianapolis Motor Speedway for 85 years. The oil-based, non-hardening clay produced by this company has been used in schools since 1919. This landmark was leveled in spring of 2004, but the company continues in a new location. (Courtesy of Don Katterhenry.)

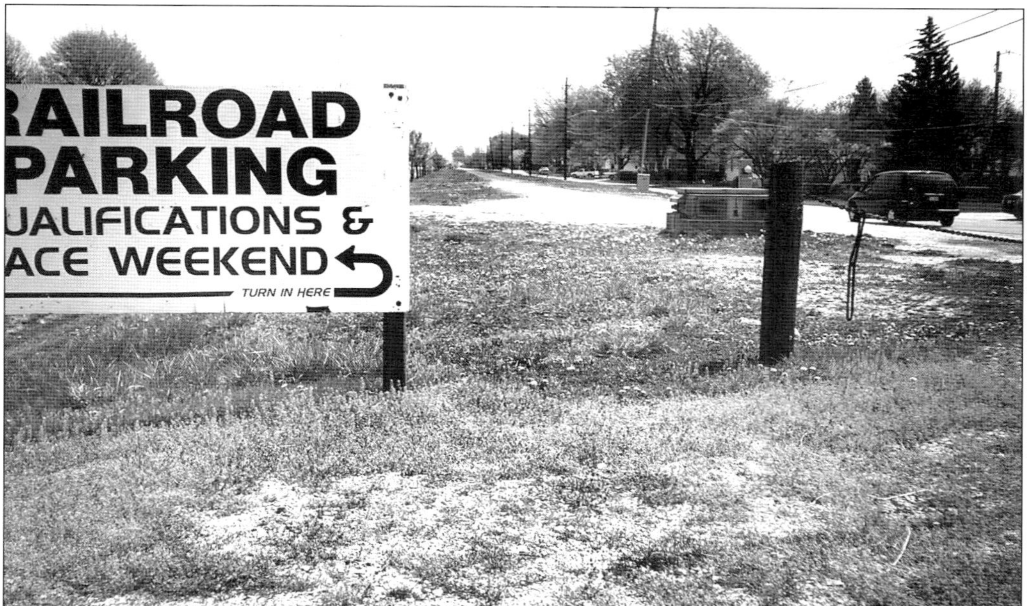

All that remains of the old Ben Hur line interurban that carried race fans from Indianapolis and Crawfordsville is an empty rail bed used by today's race fans as parking.

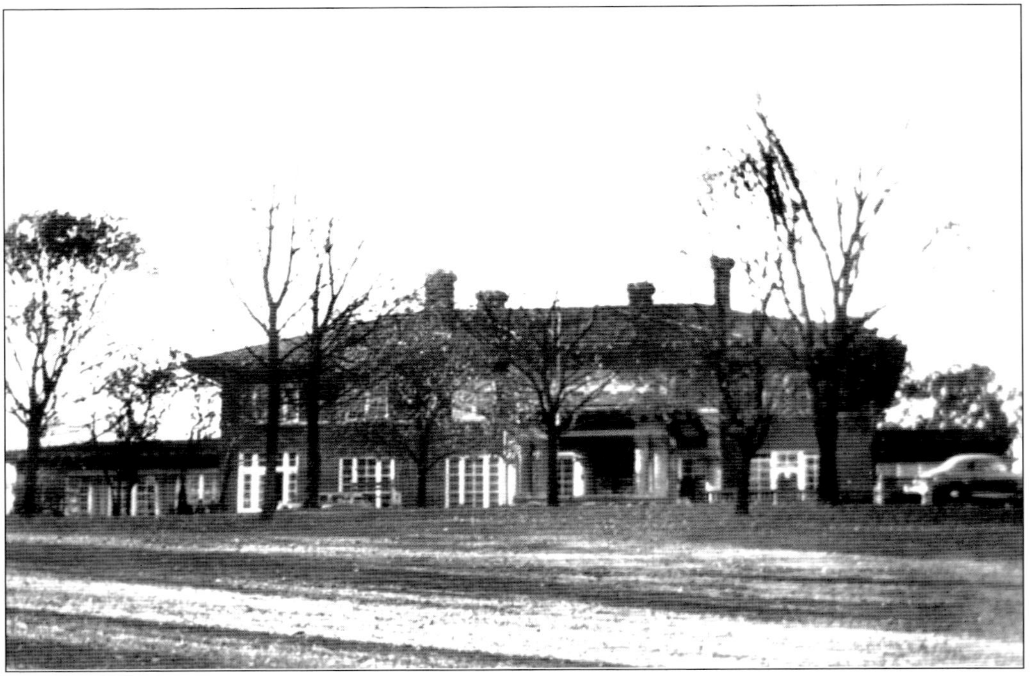

Riverdale, built in 1911, was the mansion home of James Allison, one of the founders of Speedway. Here the mansion is shown as it appeared in 1936. The mansion is now on the property of Marian College in Indianapolis. (Courtesy of Marian College Archives.)

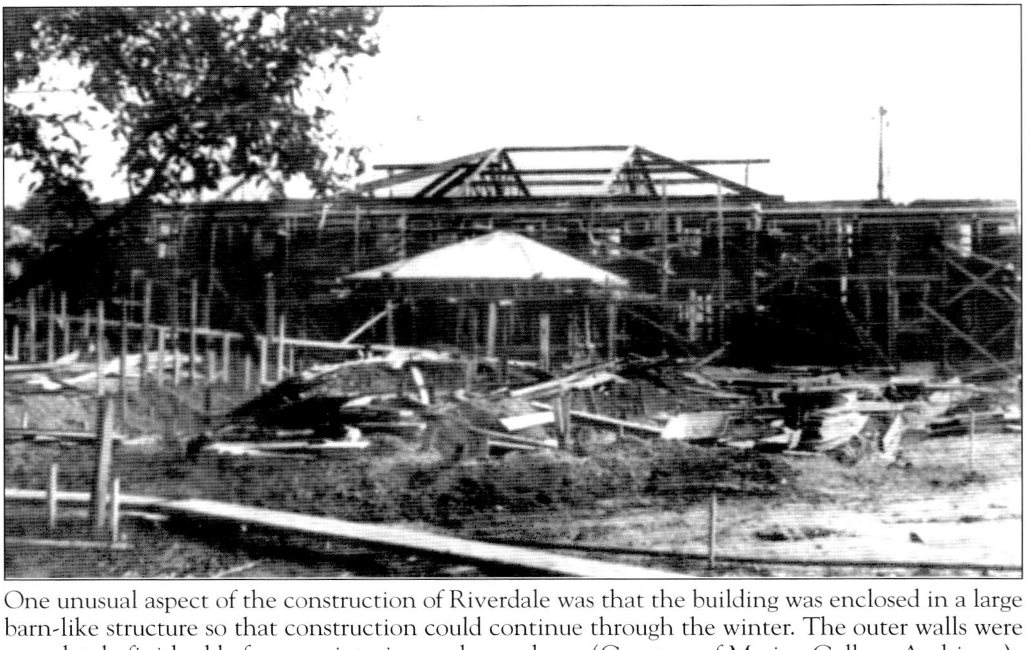

One unusual aspect of the construction of Riverdale was that the building was enclosed in a large barn-like structure so that construction could continue through the winter. The outer walls were completely finished before any interior work was done. (Courtesy of Marian College Archives.)

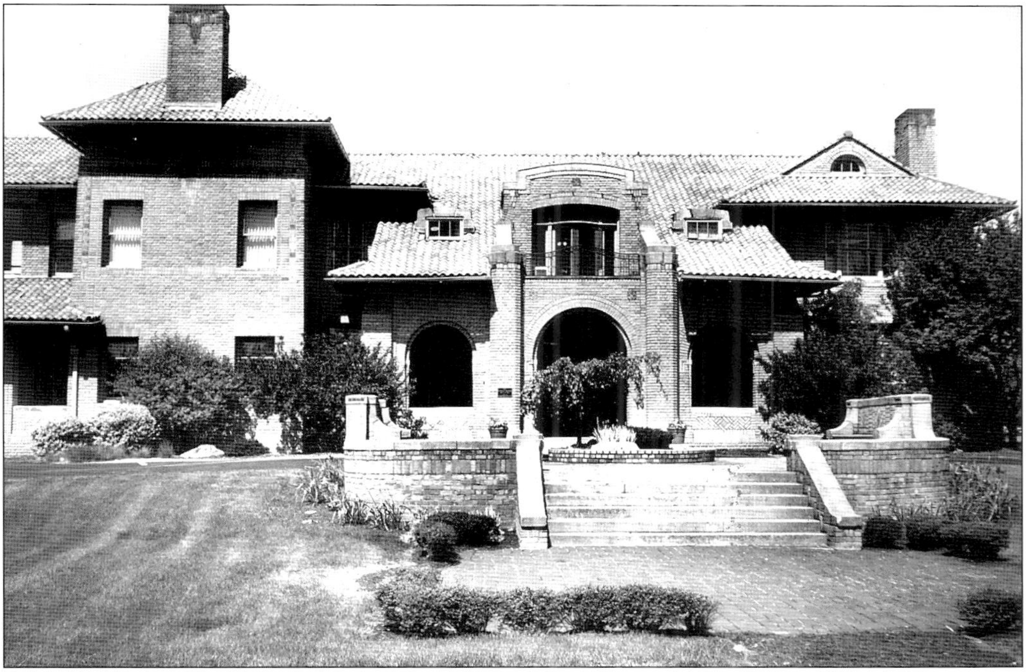

Hawkeye was the spacious home of Frank Wheeler, one of the founders of the Indianapolis Motor Speedway. The estate originally included a man-made lake complete with an island and a Venetian gondola. The home was later sold to William B. Stokely of the Stokely-Van Camp Company. The house was sold to Marian College in 1963.

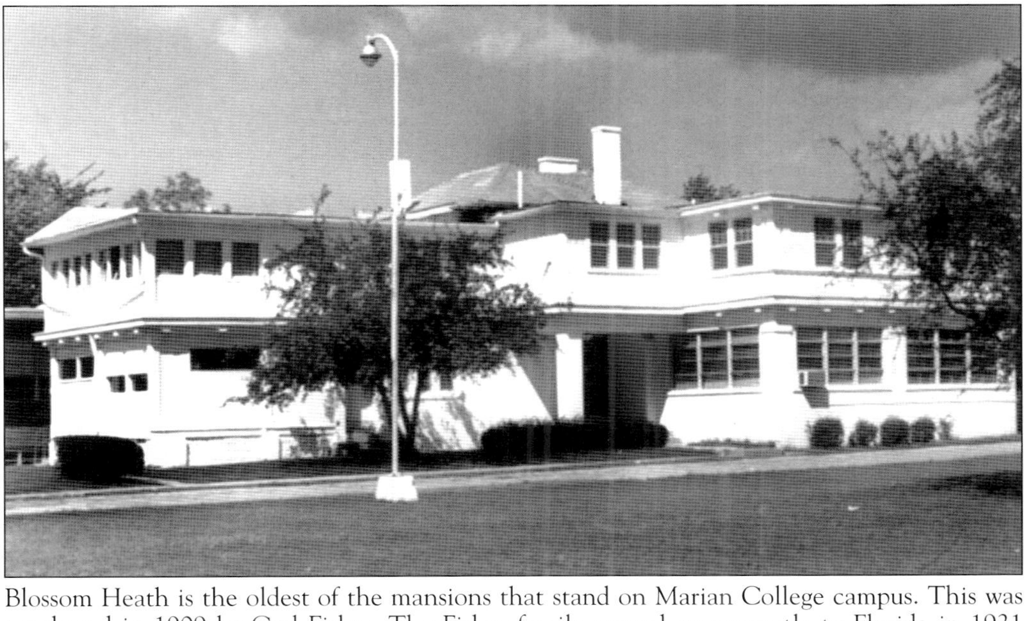

Blossom Heath is the oldest of the mansions that stand on Marian College campus. This was purchased in 1909 by Carl Fisher. The Fisher family moved permanently to Florida in 1921 where Carl Fisher developed Miami Beach. This picture was taken in the 1970s. (Courtesy of Marian College Archives.)

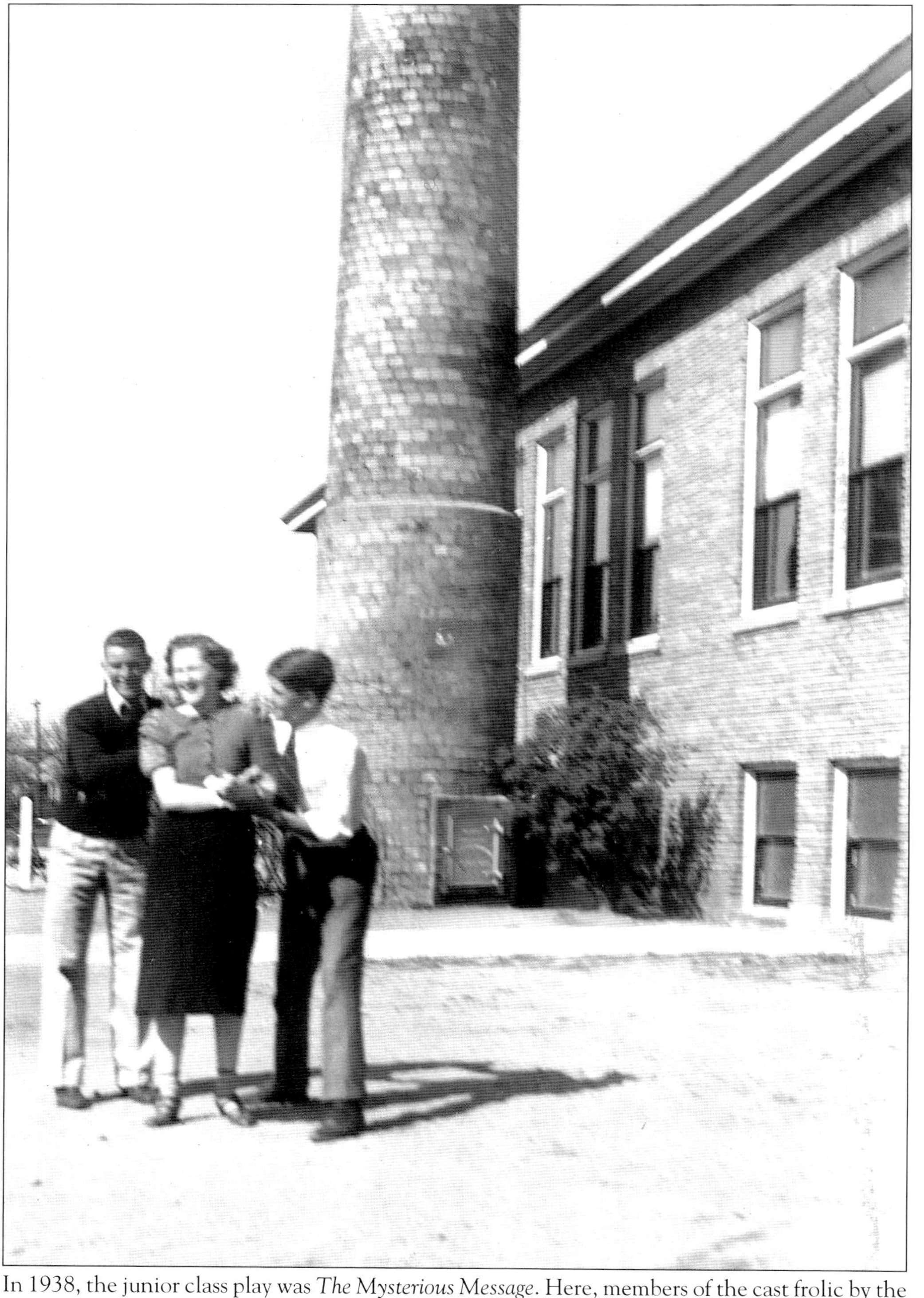

In 1938, the junior class play was *The Mysterious Message*. Here, members of the cast frolic by the chimney that used to stand behind the old Speedway School. (Courtesy of Edith Spencer.)

Six

People Remembered

The story of any town is written by the people who live there. The success of a community depends upon the strengths of its citizens. The success of Speedway is in no small way the result of its founders and the people who have made the town their home for generations.

The original idea behind the planning of Speedway was to give the working class a comfortable place to live close to the factories that provided their income. The philosophy worked well in this small Indiana town. The fact that Speedway was carefully planned, and that the town has managed to keep its individuality in the face of the expansion of the metropolitan area of Indianpolis, speaks well for the founders and the citizens who have followed through the years.

We can look back and remember people who contributed to the building of the community.

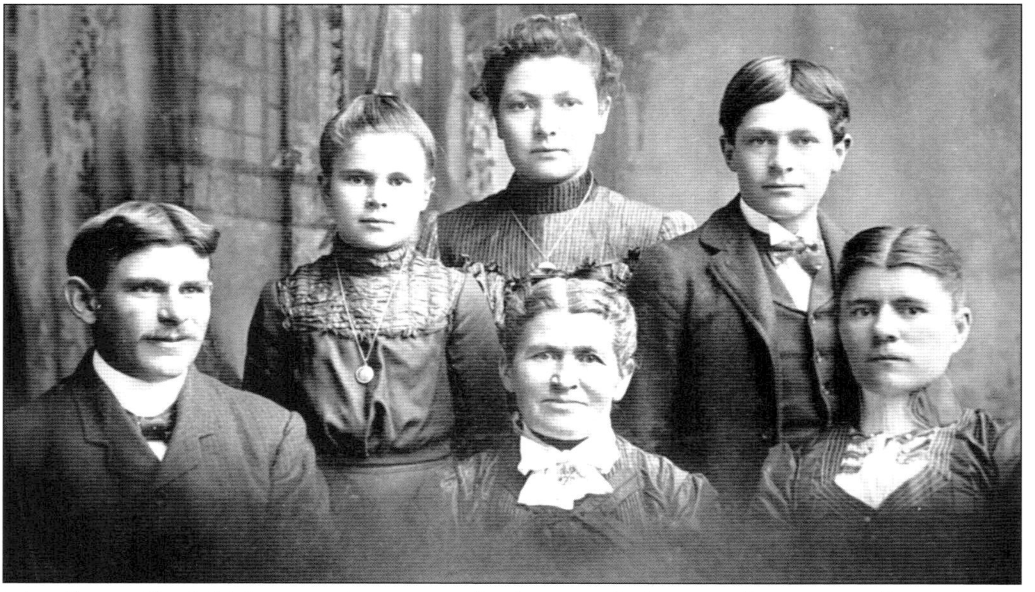

John Eppen (far left) became the owner of a large truck farm on Georgetown Road. In the center is his mother, Friedericka Webber Eppen Wenzler, a German immigrant. On the right is Caroline Wenzler, who later married Herman F. Pieper. The back row includes (left to right) Emma Wenzler, Katie Wenzler, who later married William Ziegelmueller, and Christian Wenzler. (Courtesy of Carl Pieper.)

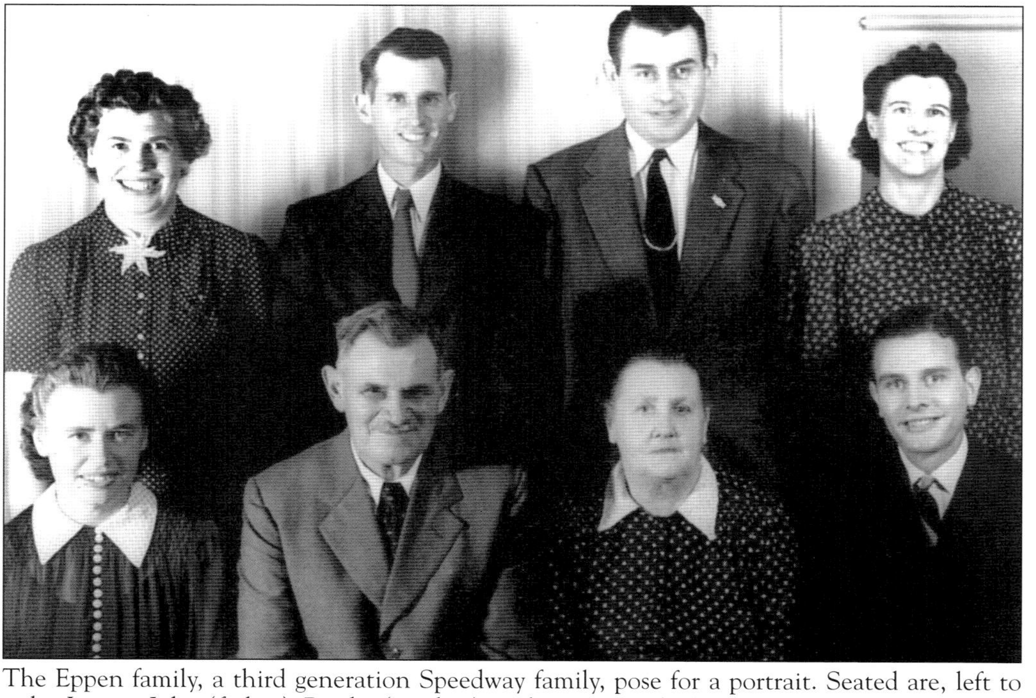

The Eppen family, a third generation Speedway family, pose for a portrait. Seated are, left to right, Louise, John (father), Bertha (mother), and Ernest. In the back row are Frances, Herman, Reinhart, and Henrietta. (Courtesy of the Eppen Family.)

Friedericka Webber Eppen Wenzler came to the United States when she was 19 years old. She decided to leave Germany when her parents wanted her to stay home and take care of her younger siblings. She first married Mr. Eppen and had one child, John. When her first husband died, she married Mr. Wenzler. (Courtesy of Carl Pieper.)

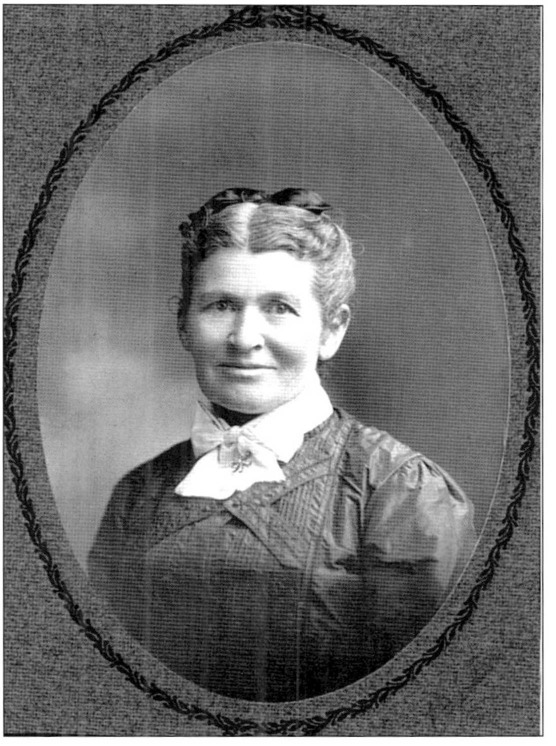

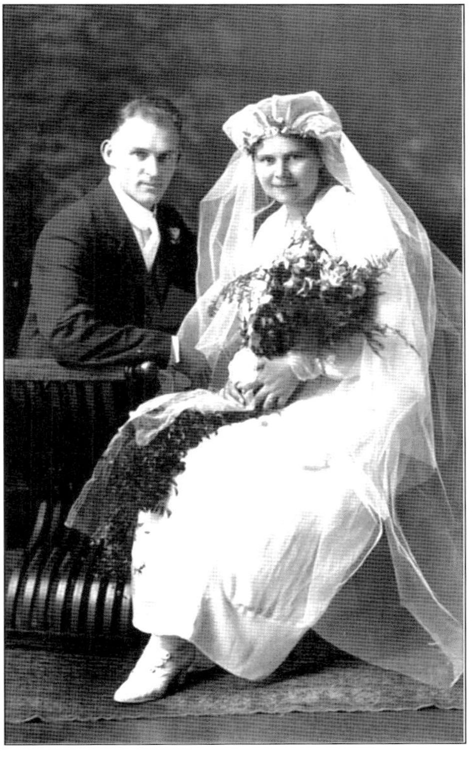

When Carolyn Wenzler (1891–1972) married Herman F. Pieper (1885–1959) in 1918, she rented a wedding dress to wear for her formal wedding portrait. The couple could not afford to purchase a wedding dress. (Courtesy of Carl Pieper.)

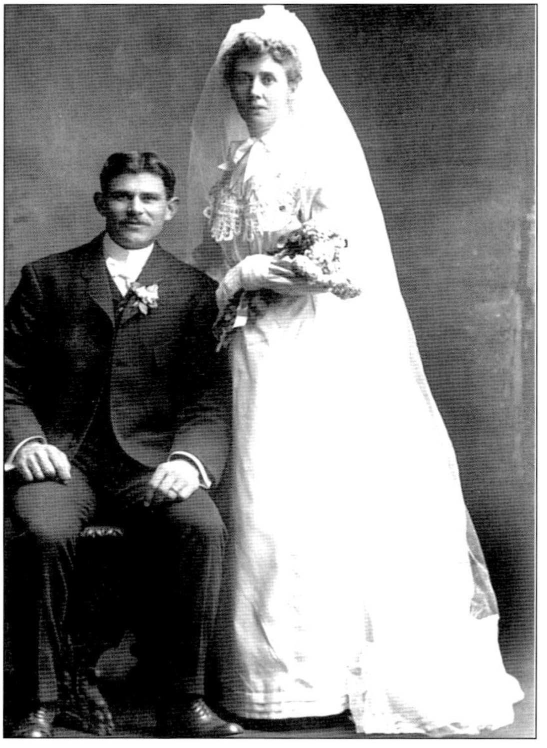

John Eppen and his new bride Bertha Ziegelmueller pose for their formal wedding portrait. (Courtesy of Carl Pieper and the Eppen Family.)

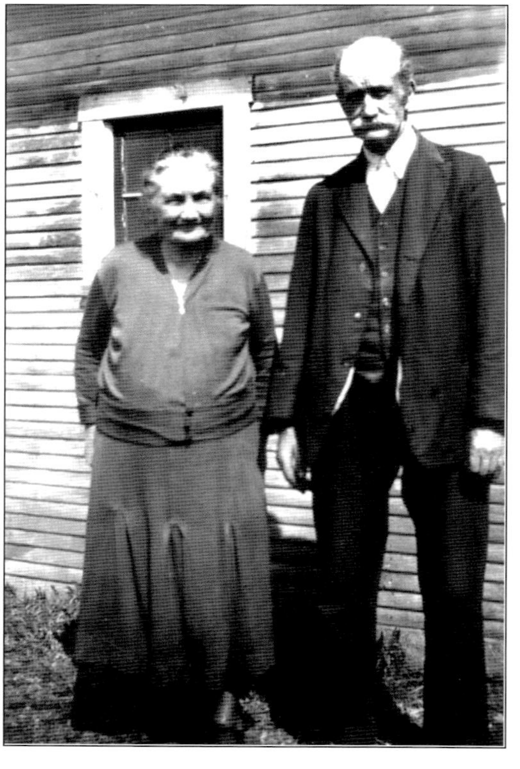

Herman Ziegelmueller, the brother of Bertha Ziegelmueller Eppen, and his wife Lydia Thornmeyer Ziegelmueller pose on the farm. (Courtesy of the Eppen Family.)

During the Great Depression, Ray Gates lived in one of the outbuildings on the Eppen farm. Ernest Eppen described him as "one of the finest men who ever lived." (Courtesy of the Eppen Family.)

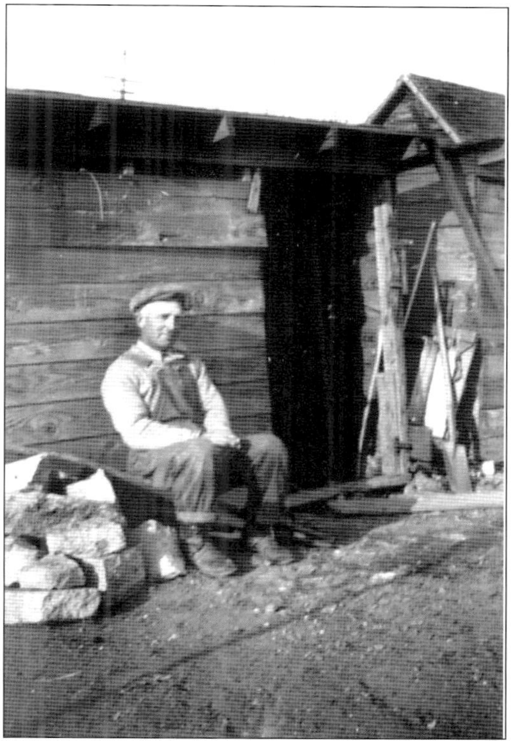

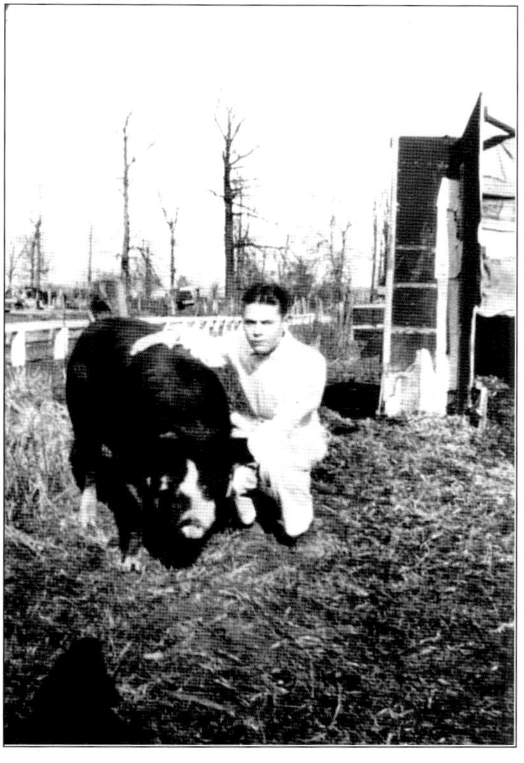

Earnest Eppen poses with his blue ribbon Berkshire hog on the family farm. They won first place at the Indiana State Fair in 1927 and 1928. (Courtesy of the Eppen Family.)

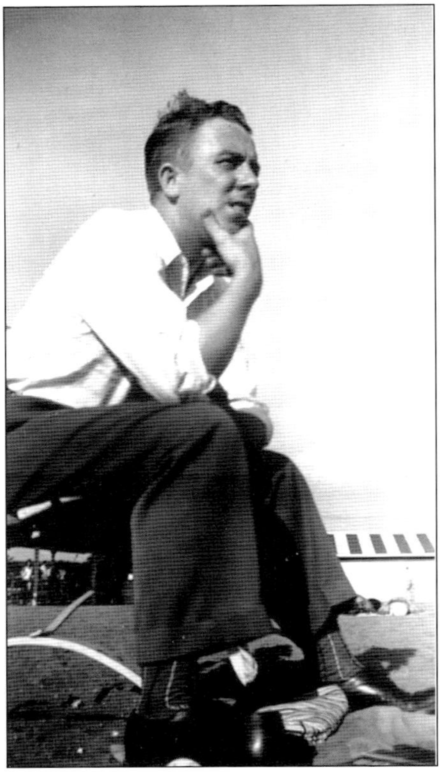

Frank Woodlock, who became superintendent of Allison engineering, muses over the activities during a Westlake outing. (Courtesy of the Eppen Family.)

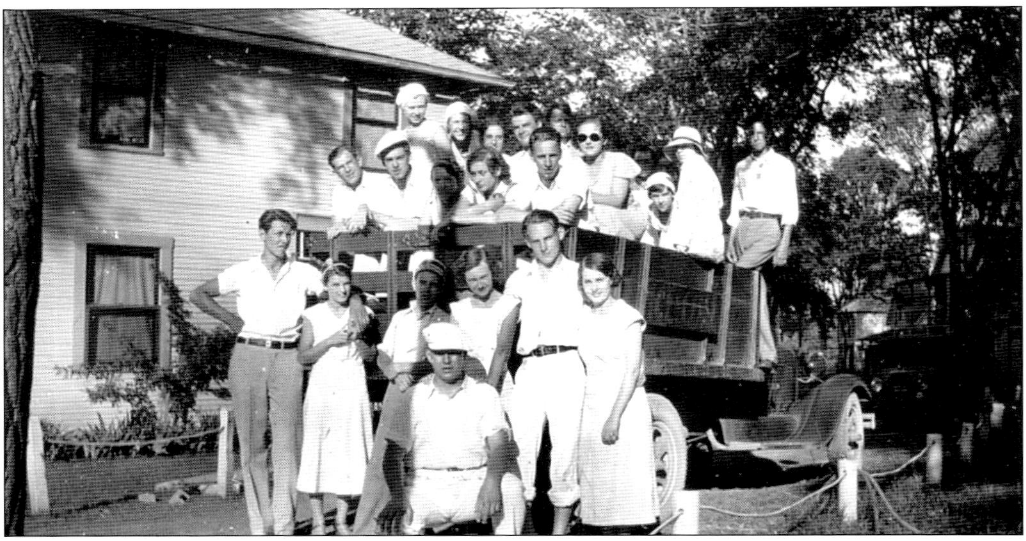

After church, a group of young people from the Speedway Christian Church load onto a truck at the Eppen farm to go to a park for a picnic. (Courtesy of the Eppen Family.)

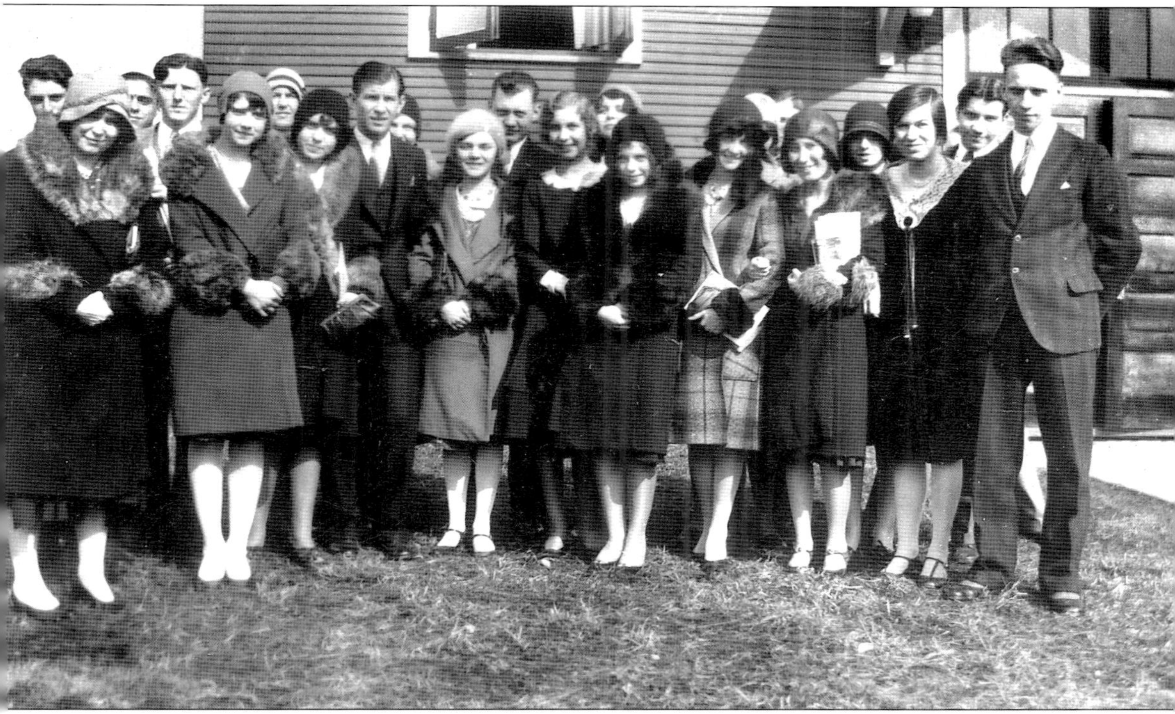

A Speedway Christian Church group poses outside of "the church that was built in a day." On September 18, 1926, 100 men built the church, and the next day services were held in the sanctuary. That building stood on that site until 1955. (Courtesy of the Eppen Family.)

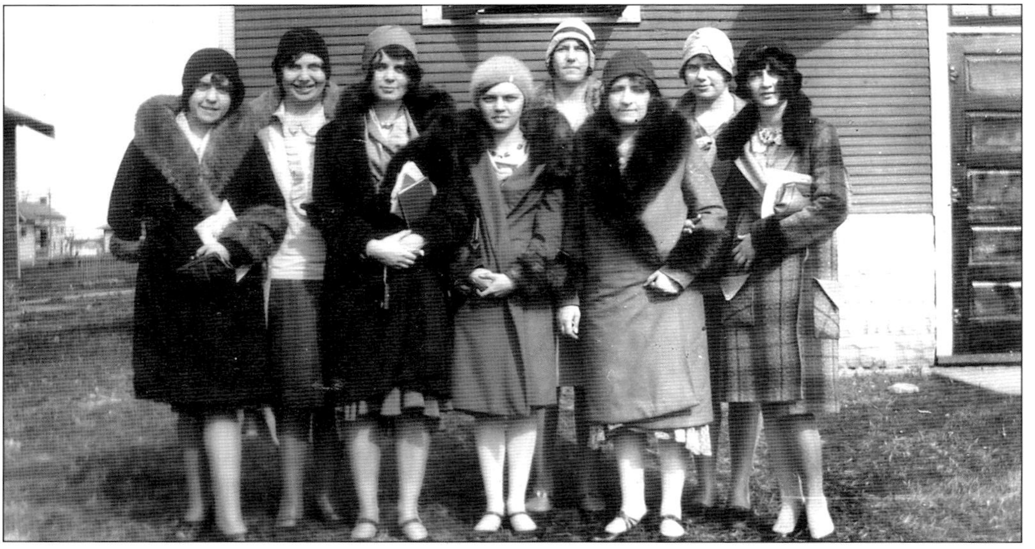

The Semper Fidelis Sunday school class poses outside of the Christian Church. Pictured here, from left to right, are: unknown, Francis Eppen, Mabel ?, Mary ?, Henrietta Eppen, Mrs. Hammer (teacher), Louise Eppen, and Flora ?. (Courtesy of the Eppen Family.)

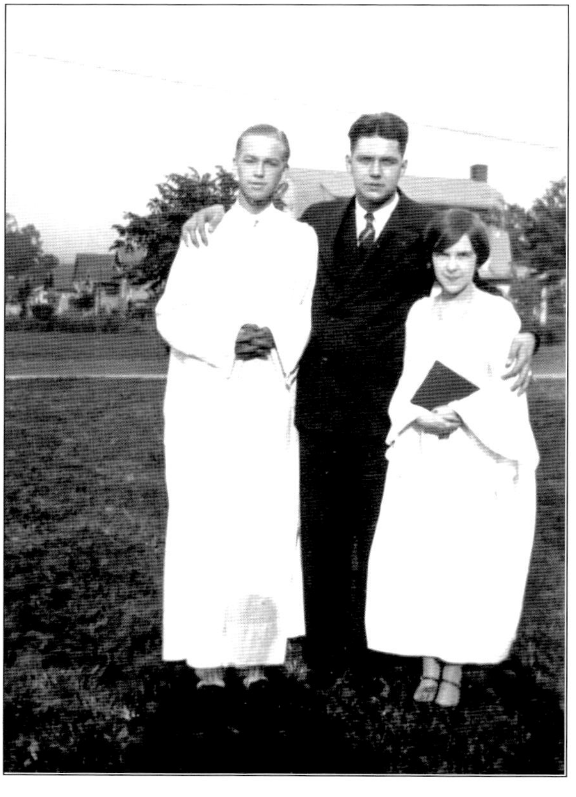

Rev. Howard Anderson poses with his arms around John Wilson and Mrs. Anderson. Rev. Anderson was the pastor of the Speedway Christian Church from 1927 until 1945. (Courtesy of the Eppen Family.)

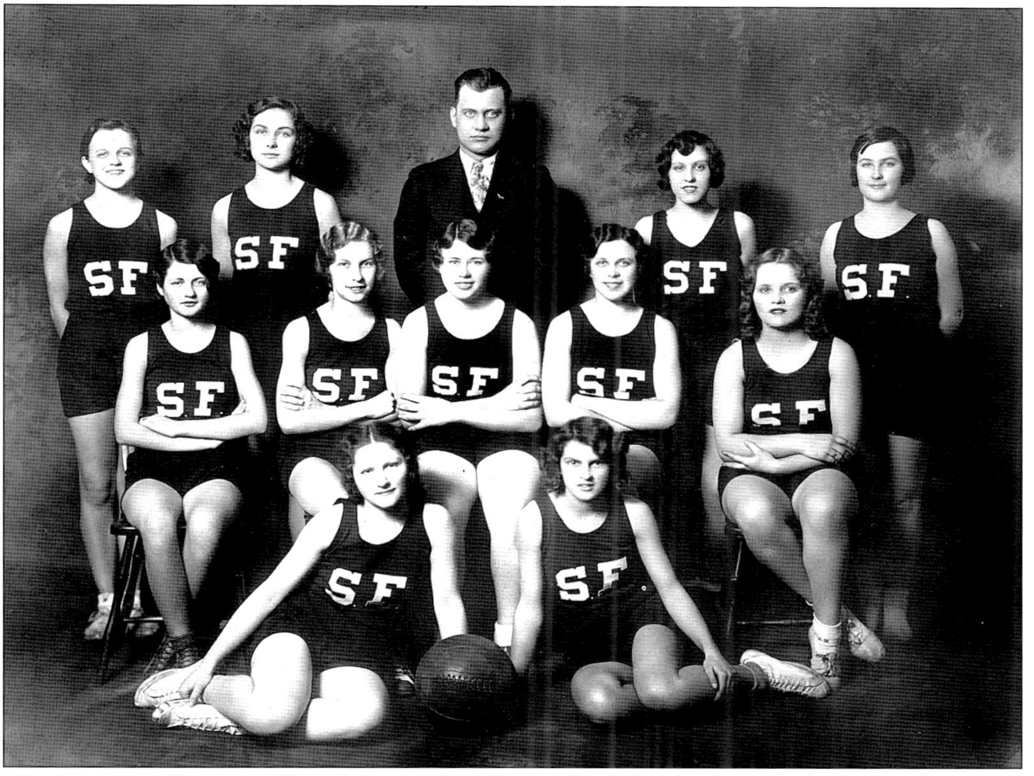

The Speedway Christian Church Semper Fidelis Sunday School girl's basketball team poses for a formal picture. Louise Eppen sits in front of the team coach. (Courtesy of the Eppen Family.)

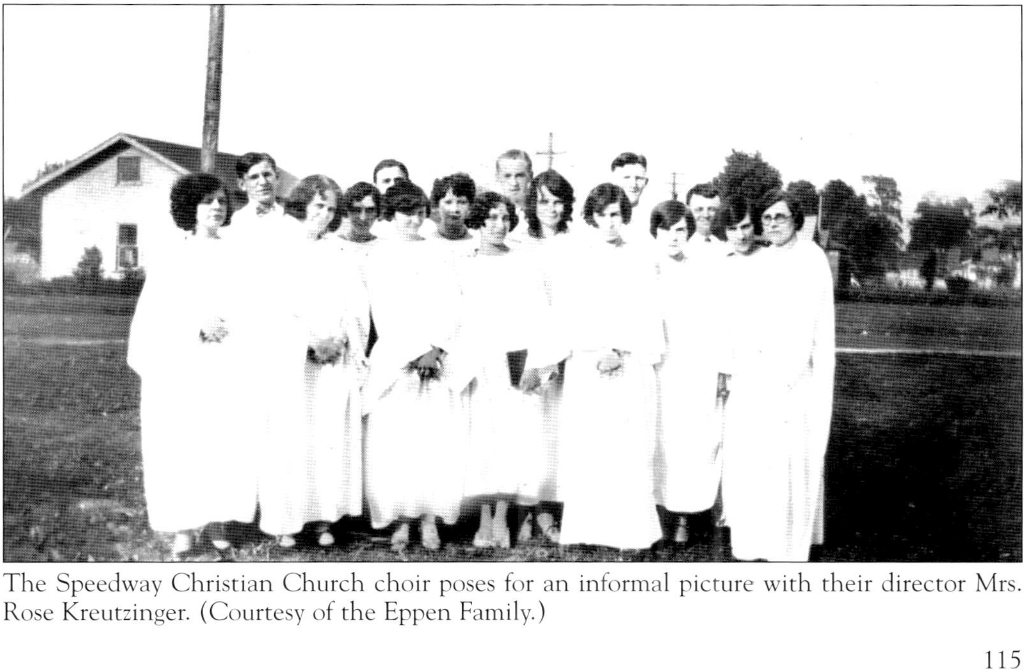
The Speedway Christian Church choir poses for an informal picture with their director Mrs. Rose Kreutzinger. (Courtesy of the Eppen Family.)

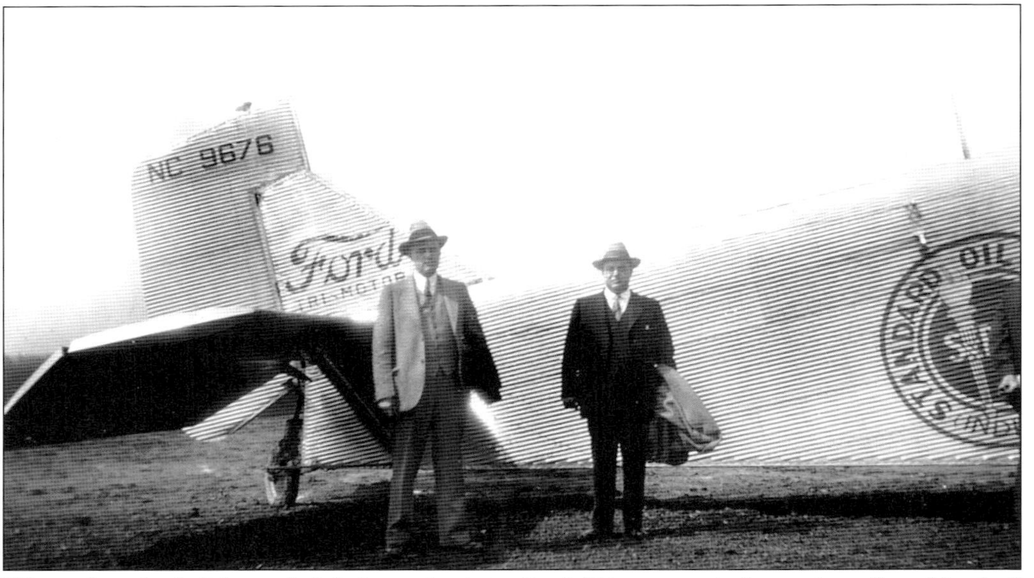

When Standard Oil needed help with their Ford Tri-motor airplane, they flew Marshall Spencer and others from Electric Steel Castings to Chicago to find the problem. Here the men get ready to leave Capitol Field on April 30, 1930. (Courtesy of Edith Spencer.)

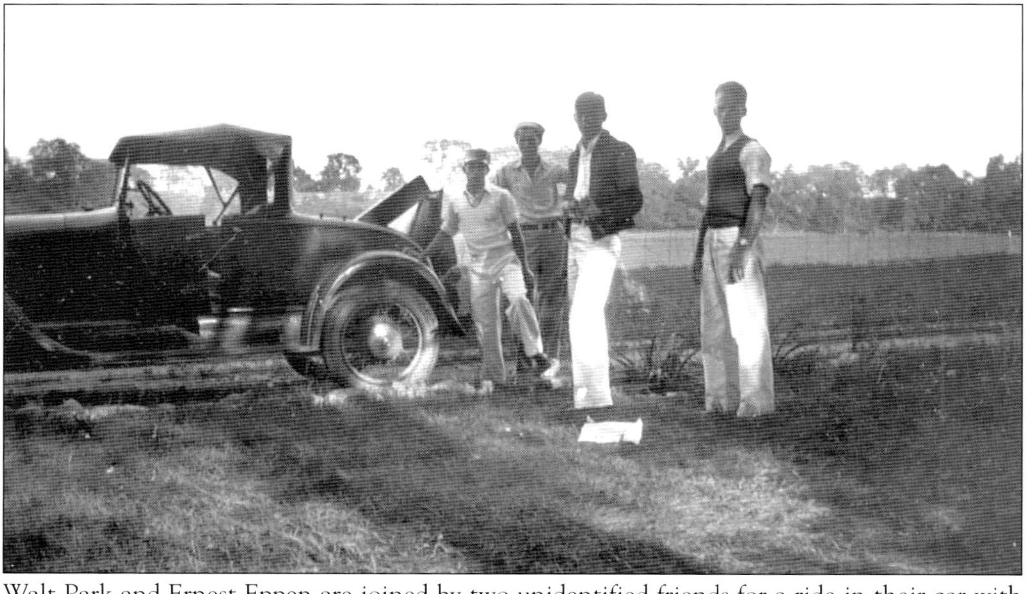

Walt Park and Ernest Eppen are joined by two unidentified friends for a ride in their car with a rumble seat. (Courtesy of the Eppen Family.)

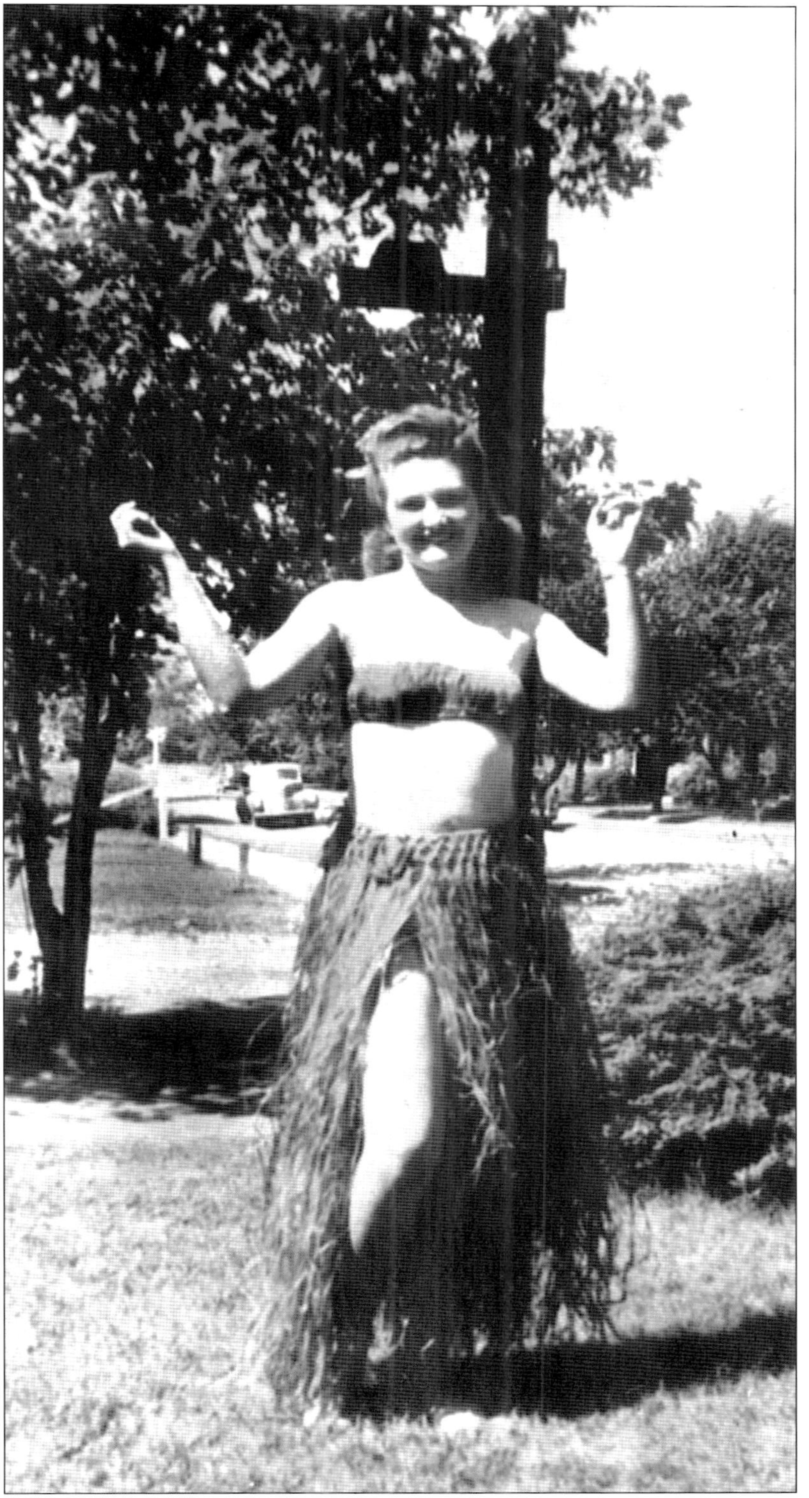

Rosemary Pieper was elected pinup queen in 1945. Her grass skirt was a present from her husband Carl who had returned from the South Pacific in WW II. The following is a poem of tribute composed for her by Edward Moyer. (Courtesy of Carl Pieper.)

A New Queen

The curtain goes up—the lights go on
The spotlight throws its beam
On a vision of feminine loveliness
As fair as any dream.
The star of nineteen forty-five
Our new crowned pin-up queen!

Let us go over her good gifts
Please follow our description
Brown hair, blue eyes and shapely limbs;
Height and weight we'd call perfection.
Add these up and I think you'll find
We have made a wise selection.

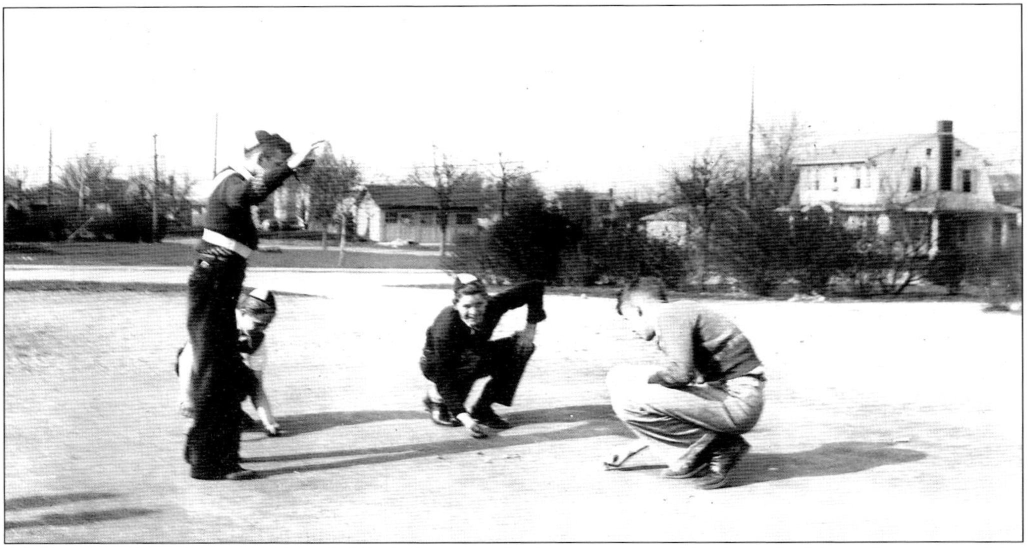

Four boys play marbles in the schoolyard of Speedway School in 1935. This is the southeast corner of Winton Avenue and 14th Street. (Courtesy of Edith Spencer.)

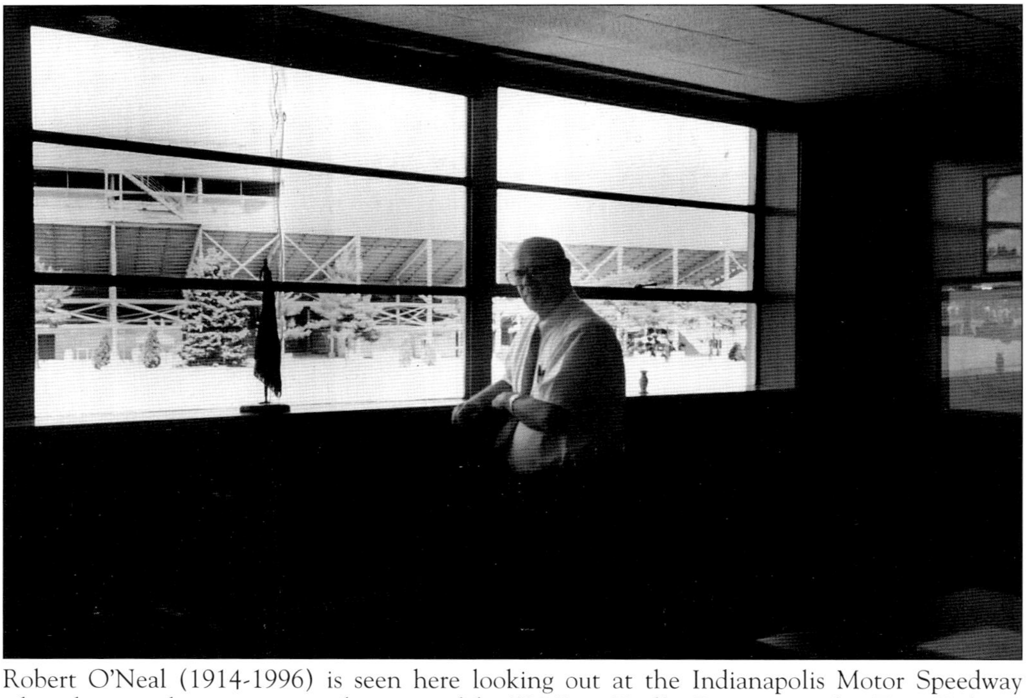

Robert O'Neal (1914-1996) is seen here looking out at the Indianapolis Motor Speedway where he served many years as chairman of the 500 Race Traffic Committee after Tony Hulman bought the track in 1945. He was the track safety director from 1988 until 1994. (Courtesy of the O'Neal Family.)

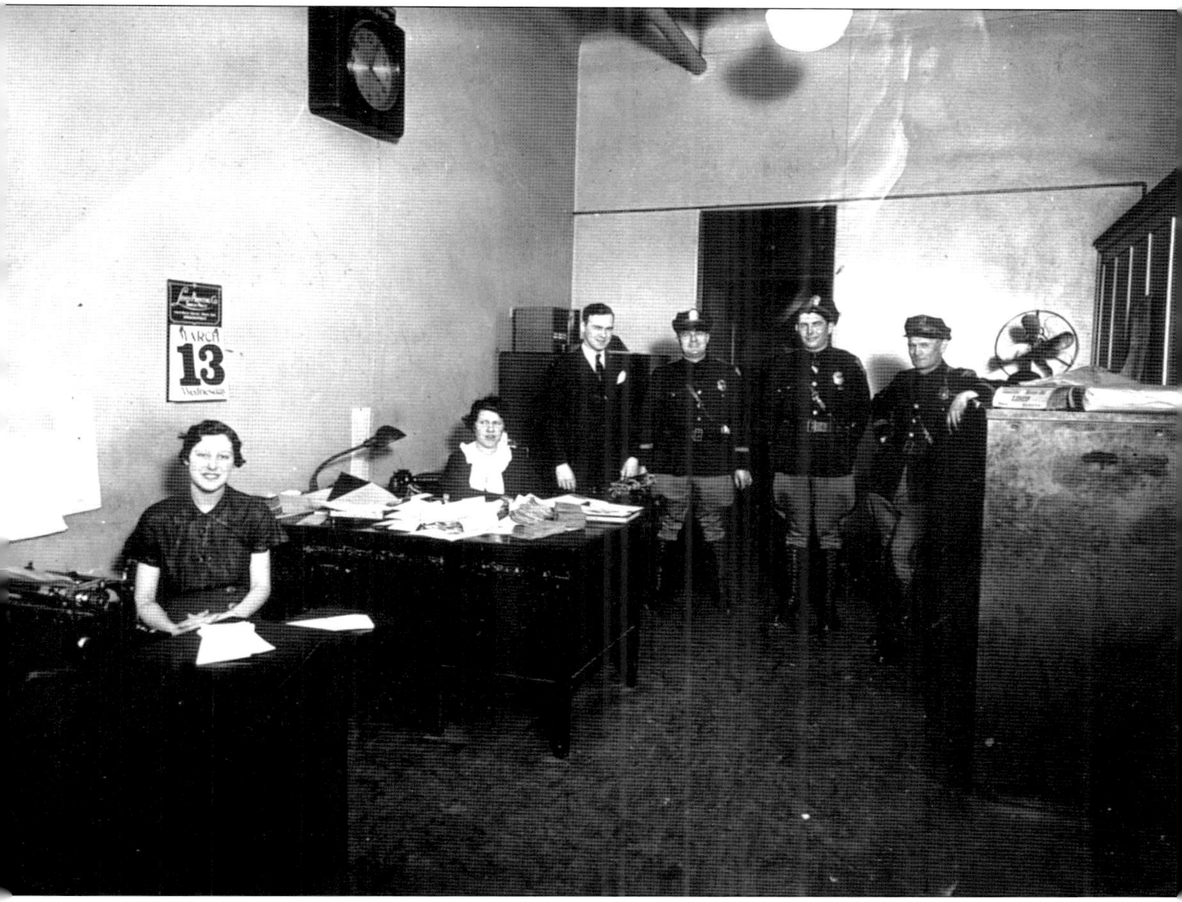

Longtime Speedway resident, Robert A. O'Neal (first man on the left) was inducted in to the Indiana State Police on March 13, 1935. He went on to become the superintendent. In 1954, he became the Marion County Sheriff, and in 1962 was named U.S. Marshal by John F. Kennedy. He was Police Commissioner of Speedway for three terms, 1969-71, 1980-82, and 1983-85. Pictured here, from left to right, are: Inez Coogan, Nell McArthur, Robert O'Neal, Troopers Oscar Bunkett and John McCormick, and Sgt. Ernie Pierce. (Courtesy of the O'Neal family.)

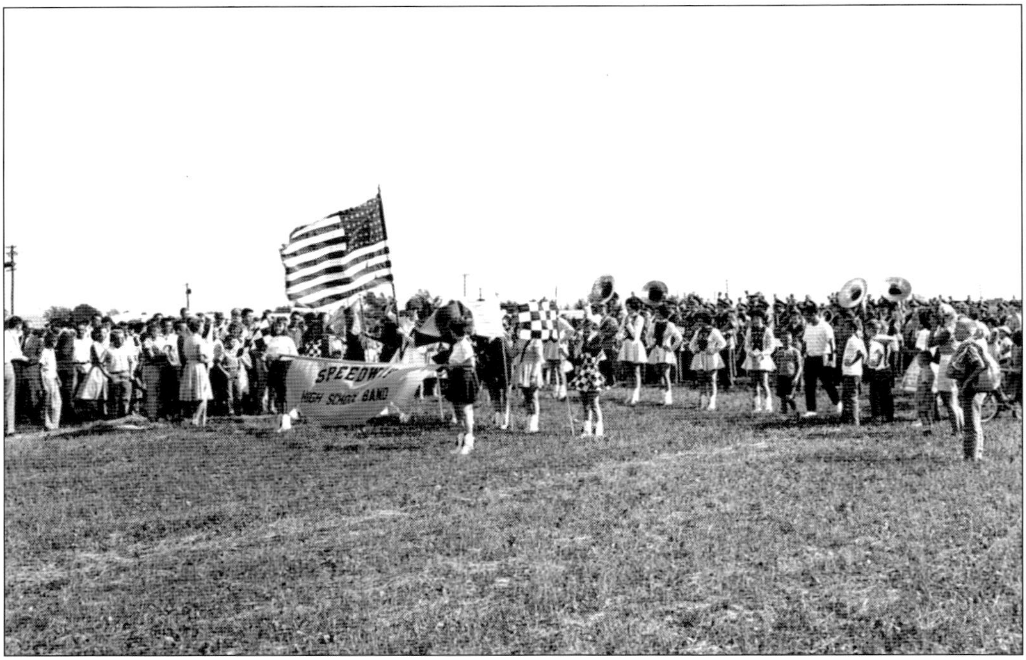

The Speedway High School band is seen here lining up for a parade in 1960. (Courtesy of Edith Spencer.)

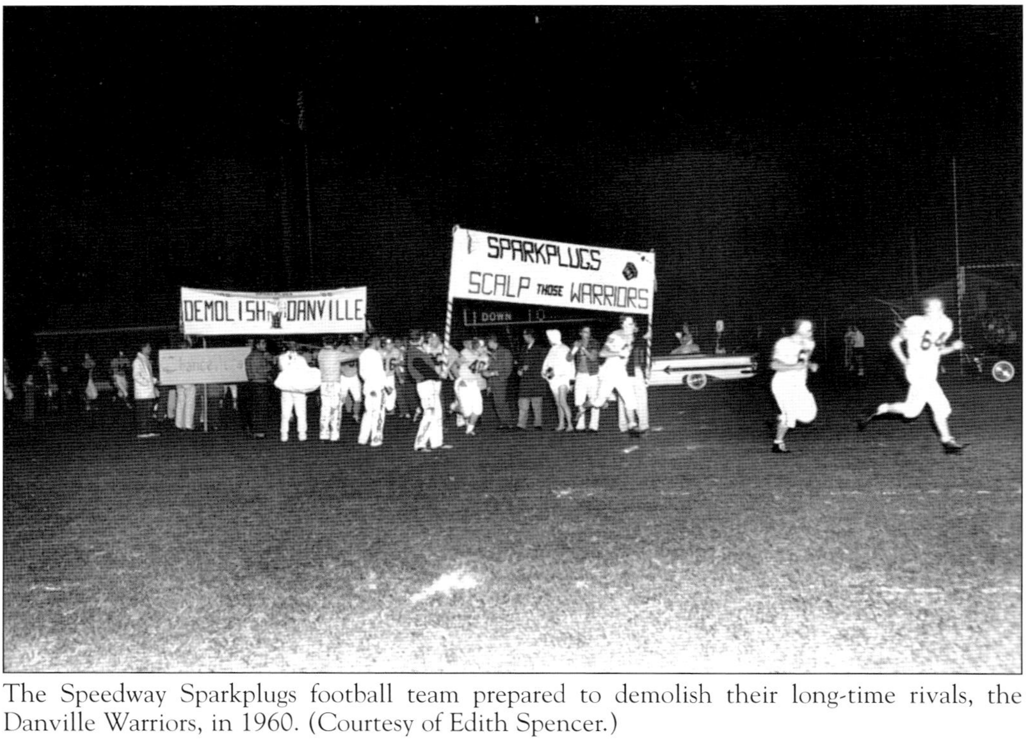

The Speedway Sparkplugs football team prepared to demolish their long-time rivals, the Danville Warriors, in 1960. (Courtesy of Edith Spencer.)

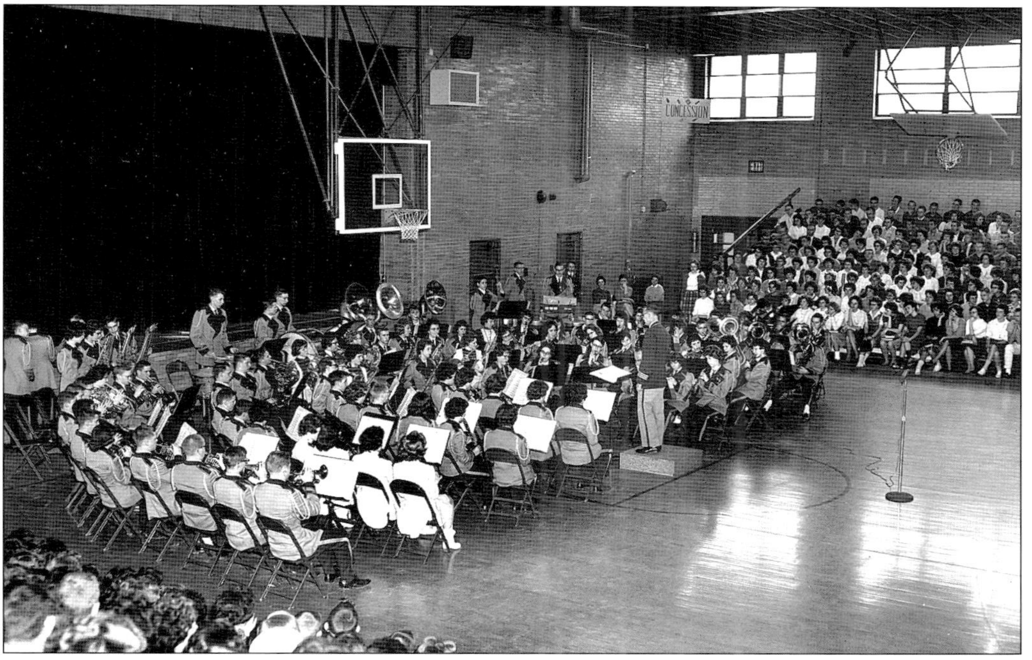

The old high school gym served for many functions. Here the band performs in 1960 to a packed house. (Courtesy of Edith Spencer.)

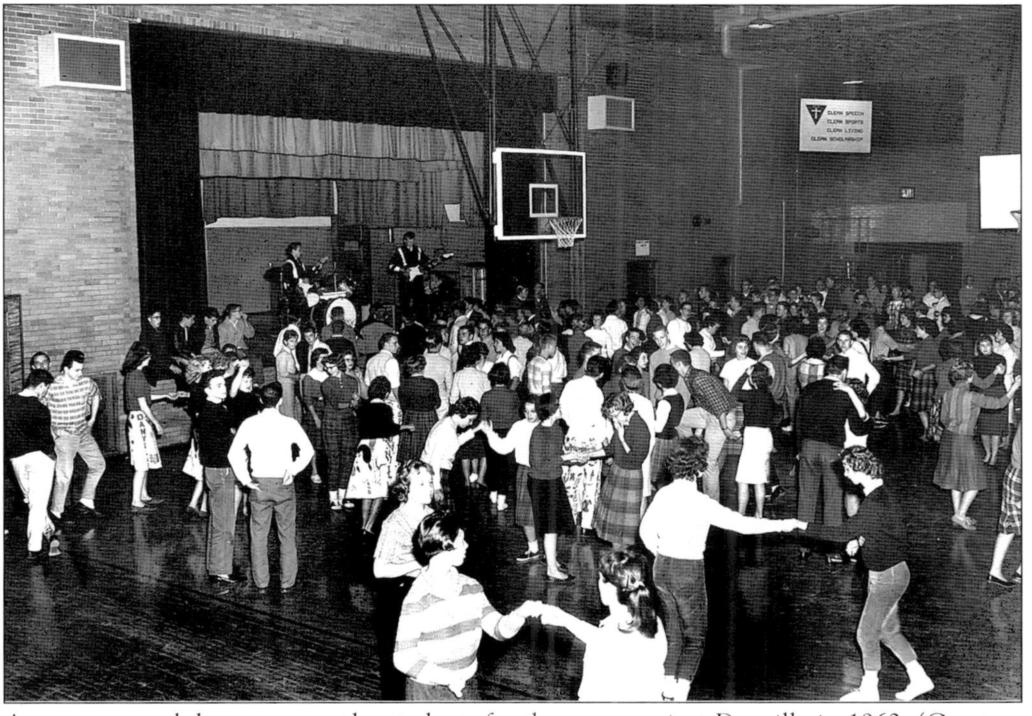

A pre-game sock hop prepares the students for the game against Danville in 1960. (Courtesy of Edith Spencer.)

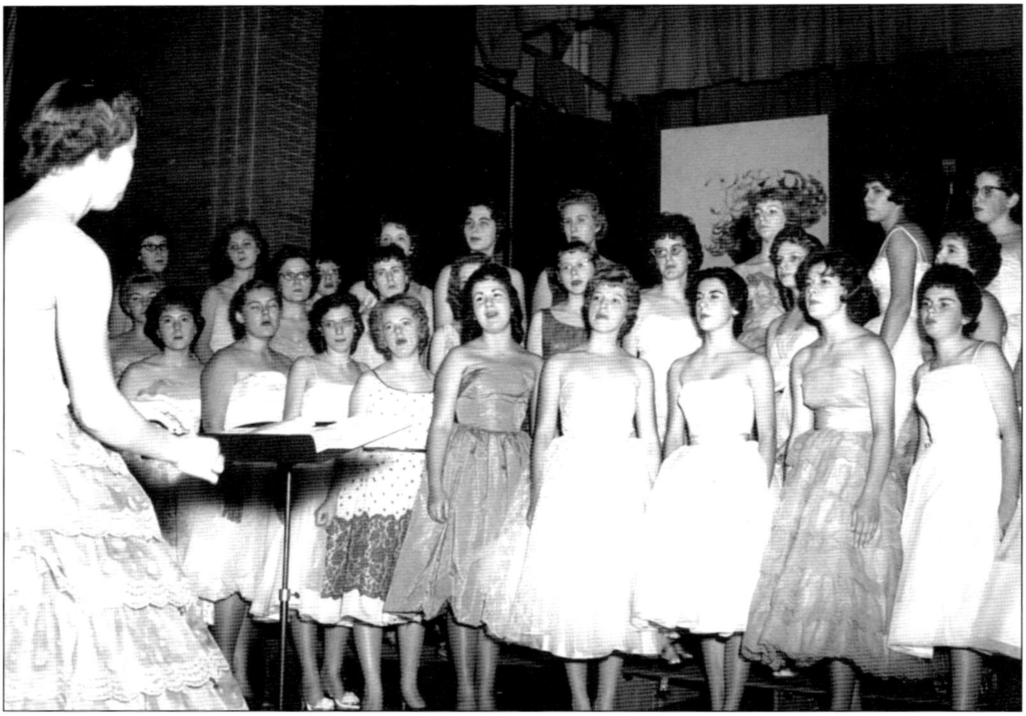

Here the Modern-Aires perform before the school in 1960. (Courtesy of Edith Spencer.)

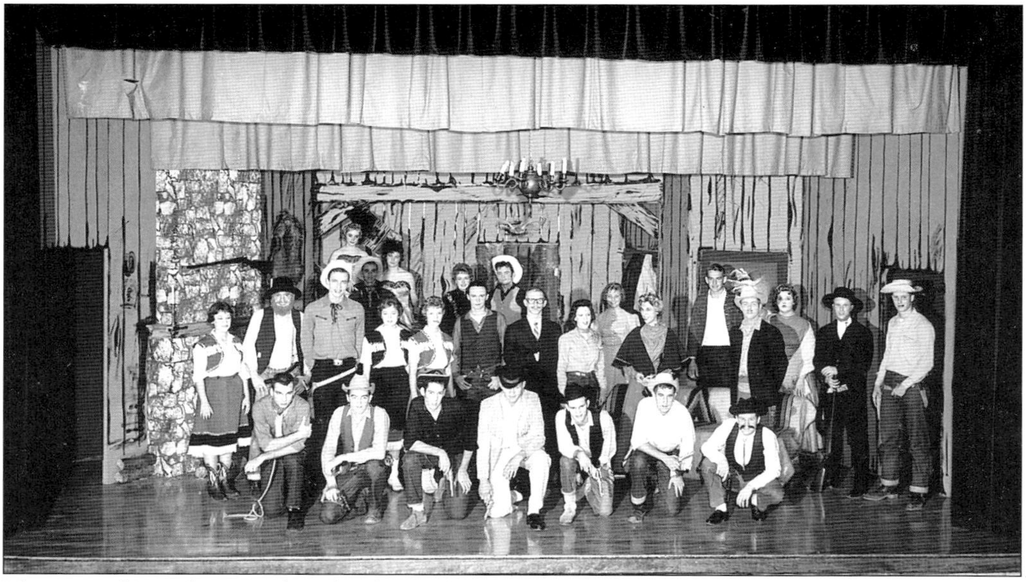

The cast of Speedway High School's production of *Oklahoma* pose for a formal picture in 1964. (Courtesy of Edith Spencer.)

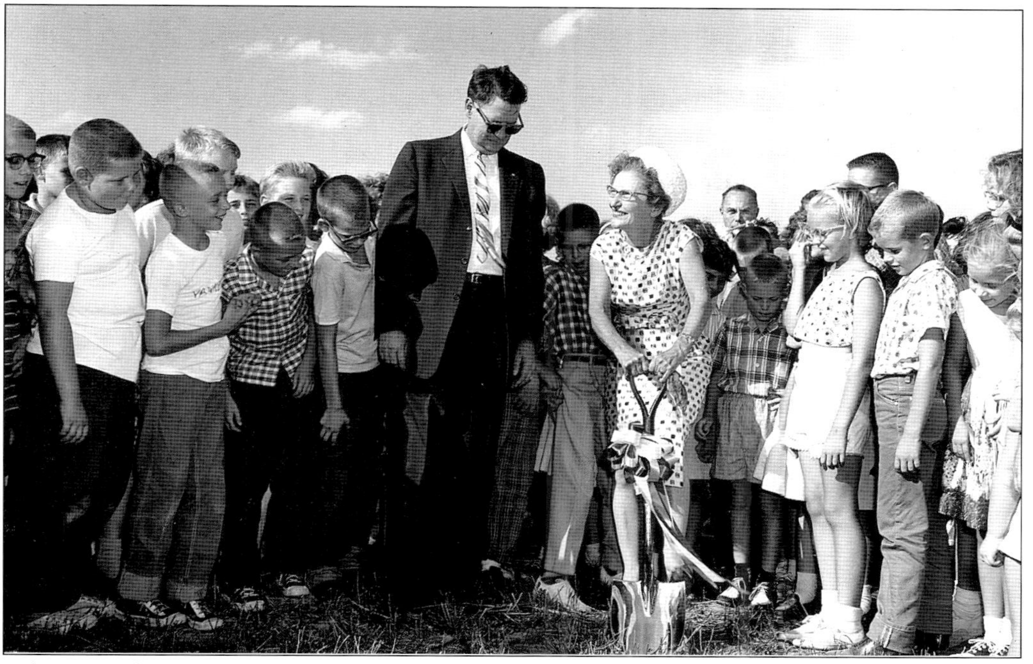

When Speedway prepared to build the new Speedway High School in 1961, Mrs. Howard J. Lacy II broke the ground for the school that would be named for her late husband. Here, Ross Swords, president of the Speedway School Building Corporation, watches. (Courtesy of Edith Spencer.)

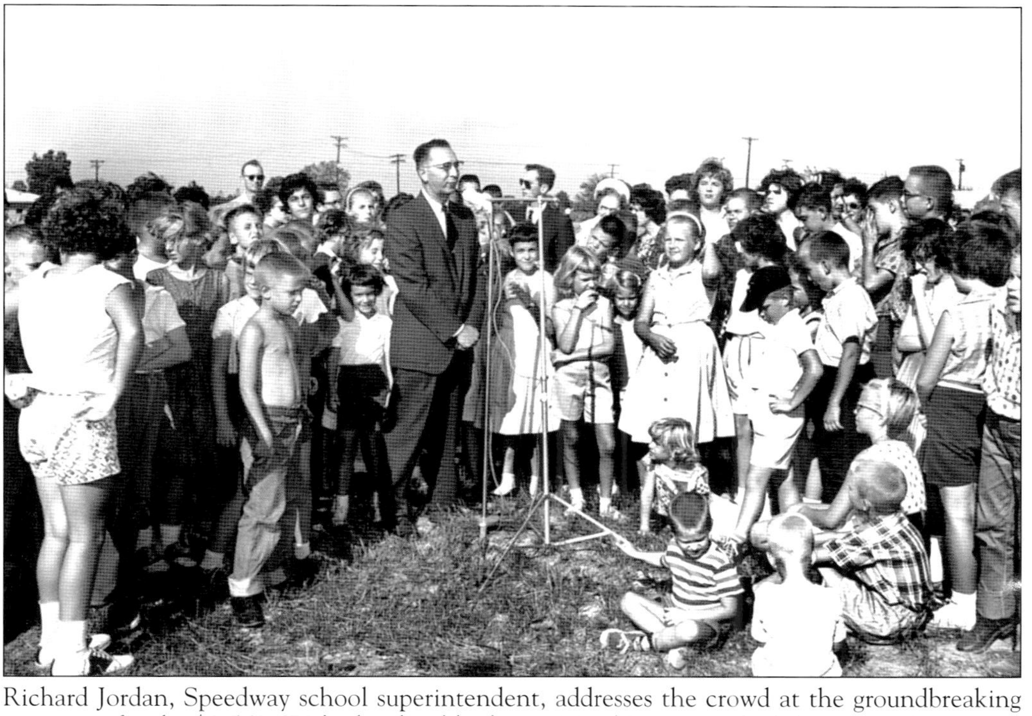

Richard Jordan, Speedway school superintendent, addresses the crowd at the groundbreaking ceremony for the $3,563,678 high school built in 1961. (Courtesy of Edith Spencer.)

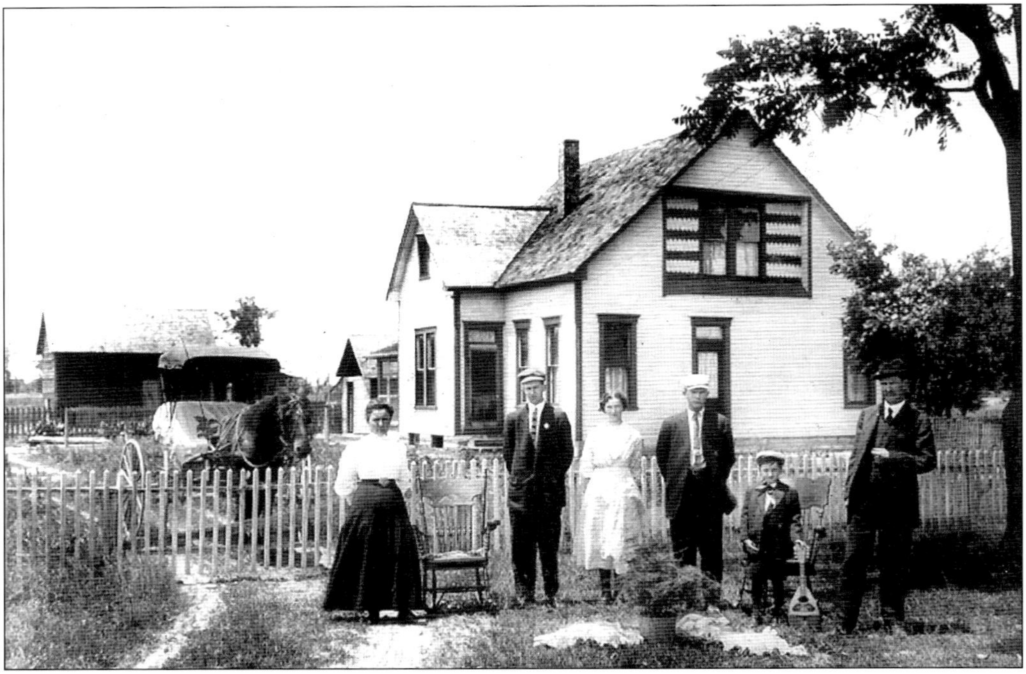

This house once stood where the Speedway Baptist Church now stands. This picture was taken around 1914. Pictured with some of their favorite possessions are, Eva Daupert, Harry Daupert, Ethel Daupert, Owen Daupert, Alfred Daupert, and Elmer H. Daupert. (Courtesy of Charles Bennett.)

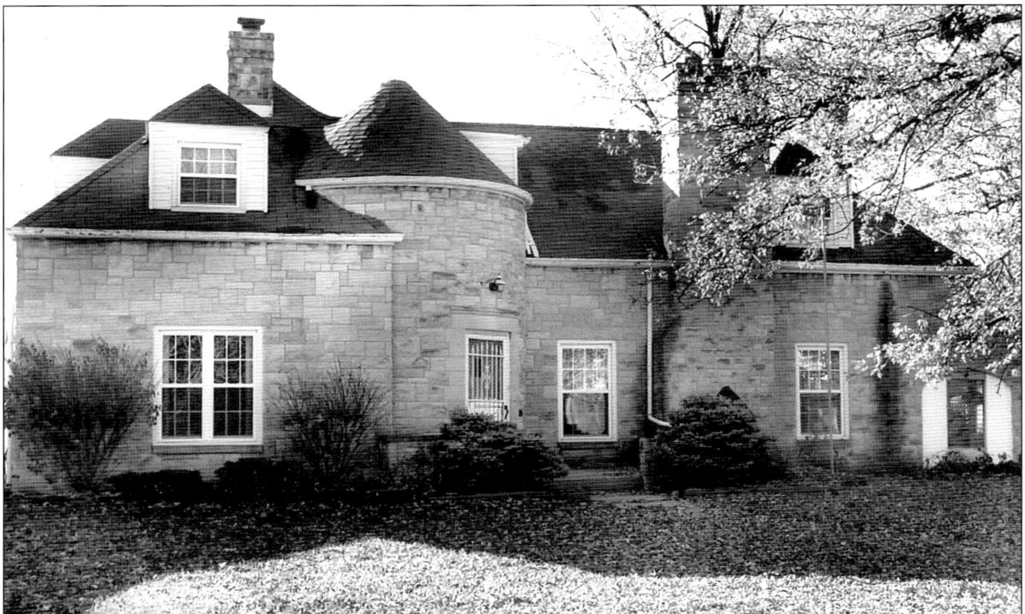

This Norman Cottage style house was the home of Dr. Hanna, the Indianapolis Motor Speedway doctor in the 1920s. (Courtesy of Charles Bennett.)

Seven

History Looks Forward

Charles Bennett, a social studies teacher at the Speedway Junior High School, is making sure that the history of his hometown is not lost on the younger generation. He and his students are working with the Old Speedway Neighborhood Association to have the oldest section of Speedway entered into the National Register as an historic district. The project was started with the 2001-2002 school year. The date for completion of the application is October 2004, but the project itself has already expanded far beyond the original borders into other neighborhoods of Speedway.

In order to instill a love of history in his eighth grade United States history students, Mr. Bennett took them into the streets of their community to "adopt" houses. Each student was then responsible for contacting the owners and learning as much as possible about the architecture and history of the home. The students then created a record of their investigations by storing the information on computers and by making Powerpoint presentations. The information gathered by the students was used to complete the application for the historic neighborhood application. The neighborhood will be called the Speedway Historic District.

Other efforts are being made by the Old Speedway Neighborhood Association to preserve the history of their community. Such a unique history deserves to be preserved and protected. Speedway, the town around the track, is indeed a town of distinction.

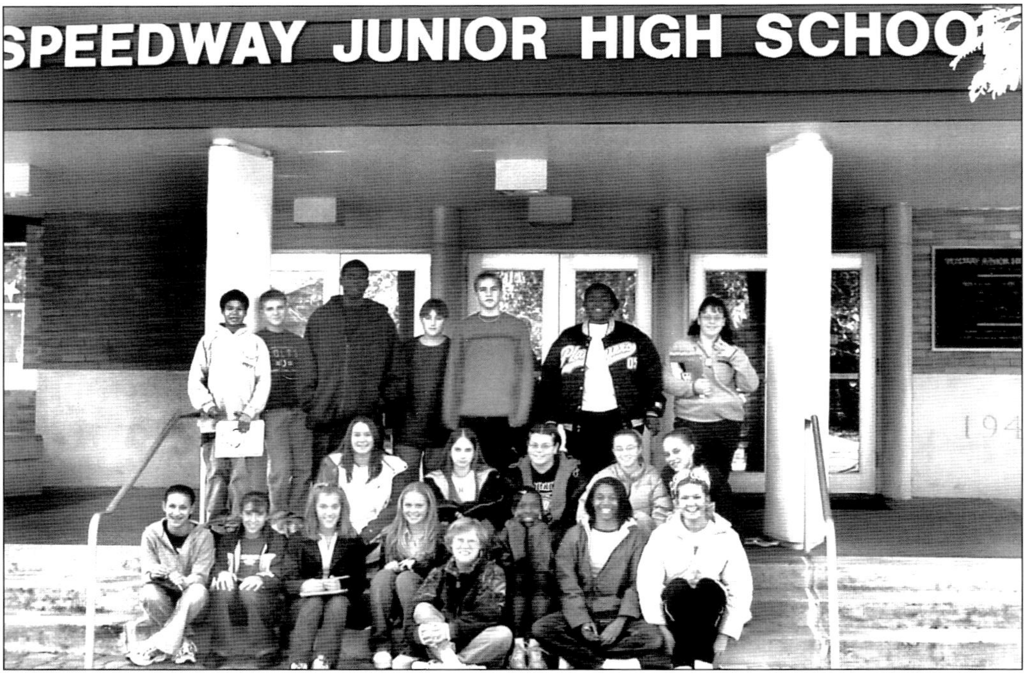

This group of students from Speedway Junior High School pioneered the history project which started during the 2001-2002 school year. These eighth grade United States history students were in Mr. Bennett's third period class. Here they pose with local columnist, Sara Sanderson (center, front). (Courtesy of Charles Bennett.)

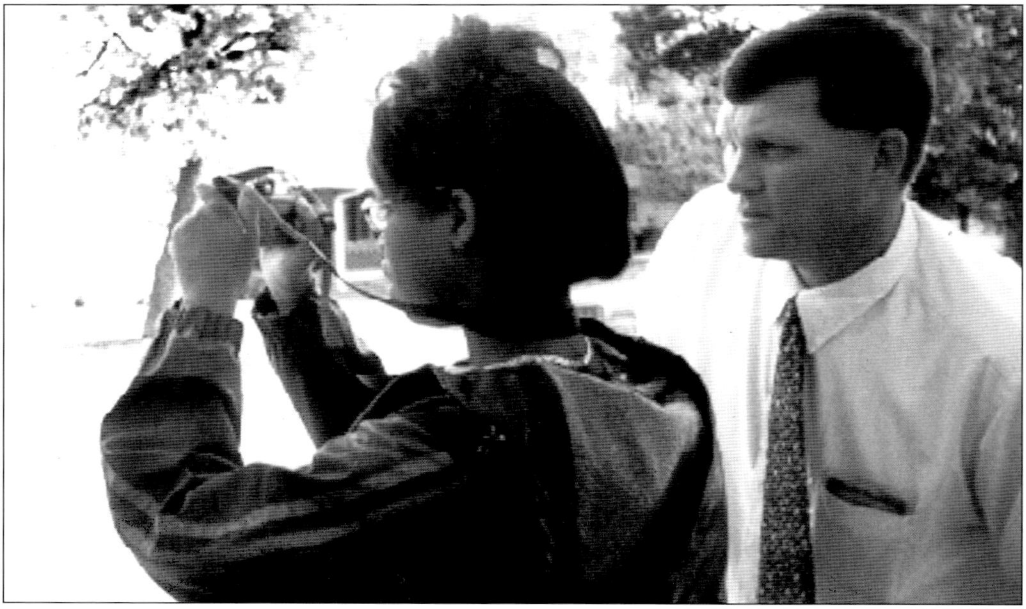

Here Mr. Charles Bennett, social studies teacher at Speedway Junior High School, helps a student get a focus on her house, and on history. Students studied the varied styles of architecture that help to make Speedway an interesting and unique town. (Courtesy of Charles Bennett.)

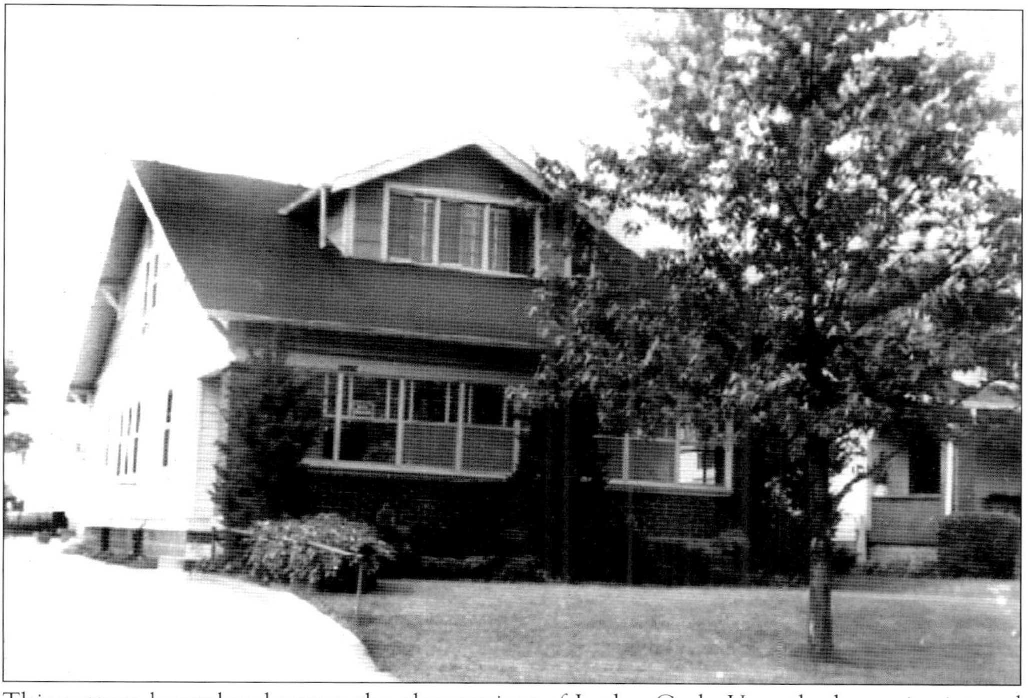

This cottage bungalow became the class project of Jordan Cork. Here the house is pictured as it appeared in 1960. This type of house is common in the Speedway area. (Courtesy of Charles Bennett.)

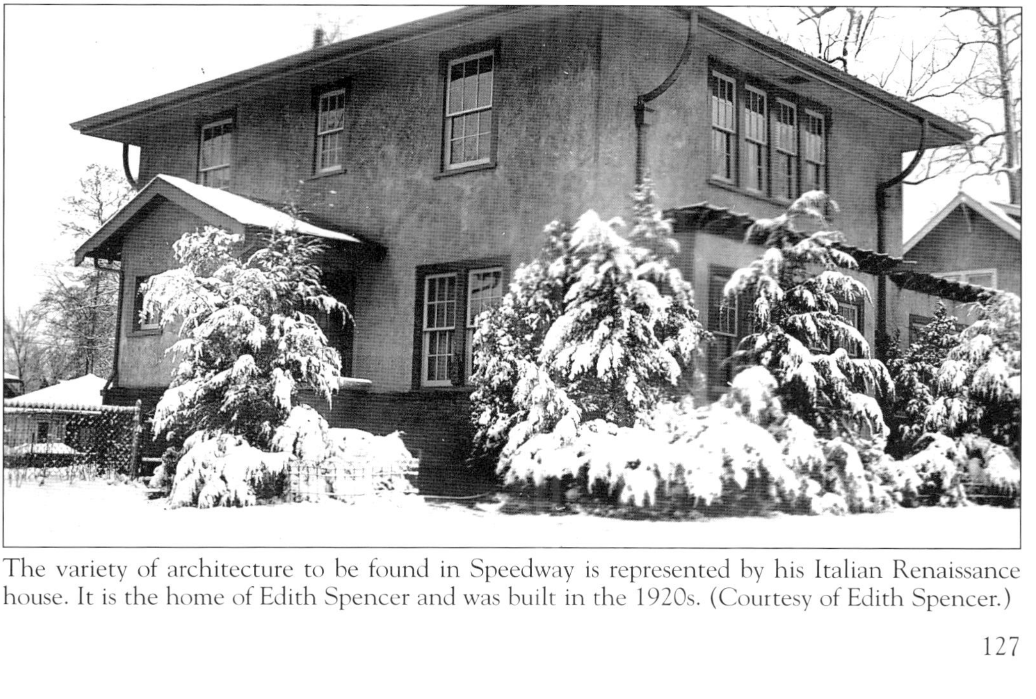

The variety of architecture to be found in Speedway is represented by his Italian Renaissance house. It is the home of Edith Spencer and was built in the 1920s. (Courtesy of Edith Spencer.)

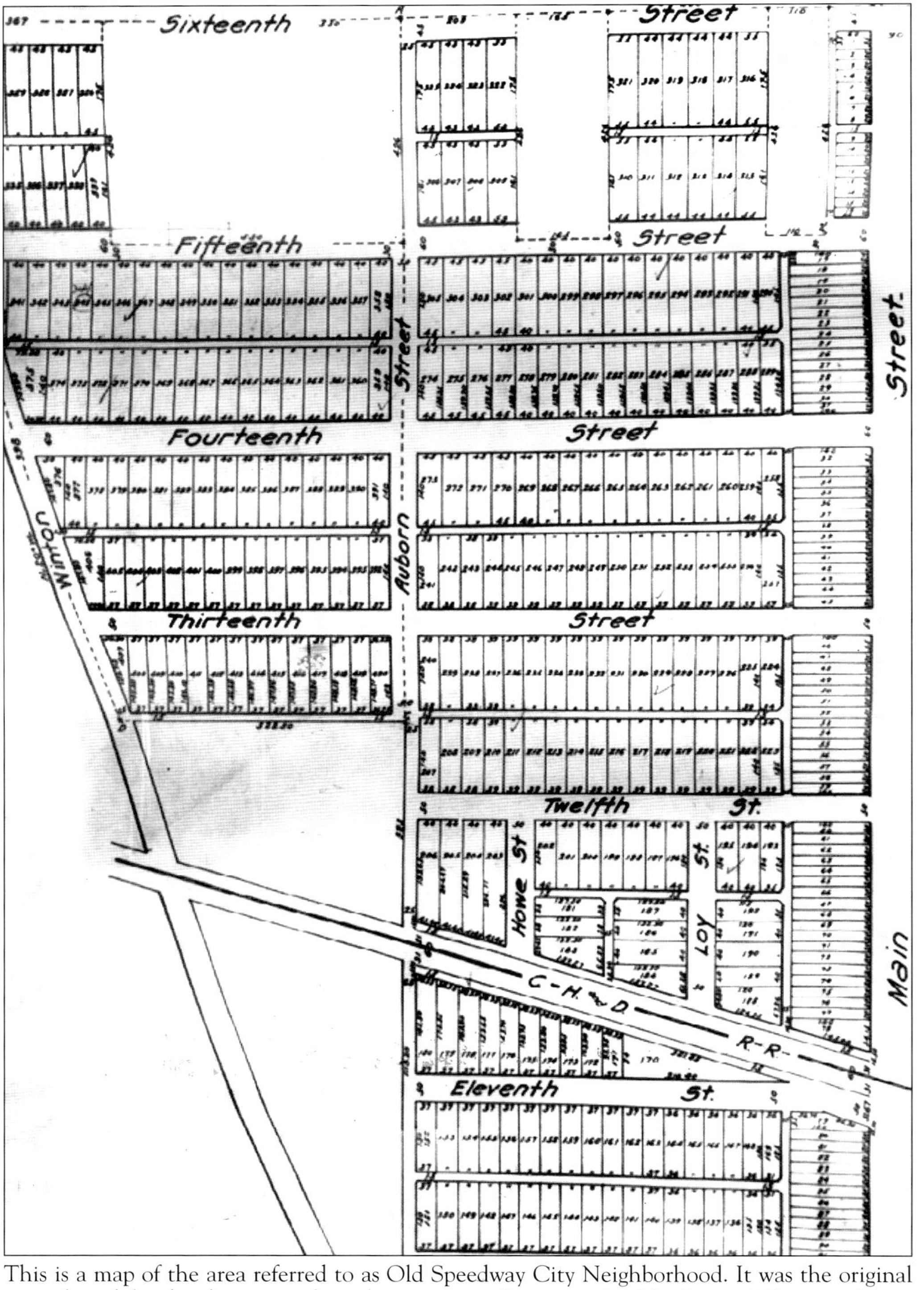

This is a map of the area referred to as Old Speedway City Neighborhood. It was the original area platted for development when the town was first conceived by James Allison and Lem Trotter. (Courtesy of Charles Bennett.)